Gunfighter in Gotham

this book is supported by a grant from

Figure Foundation

Gunfighter in Gotham

BAT MASTERSON'S
NEW YORK CITY YEARS

Robert K. DeArment

UNIVERSITY OF OKLAHOMA : NORMAN

Library of Congress Cataloging-in-Publication Data
DeArment, Robert K., 1925–
Gunfighter in Gotham : Bat Masterson's New York City years / Robert K.
DeArment.
p. cm.
Rev. ed. of: Broadway Bat. Honolulu, HI :Talei Publishers, 2005.
Includes bibliographical references and index.
ISBN 978-0-8061-4263-0 (hardcover : alk. paper)   1. Masterson, Bat,
1853–1921.   2. New York (N.Y.)—Biography.   3. Journalists—New York
(State)—New York—Biography.   4. Masterson, Bat, 1853–1921—Homes
and haunts—New York (State)—New York.   I. DeArment, Robert K.,
1925– Broadway Bat. II. Title.
Fl28.5.M37D43 2013
974.7'1 04092—dc23
[B]

2012022701

The paper in this book meets the guidelines for permanence and durability
of the Committee on Production Guidelines for Book Longevity of the
Council on Library Resources, Inc. ⊗

1 2 3 4 5 6 7 8 9 10

Contents

Illustrations

Acknowledgments

In 2005 *Broadway Bat* was published in a very limited edition, and few of those interested in the remarkable life of Bat Masterson have been able to read of his New York City career. I want to take this opportunity to thank Charles Rankin, editor-in-chief and associate director of the University of Oklahoma Press, and his staff for making that story available in this reprint, in which newly discovered information has been added. I also would like to express my gratitude to the following people who contributed in many ways to making the book possible: Phil Earl, Reno, Nevada; Craig Fouts, San Diego, California; Elnora Frye, Laramie, Wyoming; the late Arthur Goldberg, Rockville, Maryland; Penn Jones, La Mesa, California; Leo N. Miletich, El Paso, Texas; Jeff Morey, Long Beach, California; Roger Myers, Larned, Kansas; Bob Palmquist, Tucson, Arizona; Chuck Parsons, Luling, Texas; Gary Roberts, Tifton, Georgia; Nancy Samuelson, Sacramento, California; Johnny Spellman, Austin, Texas; Mark Sweeney, Library of Congress, Washington, D.C.; Casey Tefertiller, San Bruno, California; Jeannine Wilbarger and staff at the Toledo–Lucas County Public Library, Toledo, Ohio; and especially Jack De-Mattos of North Attleboro, Massachusetts, who generously turned over his extensive files on Bat Masterson and Teddy Roosevelt to me and shared other important information; Lou Grafton of New York City, who spent untold hours digging out elusive bits of information for me in the libraries, archives, and court records of Manhattan; and Chris Penn of Marsham, England, a tireless researcher who continues to amaze me with his ability to ferret out previously unknown gems of Masterson lore.

Gunfighter in Gotham

W. B. "Bat" Masterson, the "Ham Reporter," a "Broadway Guy."
(Courtesy Western History Department, Denver Public Library)

2

INTRODUCTION

I am a ham reporter, a Broadway guy.

W. B. "Bat" Masterson

Thanks to the magic of modern mass media the name Bat Masterson is widely recognized in America and many foreign lands. After more than a century of newspaper and magazine articles, novels and biographies, and motion pictures and television dramas, the image of Masterson as a deadly man-killing gunfighter of the American frontier West is firmly embedded in the public consciousness.

But the truth is that the popular perception of William Barclay Masterson, better known as Bat, has little basis in fact and had its genesis in a prank pulled on a gullible easterner by a mischievous westerner in the time-honored practical-joke tradition of the frontier.

In August 1881 *New York Sun* correspondent William Young was in the booming Colorado mining town of Gunnison looking for a sensational shoot-'em-up western story to titillate his eastern readers. When he asked Dr. W. S. Cockrell, a frontier veteran, where the western man-killers and "bad men" were of whom easterners had heard so much, Cockrell pointed to a young man standing nearby. That fellow, W. B. Masterson of Dodge City, Kansas, said Cockrell, was only twenty-seven years old, but had already killed twenty-six men. The doctor went on to spin lurid tales of the young man-killer's sensational adventures. One time, he said, Masterson shot seven men dead to avenge the murder of his brother. On another occasion, at a remote mountain hideout, he killed two Mexican half-breed outlaws for whom rewards were offered. Cutting off their heads, he started back, but a two-day ride under a hot sun swelled and disfigured the heads so that they were unrecognizable, and he failed to collect the rewards.[1]

When Cockrell's stories appeared in the *New York Sun*, they were picked up, reprinted, and expanded upon in newspapers around the country and became the foundation of the Bat Masterson gun-fighting legend. The fiction of the deadly killer "entering on his third dozen" of victims found its way into magazine articles, novels, and purportedly factual books. The legend would follow Masterson throughout his life and prove both a blessing and a curse.

Not only were Cockrell's yarns untrue, but the man he pointed out to the *Sun* newsman was not Bat Masterson at all. He was not even in Gunnison at the time, Masterson later insisted. It was all "a newspaper canard," a joke played on Young by Cockrell. When they met later, Cockrell apologized to Bat for having used his name to "guy" the easterner.[2]

Over the next century the frontier exploits of Bat Masterson were told with varying degrees of accuracy: how he left home as a teenager to hunt buffalo in Kansas; how he gained Indian-fighting renown after participating in the famous Battle of Adobe Walls in Texas, when a handful of intrepid buffalo hunters repulsed an attack by hundreds of Indian warriors; how he served as an army scout in the ensuing Red River War, became a peace officer in wild and wooly Dodge City, was elected sheriff there when only twenty-three years old, won fame as a lawman in Kansas and Colorado, turned to professional gambling as a career, and associated with and was the peer of such six-shooter notables as Wyatt Earp, Doc Holliday, Ben Thompson, and Luke Short.

Aside from his Indian-fighting experience, Bat Masterson actually used a firearm against a fellow man on only six occasions. In January 1876 he shot and killed army corporal Melvin King at Sweetwater, Texas, after King killed a woman and wounded Bat in the groin. As lawmen in Dodge City, Bat and brother Ed fired at a rampaging cowboy named A. C. Jackson and succeeded in killing his horse. Jackson was unhurt. In April 1878, after cowboys Jack Wagner and Alf Walker shot and killed Ed Masterson, Bat downed them both. Wagner died. James Kenedy, a fugitive wanted for the murder of a woman at Dodge, was pursued by a Masterson-led posse, brought down by a bullet from Bat's rifle, and captured in October 1878. Bat wounded saloon man Al Updegraff in a wild shootout in the Dodge City plaza in April 1881, and he nicked a man named C. C. Louderbaugh during a polling place altercation in Denver in April 1897.

Masterson always believed he had killed King, Wagner, and Kenedy and so testified in two separate court trials. The deaths of King and Wagner at Bat's hands have been well established, but he was mistaken about Kenedy. Although one Dodge City pioneer reported that young Kenedy returned to Texas, where he killed several men before he "finally met his death by someone a little quicker on the trigger than himself,"[3] Bat chose to believe Dr. Henry Hoyt, who claimed Kenedy returned from Dodge to the Texas Panhandle with "one arm and shoulder all shot to pieces" and died a year or two later from the wound.[4] Actually, neither story is correct. After a preliminary-examination acquittal on the murder charge, probably as a result of some well-placed monetary exchange by his wealthy father, Jim Kenedy returned to South Texas and eventually recovered from his wound. He died of tuberculosis on December 29, 1884.[5]

The Bat Masterson story is replete with ironies.

The enduring myth that he was a killer who left corpses scattered across the West is based on a practical joke at which he was not even present.

A New York newspaperman was responsible for creating the myth, and Masterson spent the last two decades of his life as a New York newspaperman.

Although Masterson publicly and repeatedly renounced his gunfighting notoriety, that very celebrity attracted the interest of Theodore Roosevelt and journalist brothers Alfred Henry and William E. Lewis, men of influence who promoted and abetted his later career and in large measure were responsible for the success of his mature years.

Masterson is remembered today as a western lawman, yet his service as a deputy U.S. marshal in New York was far longer than the total time he spent as a peace officer in the West.

He became famous as a character of the Old West, but almost a third of his life was spent on the East Coast, and he lived in New York City twice as long as any place in the West.

Bat Masterson's adult life spanned exactly fifty years, from the fall of 1871 when he left his father's farm for the buffalo plains of western Kansas to the fall of 1921 when he wrote his last column and died at his New York City desk. During that half century his life was divided into two distinct periods of twenty-five years each. The first was spent on the frontier, primarily in small cattle or mining towns, and it was during this time that his enduring legend as a fearless lawman and deadly gunfighter emerged. But about the time historian Frederick Jackson Turner announced the closing of the American frontier,[6] Masterson turned a lifelong interest in prizefighting into a journalistic career. The former frontiersman spent the last quarter century of his life as a city dweller, first in Denver, then in the nation's largest city, New York, where he achieved new fame as a ring historian and boxing authority.

His pursuit of matters fistic took him to all corners of the United States, from San Francisco Bay to the bright lights of Broadway, from the Pacific Northwest to the Florida Keys, and from Langtry, Texas, to Minnehaha Falls, Minnesota. He would witness the growth of pugilism in the United States from title matches held in grass-covered fields, with attendance numbering in the dozens and purses in the hundreds of dollars, to bouts in huge stadiums and million-dollar gates.

During his twenty-year residency in New York the city's population would grow by over two million, and he would see horsecars, carriages, and hansom cabs disappear from Broadway, to be replaced by electric trams and motor cars. The man who had spent days in the saddle chasing bandits across desert wastes would live to admire the beauties of Alexandria Bay, New York, from a seat in the cockpit of an airplane flying high above.

For eighteen years, from 1903 until 1921, Masterson authored a lengthy thrice-a-week sports column for the *New York Morning Telegraph* that came to be titled "Masterson's Views on Timely Topics." Those columns, totaling almost four million words, dealt primarily with pugilistic events and figures, but often reflected the man's outspoken, often belligerent, iconoclastic opinions on war, crime, politics, and societal changes. With the growth of his renown as a boxing expert, his opinions were picked up and reprinted in this country and abroad. Many of the topics Bat found timely almost a century ago are no less timely today.

The first two decades of the twentieth century, when Masterson lived, worked, and recreated in the Broadway district of New York City, were probably the most exciting period in the history of that storied sector. There he hobnobbed with the Broadway characters immortalized in the stories of Damon Runyon and became one of those memorable characters himself.

This, then, is the story of Bat Masterson's other life, one played on a stage far removed from the sweeping western plains and dusty cowtown streets of his youth—when he became, in his own words, "a ham reporter, a Broadway guy."

BATTLING MASTERSON

Sheriff, nut, crook, sport, regular guy, gambler, peace officer, buffalo killer.

> Note on the back of a photo of Bat in the Walter Noble Burns papers, Arizona Special Collections, Tucson

One hundred and thirty years ago the name of Bat Masterson was familiar to many Americans from their reading of their daily papers. He was, they knew, a hero of the western frontier, at the age of twenty the youngest member of a fearless little band of buffalo hunters who withstood repeated attacks by hundreds of Indians in the famous Battle of Adobe Walls; sheriff of Ford County, Kansas, headquartered in the wild cattle town of Dodge, when he was only twenty-five; and by the age of thirty a deadly gunfighter who had downed more than a score of men.

One hundred years ago members of another generation, readers of the sports pages throughout America and parts of the English-speaking world, recognized the name Bat Masterson as a leading expert on boxing and the fistic scene.

Fifty years ago the name Bat Masterson became familiar to yet another generation when the new medium of television introduced a highly fictionalized depiction of his western exploits into their homes with a popular weekly series.

A few years ago my wife, a friendly, garrulous sort, struck up a conversation with the man seated next to her on a cross-country commercial plane flight. It turned out the fellow was a coach for a big-league baseball team, and he enlightened her for some time with stats and records of the current teams and players. My wife, not a baseball fan, finally attempted to change the subject.

"My husband wrote the definitive biography of Bat Masterson," she offered.

The man turned and looked at her blankly before asking, "Who did he play for?"

One of the reasons for the several incarnations of Masterson fame was the nickname "Bat." Like the sobriquets of other highly publicized western figures—the "Bills" for instance: "Buffalo Bill" Cody, "Wild Bill" Hickok, and "Billy the Kid" Bonney—the name "Bat" Masterson was catchy and easily remembered.

How Masterson acquired the nickname has been the subject of much conjecture. He did not get it from his prowess with a Louisville Slugger, as the baseball coach presumed. Nor did he get it by shooting flying bats in caves in order to sharpen his quickness and skill with a six-shooter, as envisioned by western novelists. In his 1905 semifictional biography of Masterson, Alfred Henry Lewis suggested that his subject acquired the name through his prowess as a hunter, reminding frontier veterans of the feats of Baptiste "Bat" Brown, an intrepid frontiersman of an earlier day.[1] Other writers have surmised that citizens of Dodge City tagged the young lawman with the name when he batted miscreants over the head with a walking stick he carried as a result of a gunshot wound.[2]

Actually the appellation derived from his baptismal name, "Bartholomew," shortened by the family to "Bart" and eventually to "Bat." Masterson found no fault with "Bat" but disliked "Bartholomew" and as a young man discarded it for "William Barclay," the name he would use throughout his adult life.

Strangely, no one seems to have suggested that he picked up the sobriquet "Bat" as a shortening of "Battling" because of his pugnacious nature, as did several pugilists of the day, most notably Oscar Matthew "Battling" Nelson, lightweight champion, 1908–1910. It would have been a logical assumption, for Masterson was indeed a battler. Quick to take offense, with a short-fused temper, he carried grudges for years, and did not hesitate to back up bitter words with violent physical action. In his early years he engaged in a number of brawls.

His earliest recorded fistfight occurred at Adobe Walls when the buffalo hunters, having beaten off the Indians in the famous battle, began to fight among themselves, and Masterson tangled with another hunter named Frank Brown.

At Dodge City in 1877 he became embroiled in two fights within a month. The first occurred on June 6 when, objecting to city marshal Larry Deger's rough handling of a drunken prisoner, he took on the 300-pound Deger, a deputy, and a number of bystanders, and allowed the prisoner to escape. Although beaten over the head by the officers' pistols, Masterson "seemed possessed of extraordinary strength," according to a news account, and fought every foot of the way to the calaboose. After a night in the cooler, nursing his battered head and wounded feelings, he paid a $25 fine for disturbing the peace.[3]

Bat was running the Lone Star Saloon and Dancehall in Dodge at this time. Charlie Siringo, later renowned as a Pinkerton detective and writer, was in the place on the Fourth of July when a free-for-all broke out between Texas cowboys and buffalo hunters. Bat began pitching heavy beer mugs, and when he ran out of glassware, he waded into the fray with an ice mallet. Then, said Siringo, "the blood flew."[4]

In 1884 Bat engaged in what a local newspaper editor called "a little melee" in a Dodge City saloon. When a man named A. J. Howard attacked him with a long carving knife, "the stalwart form of Masterson rose in its majesty." Seizing a chair, Bat knocked his assailant down. The intervention of bystanders prevented him from administering more punishment, which, according to the editor, "was well for the safety of the chair and Mr. Howard's head."[5]

By 1886 Masterson was spending most of his time in Denver, where his dalliance with variety hall singer Nellie McMahon led to two more clashes. Nellie was married to Lou Spencer, a vaudevillian appearing at Denver's California Hall. On the night of September 18 Spencer entered one of the theater boxes to find his wife perched on Masterson's knee. A fight broke out, and both men were arrested. Three days later Nellie filed suit for divorce and left town with Masterson. The cuckolded husband attempted to allay his anguish with narcotics. Arrested in an opium den on October 3, he was bailed out of jail by a friend named Bagsby. Bat, who had returned to Denver, ran into Bagsby later that night in Murphy's Saloon and attacked him with a cane. Patrons, fleeing the scene, heard a shot. When police arrived, they found Bagsby sponging blood from his face and Masterson in a back room with a gunshot wound in the calf of his leg. Bat explained that he had been hit by a bullet accidentally discharged from a gun dropped by a saloon customer in his mad rush for the exits. No charges were filed.

His natural combativeness drew Masterson inexorably to pugilism, the "manly art." Prizefighting as a sport in the nineteenth century was developed and controlled by professional gamblers; many of the early boxers followed the calling themselves. Although Masterson never fought in the ring, by the early 1880s, having turned to gambling as a profession, he had forged close ties to members of the boxing fraternity and was becoming increasingly identified with the sport. The qualities exemplified in the best ring gladiators—courage, aggressiveness, and manly prowess—were those attributes he held in the highest regard in himself and other men. Over the next forty years he attended almost every important fistic event held in the United States and was personally involved in many of them.

The ring's first national celebrity was John L. Sullivan, a flamboyant, hard-drinking saloon brawler from Boston who defeated Paddy Ryan for the heavyweight title in 1882. Due primarily to fawning accolades in the pages of the *National Police Gazette*, the barbershop bible, Sullivan was widely believed to be invincible, a fighting man nonpareil. (Bat Masterson consistently held a minority opinion. The celebrated "Boston Strong Boy" was, he insisted, "the poorest excuse for a champion the American prize ring ever had," and his celebrity was a creation of sycophantic sportswriters.)[6]

One of Sullivan's several managers was gambling house proprietor and fight promoter Charles E. "Parson" Davies of Chicago, who became a lifelong friend of Masterson's. In 1883 Bat induced Davies to bring two of the pugs in his stable, Fred Plaisted and Jimmy Elliott, to Dodge City and put on a match. This first Masterson promotion was billed as a gentlemanly "boxing exhibition," but quickly degenerated into a slugging roughhouse with fighters and referee Davies flailing away to the delight of the Dodge City spectators.

Other sports drew Masterson's attention during this period as well. He was a founder and vice president of Dodge City's first baseball club, served on the town's foot-racing committee, and officiated at football games. It was while referring a football scrimmage that he suffered a humiliating accident. The man who could "face a six-shooter without flinching," said a local paper, had to withdraw "when a football pasted him a gentle reminder under the left ear."[7] Bat disliked football thereafter, likening the game to "organized rioting." He thought football was more dangerous and brutal than bull fighting, and it did not approach boxing as a "manly, decent, healthful sport."[8] In the East he refused to attend the much-publicized Yale-Harvard games, saying he had seen many illegal riots and had no desire to watch a legal one. An observer remarked that he might disagree with the sentiment, but certainly admired Masterson's way of saying things.[9]

Bat's first known attempt at written sports commentary was in the form of a letter to the editor, castigating two judges of a horse race held at Dodge in the summer of 1884. Its vituperative, accusatory rhetoric would become a distinctive element of his style in later years. A winner had been announced in a very close race Bat thought should have been called a dead heat. He called the judges "fop-eared nonentities" who "were willing to stultify their honor and manhood" and accused them of betting on the horse they said had won.[10]

The following November Masterson made his first real effort in the journalistic field with the publication at Dodge City of a four-page newspaper he called the *Vox Populi*. There was only one issue, as the paper's sole purpose was to influence the November election. In this political screed Bat viciously attacked his political opponents with epithets like "scum and filth, crawling reptile, thief, liar, murderer, rapists, barn burner, and poisoner of horses." He counted the effort a success, for on Election Day his favored slate of candidates handily defeated his political enemies. In a letter to a Dodge City paper he announced that his "brief sojourn in the journalistic field" was ended and boasted that "the blows [*Vox Populi*] dealt to the venomous vipers whom it opposed had a telling effect."[11]

Masterson's writing talents impressed at least two newspapermen. In a classic understatement a Dodge City editor remarked that Bat's views seemed to be "somewhat of a personal nature," but thought his writing held promise and he might accomplish much in the journalistic field.[12] Olney Newell, editor of the *Trinidad (Colorado) News*, thought Bat "an easy and graceful writer [of] real journalistic ability."[13]

During the 1880s, as public interest in boxing was heightened by the ascendancy of the ring's first charismatic superstar, heavyweight king John L. Sullivan, Masterson became increasingly involved in the sport. One of his first mentors was Billy Madden, a clever middleweight who introduced Bat to some of the complexities of ring strategy and became a friend for life. Madden helped train and manage Sullivan and, Bat always maintained, was largely responsible for making John L. a national ring idol.

In the summer of 1883 Madden introduced Bat to Charlie Mitchell, the prizefighter Bat came to admire above all others. Mitchell, a young Englishman weighing no more than 150 pounds, had defeated the best heavyweights in his own country and was angling for a shot at Sullivan's American title. In Denver Bat showed his friends around town and then accompanied them to Leadville, where Mitchell took on all comers in four-round bouts.

Inspired by the example of Billy Madden, Masterson took up management of prizefighters. His first protégé was a youngster named John P. Clow, who Bat fondly remembered years later as weighing about 150 pounds and being built on the order of Bob Fitzsimmons, "with powerful shoulders and light underpinning."[14] In August 1885 Bat matched Clow against heavyweight Harry Hynds in a bout at Rawlins, Wyoming. Special trains brought sporting men from around the country who wagered no less than $20,000 on the outcome. After Clow knocked out his opponent in the sixth round Masterson claimed the heavyweight championship of the Rocky Mountains for his fighter and toured Kansas and Colorado with him, setting up matches with local battlers. In 1886 Bat and Clow helped train and condition Charlie Mitchell and worked his corner in winning bouts against highly rated heavyweights Jack Burke in Chicago and Patsy Cardiff in Minneapolis.

Prizefights during this period were fought under London Prize Ring rules with the contestants bare-knuckled or wearing skin-tight gloves. A round lasted until one of the combatants went to the ground from the effects of either a blow or a wrestling move. With the aid of his handlers he then had thirty seconds to "toe the mark," a line drawn in the center of the ring, and resume fighting. The battle continued until one of the fighters could no longer continue. In these bare-knuckle fights emphasis was on physical strength and ability to withstand punishment. The description in a Dodge City paper of one such bout between two pugs named Nelson Whitman and "Red" Hanley was undoubtedly long on hyperbole, but gives an idea of the brutality of the early matches. At the conclusion of the forty-second round, ran the story, Hanley had to "put his right eye back where it belonged, set his jaw bone and have the ragged edge trimmed off his ears where they had been chewed the worst." In the sixty-first round Red "squealed unmistakable," and Whitman was declared the winner. Injuries sustained, reported the paper, included "two ears chewed off, one eye bursted and the other disabled, right cheek bone caved in, bridge of the nose broken, seven teeth knocked out, one jaw bone mashed, one side of the tongue chewed off, and several other unimportant fractures and bruises."[15]

Masterson refereed many of these affairs, including a notable 1888 bout promoted by Jefferson "Soapy" Smith, Ed Gaylord, and other prominent Denver gamblers in which John C. Sterling of Cheyenne and W. A. Ross of San Francisco were matched for a $300 purse. Boxing was banned in Denver at the time, so a special train conveyed the fighters, their attendants, the officials, and about 400 sporting men into neighboring Douglas County, where a ring had been prepared in a field beside the track. Referee Masterson declared Ross the winner when, after one hour and fifteen minutes of slugging, kicking, throttling, eye-gouging action, Sterling could not toe the line for the twenty-seventh round.

When not managing or refereeing, Bat often acted as timekeeper and/or bodyguard for principals at important fights. He served in this dual capacity for Jake Kilrain in 1889 when Kilrain challenged Sullivan for the heavyweight title. Others in the challenger's entourage were Mike Donovan, one-time American middleweight champion, and Charlie Mitchell. Although Bat was Kilrain's official bodyguard, Mitchell also carried two revolvers, according to ring historian Nat Fleischer. "Gunmen were an important part of the pugilistic picture in those rough-and-ready days, when fair play was best maintained by a judicious display of force on both sides."[16]

The fight had been planned for New Orleans, but when antiboxing religious leaders raised an uproar and the Louisiana governor threatened to use militia to prevent the bout, the fight crowd and press representatives boarded special trains and crossed the state line to Richburg, Mississippi. There, on a steamy hot day in a clearing of tall Mississippi pines, the gladiators battled for two hours and sixteen minutes in what would be the last bare-knuckle championship bout fought under London Prize Ring rules in America. After seventy-five rounds Donovan tossed in the sponge, conceding Kilrain's defeat. The fight has come down in history as one of the great ring battles of all time, but Bat Masterson always dissented from that view, contending that it was the worst exhibition of fighting ineptitude by two pugilists he ever witnessed. The fact that he lost a bundle on the fight no doubt contributed to this harsh appraisal. He had never previously seen Kilrain in action, but based on Mitchell's repeated assurance that the challenger was "the real thing" and his own conviction that Sullivan was highly overrated, Bat backed Kilrain with his purse and lost.

At the conclusion of the fight, reporters, anxious to wire their stories from New Orleans, made a rush for the trains. An Associated Press (AP) special was the first to depart, and just before it pulled out, the Kilrain party attached their special car to the end. According to the *National Police Gazette*, the train was traveling at "lightning speed" when the AP men discovered their uninvited traveling companion and attempted to pull the pin connecting the cars. "Bat Masterson then came to the fore. With a merry twinkle in his eyes, he said he would give $50 to anyone who would pull the pin. As he made this remark, he drew a formidable-looking revolver, cocked it, and pointed it at the bumper pin. No one seemed anxious to win the money, and Kilrain's party was permitted to keep on."[17]

A month later Masterson made his first visit to San Francisco, then becoming a center of prize ring activity, to witness another highly touted title match, a fight between middleweight champion Jack Dempsey, "the Nonpareil," and George LaBlanche, the Canadian challenger. It was one of the first championship bouts fought under the Marquess of Queensberry rules, just coming into general acceptance. Under the new rules boxers wore gloves and fought in three-minute rounds with one-minute rest periods. A knocked-down fighter had ten seconds to regain his feet before being counted out by the referee. If both fighters were still capable of continuing at the conclusion of a prescribed number of rounds determined by previous agreement, the referee or judges could announce a winner or declare the bout a draw.

In 1890 John Clow developed tuberculosis and quit the ring. As the disease ravaged his body he drank heavily and became increasingly quarrelsome. In May of that year a man named Garret Hughes shot and wounded him in Denver's notorious Exchange Saloon. Seven months later Frank Marshall, son of a former Kansas governor, shot Clow to death in the same establishment. A jury acquitted Marshall, apparently taking the view, as Bat later bitterly commented, "that it was no crime for the degenerate son of wealthy parents to kill a prizefighter without cause or provocation."[18]

With Clow's departure, Bat began looking for a new young prospect. A middleweight from Cleveland, Ohio, named Patrick R. Gallagher, nicknamed "Reddy" for his flaming locks, turned up in Denver about this time. Well-built and flashy in his workouts, Gallagher claimed to have cleaned up all the competition in the Midwest. Masterson took him to San Francisco and matched him with Johnny Herget, a promising middleweight fighting under the name "Young Mitchell." The bout aroused much interest among the Bay Area sporting crowd, and some of the greatest ring names of the era became involved. Jack "Nonpareil" Dempsey was Mitchell's chief adviser. Seconding Gallagher were English lightweight Jimmy Carroll and Ruby Bob Fitzsimmons, the big-shouldered, spindly-legged Australian who the following year would knock out Dempsey to win the first of his three world championships. The great black heavyweight, Peter Jackson, refereed the match for a $5,000 purse to be split $4,000 to the winner and $1,000 to the loser.

When Jackson, after watching Gallagher work out, told Masterson he was certain his man could whip Young Mitchell, Bat placed a hefty bet on his fighter with San Francisco gambler Mose Gunst. Gallagher's performance in the bout was less than stellar, however. A disgusted Masterson later said the redhead turned out to be "the biggest false alarm" he had ever seen, a "hunk of cheese" who, after thirteen unexciting rounds "sat down on the floor until he was counted out," content to settle for the loser's purse, more money that he had ever seen.[19] Again hit hard in the pocketbook, Masterson resolved never again to back a fighter financially without first seeing him in action.

Gunfighter in Gotham

Nor would he ever fully trust Reddy Gallagher again, although he would become involved with him in an ill-fated boxing promotion venture a few years later.

A twenty-year-old heavyweight named Billy Woods was the next boxer Masterson managed. Woods was an attendant in his brother Walter's Turkish bathhouse in Denver when his splendid physique caught Bat's eye. As he was earning only $12 a week in the bathhouse, the young man quickly agreed to Bat's suggestion that he turn to boxing where he might make several hundred dollars a bout. Masterson trained Woods and eventually matched him in his first professional fight with a strapping young fellow named Bert McCormack for $200 a side and the gate receipts, winner take all. True to his resolve, Bat refused to back Billy financially until he had seen him perform in actual combat. Walter Woods came up with his brother's entry money. The gate, collected at a prairie battle site outside Denver, amounted to another $200. Although obviously short on ring skills and techniques, Woods proved to be a strong, aggressive fighter with a stout heart and put away his equally untutored but tough and willing opponent in seventeen rounds.

Bat next matched Woods with George Kessler, a Butte, Montana, fireman, for the gate receipts and a $300 side bet, but no money changed hands as after twelve rounds rowdies in the crowd started a riot. "Pistols were drawn, and while no shots were fired, the pistols were used as clubs, and a good many were badly done up in the fray," Bat remembered. "The ring was torn down during the scrimmage, and the referee was forced to stop the fight and call it a draw."[20]

In January 1891 Masterson and Woods entrained for New Orleans, where a boxing extravaganza featuring a world title bout between middleweight champion Jack Dempsey and Bob Fitzsimmons was scheduled. Accompanying them was an attractive theatrical woman who gave her name as Emma Masterson and shared Bat's sleeping quarters, but was recognized by many sports as the wife of a well-known foot racer named Ed Moulton.

In those days promoters of fistic matches, supported by law officers in districts where prizefighting was permitted, banned women from witnessing the bouts, contending that members of the weaker sex would be so shocked by the brutality displayed in the ring that they would faint dead away. But Emma insisted on attending this fight, in which she had taken a distinct interest. Bat, Woods, and others helped her. "They rigged me out in a jockey's costume," Emma related years later, "but a wisp of hair betrayed me before I got to my seat [and] I was hustled out and kept in jail for a day."[21]

The incident was noteworthy enough for several newspapermen covering the fight to expand on the details.

With her hair cut short, and dressed in a black derby hat, black coat, and light trousers, they said, she managed to pass through two sets of doorkeepers before a Captain Burnett of the police force saw through her disguise and arrested her. Taken to a precinct station, she gave her name as Emma Walters, her age as thirty, her home as Denver, and her profession as variety performer. She was held on a cross-dressing violation charge until bailed out by boxer Jake Kilrain, who, without identifying him, told officials her husband was "a prominent resident of Denver."[22]

Although he was not her husband at the time, Bat Masterson, the "prominent resident of Denver," was enthralled by the woman who could share the joys of prizefighting with him, and he would claim Emma as his wife for the thirty years remaining of his life.

Having seen both Fitzsimmons and Dempsey in action at San Francisco, Bat was convinced the Australian was the better fighter, and got down heavy wagers on him. He was able to recoup some of his earlier losses when Ruby Bob knocked out "the Nonpareil" in the thirteenth round. The purse was $11,000, of which the winner took home $10,000. In addition to the money, Fitzsimmons won many fans, including Bat Masterson, who urged Fitz to challenge Sullivan for the heavyweight belt. Both Fitzsimmons and Jimmy Carroll, his chief second, scoffed at the suggestion, believing the great John L. was much too big and strong for the Australian. But, after watching James J. Corbett destroy Sullivan in their title match twenty-one months later, Fitz admitted he should have heeded Bat's advice.

At Masterson's request, Fitzsimmons seconded Billy Woods in a bout with veteran heavyweight Mike Conley, "the Ithaca Giant," at New Orleans. Woods knocked out Conley in two rounds and so impressed Fitz that he stole the young man from under Bat's wing and took him on the road as a sparring partner. A few months later Woods and Fitzsimmons had a falling out, became bitter enemies, and Woods rejoined Bat.

The two went to San Francisco, where Bat put Woods in the ring with Jack Davis, a big Leadville miner who had scored two controversial victories over John Clow. The bout, held at the Pacific Athletic Club for a $3,000 purse, was a grudge match from the start. Masterson and Woods despised Davis because of the two disputed bouts with their friend, Clow. Bob Fitzsimmons, who had alienated both Bat and Woods, was seconding Davis. Jack Dempsey, recently stripped of his title by Fitzsimmons, refereed. After twelve bruising rounds, Woods knocked Davis down several times in the thirteenth. Fitzsimmons threw in the towel, or "skied the wipe," as the surrender sign was known in the trade, and climbed in the ring. Woods, still full of fight, rushed at him, swinging with both hands, but Fitzsimmons, always the clever boxer, fended off the attack until Dempsey finally restored order.

Bat remained in the San Francisco area about two months, staying at Sausalito across the bay, where Parson Davies was training Peter Jackson for an important fight with Jim Corbett. It was here that Masterson discovered that boat travel was terribly disruptive to his stomach. He suffered from seasickness on every one of the many five-mile ferryboat trips he made across the bay.

The Jackson-Corbett fight-to-the-finish battle for a $10,000 purse was held at the California Club on May 21, 1891. It was unusual in that the referee stood outside the ropes with two judges seated on a raised platform behind him. Both contestants were clever boxers, and neither could gain any appreciable advantage over the other. Referee Hiram Cook called a halt after sixty-one rounds and declared the match "no contest." Since the battle had not been fought to a finish, the club managers balked at dividing the entire purse, claiming the principals had not carried out their agreement, and offered each fighter $1,000 only. The fighters and their backers objected strongly to this suggestion and called on Bat Masterson to settle the dispute. The referee, not the fighters, had stopped the bout, he argued, and therefore the principals were entitled to even shares of the full prize money. But he failed to convince the promoters, who finally gave each fighter $2,500 and kept the remaining $5,000.

Masterson and Woods spent much of 1892 at the booming mining town of Creede, Colorado, where Bat managed the gambling tables in Mart Watrous's Denver Exchange while Woods handled the saloon and restaurant business. The establishment featured Saturday night prizefights, with Woods taking on all challengers and Bat acting as referee. Not surprisingly, Woods lost none of these bouts.

Billy Woods was not shot to death in Creede, as has been reported in several books,[23] but continued to fight professionally for several more years. His later career was without Bat's guidance, for the two amicably dissolved their alliance after returning to Denver. About the turn of the century Woods went to Hawaii and eventually became warden of the penitentiary at Honolulu.

In September 1892 Bat was back in New Orleans to take part in what was being billed as a "Carnival of Champions" at the Pelican Athletic Club. Title fights were scheduled for three successive nights. In the first Jack McAuliffe retained his lightweight title by knocking out Billy Myer in fifteen rounds. The next night featherweight champ George Dixon KO'd challenger Jack Skelly in eight. Then came the major attraction, a battle for the heavyweight championship between John L. Sullivan, who had held the title for ten years and was considered by many to be invincible, and "Gentleman Jim" Corbett, the flashy young "dancing master." Masterson kept time for Corbett, who entered the ring at 178 pounds, 34 pounds lighter than the champ. John L. was heavily favored in the betting. Bat, who had been greatly impressed by Corbett after seeing him fight Peter Jackson to a sixty-one round draw, and still convinced that Sullivan's fighting ability had been greatly exaggerated, got a sizable bet down on Corbett at four to one odds. His judgment, in this instance, was correct. Corbett controlled the fight from the opening bell until he knocked Sullivan out in the twenty-first round.

From that day forward Bat Masterson would always sing the praises of "Gentleman Jim" Corbett. The dancing master from California was, he said, "the swiftest and cleverest big man the prize ring ever had," a smart fighter who could move so fast "a bullet could not hit him."[24] (Only twice did he ever bet against Corbett. He had wagered on Peter Jackson in that memorable San Francisco bout, but lost no money when the affair was called a draw. Then in 1894 when Corbett faced Charlie Mitchell, Bat allowed his better judgment to be overcome by his affection for the Englishman and bet from his heart and not his head.)

GUNFIGHTER IN GOTHAM

For a short period, Masterson managed heavyweight Denver Ed Smith, a fast, clever, two-handed puncher who easily won several matches in Colorado under Bat's guidance. But Smith was unreliable and, Bat suspected, lacked sand. Their association ended when Smith ran out on an engagement and incurred the Masterson wrath.

In the spring of 1893 Bat was back in New Orleans, where Bob Fitzsimmons was to defend his middleweight title against Jim Hall, who had given Ruby Bob one of his few defeats. There he was the guest of Squire Abingdon Baird, the wealthy English patron of Charlie Mitchell. Others in Baird's party were Mitchell, Hall, Jack McAuliffe, Howard Hackett of the *New York Morning World*, and Teddy Bailey, the squire's private secretary. Baird led this crowd on a constant round of partying before the fight and insisted on picking up all bills. After all that carousing, Hall was an easy mark for Fitzsimmons, who knocked him out cold in the fourth round.

Also on the fight card at the Crescent City Club was Denver Ed Smith, now handled by John J. Quinn and Michael J. "One-Eyed Buck" Connelly. Smith was to meet Australian heavyweight Joe Goddard, who outweighed him by thirty pounds. Only hours before fight time, Quinn and Connelly called on Masterson. They said the temperamental and unpredictable Denver Ed had absolutely refused to enter the ring unless Bat Masterson was in his corner. "Tell the big bum to go to blazes," Bat snapped, but after further pleading, he agreed to discuss the matter with the fighter. They met, and a very contrite Denver Ed begged Bat to second him. Relenting finally, Masterson worked Smith's corner that night and watched Denver Ed, fighting like a tiger, batter Goddard unmercifully before knocking him out in the seventeenth round.

Billy Madden had bet on Goddard, and Bat's decision to second Smith, he said, cost him $1,250. He told Masterson he would have paid him well to work the other corner instead. "Smith, even if he had got into the ring, would have climbed out as soon as he saw you in Goddard's corner," he said.[25]

A different spin was put on this tale a few years later in an account, perhaps apocryphal, that appeared in the *Rocky Mountain News*. Bat climbed into the ring that night, according to this story, with the handle of a derringer protruding from each hip pocket. The guns were there to intimidate Smith, who was terrified of Goddard but feared Masterson's guns even more, having been warned that Bat's punishment for cowardice in the ring was instant death. "Denver Ed Smith," said the *News*, "would have jumped over the ropes a dozen rounds before he was forced into victory had it not been for Masterson and his hip pockets."[26]

By 1893 Masterson was gaining national attention as a sports figure, although his gunfighting reputation was not forgotten. The *National Police Gazette* that year crowned him "the king of Western sporting men," who could be found at every important fight. He was characterized as "a general sport [who] backs pugilists, can play any game on the green with a full deck and handles a Bowie or a revolver with the determination of a Napoleon." Only through "great presence of mind and alertness with his gun" had he avoided "being plugged with lead." Although gentlemanly in his ways, he would neither give nor brook an insult and would stand by a friend against all odds.[27]

A year later the *Illustrated Sporting West* called Masterson "one of the best judges of pugilists in America," who could pick the winner of an important fight nine times out of ten.[28]

With the introduction of Marquess of Queensberry rules, prizefights, euphemistically called "pugilistic exhibitions," were now being permitted in Denver. Early in 1893 one of these bouts turned into a wild melee when Masterson tangled with Reddy Gallagher, the fighter who had cost him dearly in the Young Mitchell bout at San Francisco three years earlier. Gallagher was matched with black middleweight Jem Smith before 3,000 spectators at Coliseum Hall. Masterson was in Smith's corner. From the opening bell Smith repeatedly dropped to the floor after receiving a light blow, only to jump up and hit his opponent while Gallagher was appealing to the referee. He was on the canvas when the round ended, and Bat climbed into the ring to assist his fighter to his corner. In a rage Gallagher struck Masterson, knocking him down. Bat jumped up, and he and Smith both attacked Gallagher. This precipitated a general brawl with fighters, seconds, and the referee all swinging wildly. When order was restored and the second round began, Smith continued his tactics. His Irish temper at a boiling point, the redheaded fighter reacted to shouted insults from Masterson by reaching over the ropes and striking him in the face. Bat leaped back into the ring and rushed at Gallagher, but a squad of police intervened and prevented further fisticuffs. Gallagher was declared the winner of the bout on a foul. The affair received nation-wide publicity, including an account in the *Police Gazette* that ended on an ominous note: "Trouble between Gallagher and Masterson is expected when the two men come together."[29] In a letter to that publication Masterson denied that Gallagher ever got the best of him as had been suggested in some eastern press reports. The redhead could not beat him at any game on earth, he declared, "not even with his Mawleys."[30] ("Mawlies," or "Maulies," was English slang for fists.)

Bat refereed many fights in Denver, including one that resulted in tragedy. On August 4, 1893, Bobby Taylor, "The Sailor Kid," met Kid Robinson in a match at the Rambler Cycling Club. After twenty-two lively rounds, referee Masterson called the bout a draw. While dressing after the fight, Taylor suddenly fainted. He never regained consciousness and died the next day. Club manager Dock Carberry, Masterson, and Robinson were arrested. Bat issued a statement that he believed Taylor's death resulted from injuries received after the fight when he fell, striking his head on a chair. There the matter ended, but Taylor's death reinforced the view of many in Denver that prizefighting was brutal and uncivilized.

Later that year Bat was in Florida, where Charlie Mitchell was to meet Jim Corbett in a heavyweight title bout at Jacksonville on January 25, 1894, for a $20,000 purse and a $5,000 side bet. Masterson, of course, would have been delighted to see his English friend win, but odds against Mitchell's chances were running three to one, and Bat himself had reservations, which he expressed in a lengthy letter to the *National Police Gazette*. Published in the December 30, 1893, issue, it was an early attempt by Masterson at written analysis of the relative merits of two boxers and his prediction of the outcome when they met in the ring. Corbett was, he said, "a sturdy gladiator, a man [of] pluck, a first-class ring general" with decided advantages in height, weight, and reach. But he considered Mitchell without peer in a battle according to London rules, and would not have hesitated to predict his victory under the old system. Since Queensberry was to govern, he found predicting a winner difficult, especially as he was admittedly torn by his long friendship with the English fighter. He called the affair a tossup.

He did not mention that Mitchell, who weighed more than 200 pounds when he began training, had shed 40 and would enter the ring under 160. Bat feared that the drastic weight loss had sapped his strength and privately urged his friend to bow out of the match. But Mitchell's manager and father-in-law, Pony Moore, scoffed at that suggestion and assured Charlie that he would demolish the California dancing master.

In the end Bat took the odds and bet heavily on Mitchell. It was money down the drain. Corbett won easily, knocking the Englishman out cold in the third round.

Mitchell's handlers dragged the bloodied and unconscious fighter to his stool and worked feverishly to revive him. Regaining his senses after a full two minutes, Mitchell turned to Bat and mumbled an admission that he had no chance against Corbett and should have heeded his friend's advice.

Masterson took the Mitchell defeat very hard and for a time considered getting completely out of the fight game. "I'm a dead sore man, and this winds me up with prize fighters. I'll never have any business with any of them," he was quoted as saying.[31] By allowing his fondness for Mitchell to overcome his better judgment, he had suffered a severe financial setback. According to a Denver paper, having "risked his pile" on Mitchell, betting "all the money he had or could borrow," he was still working his way out of debt more than a year later.[32]

But the fight game was in Masterson's blood, of course, and he could not simply walk away from it. A few months after the Mitchell debacle he was back arranging boxing matches, promoting young fighters, and refereeing bouts. Then in May 1895 came a sharp reversal of fortune. "Bat Masterson Tumbles into the Softest Sort of Soap," announced the *Rocky Mountain News* of June 6.

George Gould, the thirty-one-year-old son of financier and railroad tycoon Jay Gould, had received death threats, and the father called on newly installed New York City police commissioner Theodore Roosevelt for protection. Seeking "a sure shot, a quick shot, and one who could be counted on not to hit the wrong person," Roosevelt thought of western sportsman Bat Masterson, whose six-shooter exploits had been widely publicized. He directed Thomas Byrnes, his superintendent of police, to wire Denver, asking Masterson to come to the big city and take employment as young Gould's bodyguard. Bat quickly boarded an eastbound train.[33]

Masterson had "at last struck it rich," said a Denver paper, "hobnobbing with George Gould and other distinguished nabobs of Gotham." For seeing that George was not "sandbagged, held up, buncoed, or kidnapped," Bat was making "an abundance of long green."[34]

In New York Masterson wallowed in a field of clover richer even than New Orleans during the heady days with Squire Abingdon Baird. In a letter to a Denver friend, he said he had gone fishing with the Goulds on their yacht and attended the races at Gravesend with George, who gave him $5,000 to play the horses. He had won $4,500 betting the nags, but lost it all the next day. He added nonchalantly that he guessed he would "have to touch George for another $5,000." He liked New York so well, he said, that he did not expect to ever return to Colorado.[35]

Masterson's initial visit to New York City was indeed pleasant, what with yachting and high-roller gambling, but his "soft snap" hobnobs with Gotham nabobs came to an end when the New York police apprehended George Gould's stalker. Bat did not remain in the eastern metropolis as he had hinted, but his decision seven years later to make Gotham his home was no doubt influenced by fond memories of that stay.

Arriving back in Denver on July 8, he was interviewed by a *Times* reporter and denied the Gould bodyguard story. "That Gould business was just foolish enough to fool foolish people," Bat said. As "a sport of high degree" he would "never stoop so low." The reporter quoted him, but suspecting Bat was just pulling his leg, noted that the "sport of high degree" had arrived in "Miss Helen Gould's special train."[36]

Early in 1896 Masterson attended one of the most bizarre promotions in the history of pugilism. Following his victory over Charlie Mitchell, Jim Corbett had announced his retirement as undefeated heavyweight champion. In November 1895 Peter Maher of Ireland and Steve O'Donnell met in a battle to claim the vacated title. Maher quickly put O'Donnell away. As Bat put it: "Peter and Steve had a brief argument one evening with the gloves over Corbett's crown. Peter whanged Steve on the jaw before you could turn around to expectorate and the Corbett title belonged to Peter."[37] But middleweight champion Bob Fitzsimmons, who had once whipped Maher, objected, saying that the Irishman held no legitimate claim to the title without facing him again. Dallas gambler Dan Stuart, seeing an opportunity for a promotional coup, signed Maher and Fitzsimmons for a bout to settle the dispute. The match, scheduled for El Paso, Texas, in February 1896, was advertised as the centerpiece of a "Great Fistic Carnival." In addition to prizefights, sports fans were to be entertained with shooting contests, baseball and football games, and even a bullfight.

Sporting men from around the country poured into El Paso. Bat Masterson, looking "suave and younger than ever," according to press reports, brought a contingent of boxers and gamblers from Denver and told reporters he had arranged for a special train to bring others from all over Colorado and as far away as Salt Lake City and Helena and Butte in Montana. The Pinkerton Detective Agency had also hired him to head a security force assigned to maintain order at the fight scene.[38]

In a letter to a friend, Bat predicted Maher was a "pipe" (a lead-pipe cinch) to win the contest, and added that he was sufficiently confident in his own judgment to back it with "a wee bit of money." Maher, he was sure, could defeat Fitz or any fighter other than Corbett, who was "simply invincible."[39] But after watching the two men work out—Fitzsimmons in Juarez across the Rio Grande from El Paso and Maher in Las Cruces, New Mexico—he lost much of his enthusiasm for the Irishman and told a reporter the winner would be the one who landed the first heavy blow.[40]

The "Great Fistic Carnival" gained more national attention when, under pressure from religious leaders opposed to boxing, Texas governor C. A. Culbertson dispatched Adjutant General W. H. Mabry and some thirty Texas Rangers to El Paso with orders to prevent the battle from occurring on Texas soil. A force of Mexican Rurales patrolled the south side of the Rio Grande to see that Stuart did not stage his fight in Juarez. To block the promoter from moving the affair over the line into New Mexico Territory, Congress rushed through a measure prohibiting prizefighting in any U.S. territory, and deputy U.S. marshals poured into El Paso to enforce the law.

Because of his gunfighting notoriety, Bat was the target of Ranger harassment in El Paso. Noting this, a local paper came to his defense, pointing out that there were "many notches on his six-shooter, but they were put there while he was in discharge of his duty in upholding the law" and gave the Rangers no reason to bother him. "If the rangers are hunting men with notches on their pistols they need not leave Texas to find them."[41]

Bat was also upset by a rumor spread by the Rangers that he, the man responsible for controlling pickpockets at the fight, lost $900 to the light-fingered gentry in El Paso. The story, heatedly denied by El Paso police chief Ed Fink, still was reported in the local press.

The entire episode left Masterson with contempt for the Texas Rangers. Still angry two decades later, he characterized the famed lawmen as "a four-flushing band of swashbucklers," and reviled their commander. W. H. Mabry was full of "affected dignity and self-importance," he said, "better qualified to superintend a public soup kitchen than to command a troop of half-civilized warriors." While on the subject of southwestern law enforcement, he took a shot at the Mexican Rurales also, dismissing them as simply "a body of armed horsemen [who] were nearly all outlaws at one time or another."[42]

In El Paso Masterson renewed acquaintanceship with George Ade, a young reporter for the *Chicago Record* whom he had first met at New Orleans in 1892 at the time of the Sullivan-Corbett fight. Ade talked Bat into writing a piece for his paper, and Masterson took the opportunity to defend the sport of boxing and attack its opponents. This would become a recurrent theme in his writing for the next quarter century. "That all this commotion has been stirred up because two men are going to box with five-ounce gloves [is] utterly ridiculous," he wrote. Boxers faced less danger, he insisted, than "jockeys [who] will be killed, football players mangled and professional bicyclists maimed." He was confident that Dan Stuart, under attack "since he launched his canoe on the tempestuous waters of the sea of pugilistic enterprises," would be successful.[43]

On February 20 a special thirteen-car train left El Paso for an undisclosed destination. Aboard were the two fighters, their entourages, Mabry's Rangers, and about 200 boxing fans. When twenty-five miles down the track it was discovered that hoodlums without tickets had clambered onto the car roofs, Bat Masterson, head of security, stopped the train and forced them off to begin a long walk back.

There is a persistent story that Bat and famed Texas Ranger Captain Bill McDonald had a tense confrontation during this trip. A stop was made at Sanderson, and many aboard, including Masterson and McDonald, crowded into a Chinese restaurant to catch a bite to eat. When a waiter incurred Bat's wrath and he moved to strike him, McDonald interfered, goes the tale, and for a moment it looked as though these two legendary western lawmen would tangle. But Masterson backed off, and nothing further happened. This story originated in a biography of McDonald authored by Albert Bigelow Paine and published in 1909. Bat chanced upon it a decade after the book appeared. In several columns he adamantly denied any such thing happened. He had seen no "Chinaman" on the trip, he insisted, nor did he have a quarrel with McDonald, whom he had known for years. He denounced the entire account as "a brazen, cowardly lie," concocted by the author to make McDonald appear heroic at Bat's expense. He called Paine "an accomplished liar, a hack writer who eked out a precarious living peddling his goulash to magazines at so much a word."[44] Despite Masterson's vehement protests, the story has become a part of the legend of both western figures.

On the afternoon of February 21 the train stopped at Langtry, Texas, almost 400 miles from El Paso, and disgorged its passengers in front of the Jersey Lily Saloon of another colorful frontier character, Judge Roy Bean, the self-styled "Law West of the Pecos." There a rude bridge led to an island in the Rio Grande, and a hastily constructed canvas wall surrounded a prize ring where the big fight was to be held.

Security chief Masterson took up his station at the arena entrance, making sure the $20 ticket price was paid by all and there were no gatecrashers. Dan Stuart convinced the Texas Rangers that the island was in Mexico and the peace and tranquility of Texas would not be disturbed. Having no tickets, the Rangers sat down on the low bluffs overlooking the river and the arena wall and waited for the show to begin.

But at this point Fitzsimmons almost brought the whole proceeding to a halt by threatening to pull out. A motion picture company had provided the winner-take-all purse of $10,000 on condition that the fighters claimed no share of the film profits. In El Paso Fitzsimmons had objected to this arrangement and threatened to back out if he wasn't given a financial interest in the pictures. Stuart had assured him that the movie company had abandoned the idea, but upon arrival at the fight site Fitzsimmons found a camera set up and ready to roll. The Australian kicked up a fuss, but finally agreed to go on with the fight, vowing "to knock Maher out so quickly that the picture will be nothing but a blur."

He made good on his threat, reducing the Irishman to unconsciousness in one minute and twenty-five seconds. The pictures were of such poor quality they were never shown, and the movie company "got nothing for its $10,000 but a lot of trouble and a blur."[45]

Bat Masterson also was handed a financial setback by the fight. He had bet on Maher and returned to Denver with his wallet once again flattened.

His fortunes did not improve later that year when Fitzsimmons and "Sailor Tom" Sharkey met in a San Francisco ring. Bat was not in attendance for this fight, but, having much greater respect for Fitz after seeing him demolish Maher, got down his limited bankroll on the Australian with Denver gamblers. Named as referee for the bout held on December 2, 1896, was Bat's old pal Wyatt Earp, who ignited a critical firestorm in the sporting world when he stopped the fight in the eighth round and awarded the victory to Sharkey on a foul. The decision created an uproar, with public charges that Earp had been bought off by gambling cronies. Investigations and hearings followed, but in the end nothing was proved or disproved, and the controversial decision remained.

Interviewed the morning after the fight, Earp scoffed at the suggestion that he or his pals had profited by Sharkey's win. He pointed to the case of the man he called "the best friend I have on earth." Said Wyatt: "If I had any leanings they would have been toward Fitzsimmons, for I know that Bat Masterson, who is in Denver tonight, had every dollar he could raise on Fitzsimmons."[46] To another reporter he said: "I am very sure that Bat Masterson lost a great deal of money on this fight, but I have always been able to decide against my own money, and my friends can stand the consequence of such a decision."[47]

For Bat, one of the consequences of Earp's controversial decision was another personal scrimmage. Shortly after the fight he tangled with a Denver politician named Felix O'Neill, who had also bet on Fitzsimmons and blamed Wyatt Earp for his loss. O'Neill was loudly denouncing Earp in a Denver saloon, calling him a scoundrel, a thief, and a bully, when he was overheard by Masterson, who defended his friend, declaring there was no fairer, squarer, straighter man on earth than Wyatt Earp. According to a newspaper account, Masterson calmly tried to reason with O'Neill, but when the furious politician cursed him, Bat ended the argument with his fists, laying O'Neill "up for repairs" in a brief fight that had no referee to create controversy.[48]

There was yet another sequel to this affair. The battered and publicly humiliated politician O'Neill plotted revenge, according to early Masterson biographer Alfred Henry Lewis. "Mr. O'Neal [sic], with a six-shooter in each overcoat pocket, and a hand on each six-shooter, sent forward a drunken ruffian to attack Mr. Masterson, with full and fell intent on Mr. O'Neal's part of 'bumping off' Mr. Masterson when once entangled with the drunken one." But Bat "knocked the drunken one senseless with his left fist, while with his right hand he abruptly acquired the drop on the designing Mr. O'Neal. With that never-erring six-shooter upon him, Mr. O'Neal's empty hands came out of his pockets, and went in the air, like winking." O'Neal pleaded for his life and Masterson's trigger finger itched, but, lowering the hammer of his gun, Bat laid the barrel across the politician's head, dropping him unconscious to the street beside his stooge. Later, O'Neal, his head swathed in bandages, sent an emissary to Bat, asking him to come to his bedside so he could apologize and "explain." Bat agreed, but told the messenger to warn O'Neal to "keep his hands outside the blankets while he's doing his 'explaining.'"[49]

As Wyatt Earp said, Masterson was able to "stand the consequences" of that controversial decision, but those consequences had been severe. Not only did Bat lose a good deal of money on the fight at a time when he could ill afford it, he almost lost his life. Although he never criticized his friend's action publicly, the fight remained a sore point in his memory two decades later. When Fitzsimmons died in 1917, Masterson wrote four lengthy articles detailing the Australian's brilliant ring career, but never once mentioned the Sharkey fight and the Earp decision that cost him dearly.

Acceding to public clamor for a clarification of the muddled heavyweight title picture, Jim Corbett came out of retirement and agreed to a championship match with Fitzsimmons to be held in Carson City, Nevada, in March 1897. Bat's record of backing losers in important prizefights beginning with the Mitchell-Corbett calamity in Florida, through the Maher-Fitzsimmons fiasco in Texas and the Sharkey-Fitzsimmons misadventure in California, was unbroken by this promotion.

He was certain Corbett could defeat Fitzsimmons. "He'll by pudding for you," he told Gentleman Jim when he stopped in Denver on his way to Carson City.[50] On his way west to see the fight a few weeks later, Bat was interviewed by a reporter in Laramie, Wyoming, and predicted a Corbett victory within six rounds.[51]

Wyatt Earp was also in Carson City to see the fight, and the two old friends had an opportunity to discuss in detail Earp's controversial decision three months earlier. The Carson City chief of police authorized Masterson to head a body of special officers charged with maintaining order at the fight, and, of course, Wyatt Earp was one of Bat's first enlistees. This security force was no doubt the basis for a wild tale spun twenty years later by Bob Edgren, an eager young reporter and cartoonist for the *San Francisco Examiner* in 1897, and later a bitter enemy of Bat Masterson in New York. Writing in 1917, Edgren said he recalled vividly "Wyatt Earp, a famous gun fighter," and his "pair of blue-barreled guns" at the head of some "twenty tough citizens, all heavily armed," at the Carson City fight scene. He illustrated his column with a drawing of gunmen seated at ringside, pistols in their hands "all cocked and primed to shoot everything in sight to pieces." Of course nothing like this ever happened, as Bat made clear in a column ridiculing Edgren.[52]

The fight was held on March 17, 1897, in the first open-air arena built especially for boxing. Fitzsimmons knocked Corbett out in the fourteenth round with a blow to the body, afterward famous as the solar plexus punch. Bat, who had backed Gentleman Jim with hard cash, lost again. But that fight had a more significant effect on Masterson's life than the damage to his bankroll, for it was at Carson City that a Denver fight fan named Otto C. Floto first met Missourian Fred G. Bonfils, owner of the *Denver Post*, a meeting that was to affect Masterson's future profoundly.

— 2 —

THE WOMEN IN HIS LIFE

*W. B. Masterson is well known in this city. He is a handsome man,
and one who pleases the ladies.*

Rocky Mountain News

One of the oft-repeated errors in the story of the life of Bat Masterson
is the place and date of his birth. He himself was largely responsible
for the confusion, as he gave conflicting and incorrect information
regarding his origins to interviewers, census enumerators, court officials, friends, acquaintances, and apparently, even his wife. Usually,
but not always, he gave Illinois as his place of birth and the year as
1854.[1] Those close to him and presumably knowledgeable about his
origins—men like his brother Tom and his close friend and fictional
biographer, Alfred Henry Lewis—repeated his inaccuracies, further
embedding them into the Masterson legend. Lewis reported in 1907
that Masterson was born in Iroquois County, Illinois, "about fifty-
three years ago," or in 1854.[2] Newspapers picked up these assertions
and repeated them.[3] In a 1937 interview, Tom Masterson said Bat
was born "on a farm near Fairfield, Illinois, November 24, 1853."[4]
Fairfield is the county seat of Wayne County, more than one hundred
miles from Iroquois County.

In 1910 Bat told George Ade that he was born in Watseka, county
seat of Iroquois County.[5] Vaudeville performer Earl "Skater" Reynolds, a close friend, in 1921 placed Bat's birthplace as "the south
bank of the Iroquois River, just over the Indiana state line, near
Momence, Illinois."[6] Momence is in Kankakee County, thirty miles

from Watseka. Richard O'Connor, the first to write a full-length biography of Masterson, simply gave Iroquois County as the site of his birth and provided no date.[7]

Bat deliberately created this obfuscation for a very good reason: to hide the fact that he was not born in the United States, was never naturalized, and, although not an American citizen, had voted, taken an active role in political activity, and held public office illegally. He was a Canadian, born in Henryville, county of Iberville, province of Quebec, on November 26, 1853, to Thomas and Catherine Masterson and christened Bertholomiew, the French spelling of Bartholomew. All of his six siblings, four brothers and two sisters, were also born at Henryville. Edward, a year older than Bat, and James, two years younger, would become, like Bat, buffalo hunters and frontier peace officers. Their younger brothers—Thomas, Jr., born in 1858, and George, in 1860—followed other career paths. The sisters, Nellie, born in 1857, and Emma, in 1862, were also younger.[8]

Soon after the birth of Emma the Masterson family left Canada for the United States and, after a short sojourn in northern New York State, began a trek westward. Through most of the Civil War decade of the 1860s the Mastersons made their home in Illinois, the land of Lincoln. Thomas, a farmer, aided by his older sons, evidently worked farms in the area either on shares or as a day laborer; no record has been found that he owned property in the state.

In 1905 a feature newspaper article entitled "'Bat' Masterson, 'Gun Fighter' and Deputy Marshal" reported that Bat was "a native of Chicago" and he and his brothers, Edward and James, attended and were all graduated from Douglas High School in that city.[9] Actually, the Masterson brothers never had the benefit of a high school education, and what formal learning they received was undoubtedly delivered by "marms" in one-room schoolhouses in the small towns of Illinois. Because a single letter composed by Jim Masterson has survived, we know that at least one brother was barely literate.[10] But Bat, an avid reader all his life, was self-educated, and, loving the English language, learned to express himself well with the written word, adopted journalism as his profession, and succeeded remarkably.

"Bartholomew," or even worse, "Bertholomiew," was too cumbersome a name to call a young boy in to do his chores, and from his earliest days the members of the Masterson family referred to the boy as "Bart" or the even simpler "Bat." Eschewing the name Bartholomew, Masterson took "William Barclay" as his legal name early in his adult life.[11] As with his citizenship, he never bothered with legalization of the name change. He signed most legal documents simply with the initials "W. B.," but his will, filed on August 3, 1907, in New York County, New York, contained the complete signature, "William Barclay Masterson." In this will Masterson did "give, devise and bequeath" to his "beloved wife, Emma," all his property, "to have and to hold the same forever."[12]

Having never concerned himself with the legality of his name or citizenship, it is not surprising that Masterson's matrimonial status was also unencumbered by legal niceties. Brother Tom said that Bat and Emma were married on November 21, 1891.[13] Bat and Emma were enumerated in the federal census of 1900 as man and wife, living in Denver. The length of the marriage was said to be ten years, indicating a union about the time given by Tom Masterson. However, to date no official record of this union has been found, and it is very likely Bat and Emma, both members of the sporting and theatrical world where common law marriage was regularly practiced, never bothered with a civil or religious ceremony, but simply lived together and called themselves husband and wife.[14]

Emma was not the first woman to attach herself to the arm of the famous western celebrity and glory in the title "Mrs. W. B. Masterson." Bat, "a handsome man and one who pleases the ladies," as a Denver paper described him, in his younger years had pleased many a lady, and some females who were not so ladylike.

Enumerated in the federal census of 1880 at Dodge City, Bat was listed as a twenty-five-year-old laborer, living with Annie Ladue, "a 19 year-old concubine."[15] There is no evidence that this relationship lasted any length of time. When Bat departed Dodge City the following year he sold his house to an "Annie," who lived on in the town for many years, but as a Dodge City historian has pointed out, "There were many Annies living in Dodge City at that time; their last names changed at regular intervals depending on whose bed they were sharing."[16]

By 1884 Bat was evidently keeping regular company with a woman calling herself his wife. The *Dodge City Democrat* of July 5 of that year referred to a visit by "guests of Mr. and Mrs. Bat Masterson," and on August 30 the *Rocky Mountain News* noted the arrival at Denver's Brunswick Hotel of "W. B. Masterson and wife." Who this woman was remains a mystery.

Until recently very little was also known about the woman who shared the life of Bat Masterson for three decades, for Emma has always remained a dim figure in the shadow of her husband's celebrity. Now, thanks to information unearthed by Lot Grafton, a resident of New York City; Chris Penn of England, a diligent and dedicated Masterson researcher; and Roy Adams, a descendent of Emma's family, a portrait has emerged of a tough and feisty woman with a history almost as unusual and fascinating as that of her famous husband.

Four years younger than Bat, Emma Matilda Walter was born on July 10, 1857, in Roxborough, a rural ward of West Philadelphia, Pennsylvania. Her father, John Walter, born at Roxborough in 1827, was the son of James and Jane Walter. Her mother, Catherine Bantom,[17] the daughter of Myers and Maria Bantom, was born a year before John in Lower Marion Township, Montgomery County, Pennsylvania.

Emma was the middle of three sisters.[18] Four months after the Civil War broke out her father, a teamster, signed on for a three-year enlistment with the Sixty-Fifth Pennsylvania Volunteers. He saw service as a picket and scout in the tidewater lowlands of Virginia. Under constant exposure to cold and damp that winter, he contracted typhoid fever and died at Camp Griffin, Virginia, on February 22, 1862. His body was shipped to Philadelphia for burial.[19]

Catherine Walter applied for a widow's pension and received it—all of $6 a month. For a time she and her three young daughters—aged seven, four, and three when their father died—lived with Catherine's brother in Montgomery County. Later they moved in with Catherine's widowed mother at her home at 65 Sloan Street in West Philadelphia. Catherine Walter never remarried, but raised her daughters alone, augmenting her meager widow's pension by taking in boarders and work as a practical nurse. She died in Philadelphia on December 21, 1907.[20]

(Bat's mother, Catherine McGurk Masterson, died at the family farm in Sedgwick County, Kansas, three months later, in March 1908. His father lived to be ninety-four, and died just shortly before Bat in 1921.)

While still in her early teens Emma left home to try her luck at theatrical work, one of the few professions open to women of the period. An attractive young girl, she soon caught the eye of Edward W. "Ed" Moulton, a professional foot racer, and the two were married in Philadelphia on January 13, 1873. Moulton was about twenty-four, and Emma was still six months shy of her sixteenth birthday.[21]

Foot racing was a popular sport at the time, especially among the gambling element, as it was an easy contest to fix, and Ed Moulton was held in high regard as a runner in the eastern states. Called "the Gopher Boy," he was rated in 1874 one of the top three men in the country in races over one hundred yards. Perhaps he was too good, for later that year racing opponents and the opportunity for prize money became scarce. By September Moulton was scheduling races against his wife, spotting her a 25-yard head start over a 125-yard course, and peddling photos of Emma and himself in their running costumes. The attraction for both race attendees and photo purchasers was the chance to see the pretty young girl clad in racing tights. There was such interest in the spectacle at the Berks County Fair in Pennsylvania, according to a newspaper report, that the race was never run because "the Grangers crowded around so to see the woman in tights that there no chance to run."[22]

When Emma beat her husband by two feet in a race at Northampton, Massachusetts, the following month, Moulton offered to back her with hard cash in a race against any other woman in the country. Challengers were not forthcoming, and Emma at seventeen retired from competitive racing, but Moulton continued to sell his photos, attempting to capitalize on the image of his wife in tights.

Emma then took up Indian club swinging, a fad popular at the time with physical culturists, and soon became so proficient at juggling and swinging the bowling-pin-shaped wooden clubs that she could demand pay for her performances. By 1877 she was engaged at theaters in Chicago, Providence, and Boston and advertised in theatrical publications as the "Queen of Clubs, in her artistic Indian club exercises, introducing new and difficult wrist motions, showing wonderful science and endurance."[23]

In 1878 Emma joined the Tony Denier "Humpty Dumpty" touring company as a supporting act for the headliner, Grimaldi, a clown. Billed as "The Champion of All Lady Club-Swingers in her artistic delineations of female physical culture—the embodiment of grace and beauty," she received excellent reviews during an extensive tour that closed with an engagement at Haverly's Theater in Chicago in the summer of 1879.

With their respective careers keeping Emma and Ed Moulton apart for most of a year, a resulting marital crisis is not surprising. As the *Chicago Tribune* reported in its August 17 edition:

> The Tony Denier company furnishes the latest scandal. The champion club-swinger, Emma Moulton, is charged with running away from her husband, E. W. Moulton, at Minneapolis, to join Frank Clifton, a horizontal-bar athlete traveling with the show. Clifton was last evening arrested upon a warrant charging him with adultery, but Mrs. Moulton could not be found. The injured husband is willing not to prosecute if Emma will return to her mother's home at Philadelphia, and quit forever the variety business, which he always objected to her entering. Clifton pleads not guilty, of course, but Moulton says he can prove that they roomed together for a week at No. 409 West Madison Street.

It appears that the Moultons reconciled after this marital contretemps. Emma left the Denier touring company, and Moulton dropped the charges against Clifton.[24]

Emma did not return to her mother's home in Philadelphia and retire from the theatrical world as her husband wished, however. She was in Philadelphia in May of the next year, but it was as a performer. She joined an all-female clog-dancing team and over the next few years appeared in engagements with theatrical units playing in the Midwest.[25]

In the spring of 1884 Ed and Emma traveled farther west and, as reported in the *Rocky Mountain News*, "Ed. W. Moulton, the well-known athlete and trainer, arrived in Denver last week, with the purpose of remaining for some time. Mrs. Moulton has an engagement for three weeks at Belmont & Hanson's rink, to give exhibitions with the Indian clubs, in which this lady is decidedly expert."[26]

Emma may have become acquainted with Bat Masterson, who was in and out of Denver frequently during this period and was a familiar figure in all the sporting and theatrical venues of the city, but if she did, she was not sufficiently enthralled to remain there, for later in the year she was again touring the Midwest with a company called Virgie Comalobo's Meteors. A reviewer for the *St. Paul Globe* thought her "wonderful club swinging" was the top attraction of the show, adding that she "also sang cleverly."[27]

Meanwhile Emma's husband, Ed Moulton, in 1886 had expanded his sports activity to include boxing and that year was involved in the promotion of a pair of Minneapolis ring contests. In one he backed Charlie Mitchell, Bat's close friend and favorite boxer, in a match with Patsy Cardiff. Since Bat attended this fight and was one of the officials, he and Moulton must have known each other by this time.

By 1886 Ed Moulton seems to have made Minneapolis his home with less frequent travel, but Emma continued to take her club-swinging act throughout cities in the Great Lakes region the following year. By early 1888 she was performing in the West again, first in Kansas City and then in the raucous mining camp at Leadville, Colorado, in March. Moving on to Denver in April, she was signed for a lengthy engagement at the Palace Theater.

An imposing two-story brick building at the corner of Blake and Fifteenth Streets in Denver's tenderloin, the Palace had been a city landmark for years. Owned and operated by Ed Chase and Ed Gaylord, leading gamblers of Denver, it provided, in addition to stage performances by some of the nation's leading vaudeville stars, seating for an audience of 750, a sixty-foot bar, and accommodation for 200 players at gambling tables overseen by twenty-five dealers. Long a target of reformers, the Palace was denounced by one cleric as a "death-trap to young men, a foul den of vice and corruption."[28]

If Emma Moulton had not met Bat Masterson in her brief Denver appearance two years earlier, she certainly got to know him well during her extended nine-month employment at the Palace, for Bat was a close friend of both Chase and Gaylord and frequented the Palace regularly.

In its issue of September 22, 1886, the *Rocky Mountain News* of Denver commented on the handsome W. B. Masterson "who pleases the ladies." One of the ladies he obviously pleased was variety theater performer Nellie McMahon, described by the paper as "a beautiful woman, with a fine wardrobe and a sweet voice." But vaudeville minstrel Lou Spencer claimed Nellie as his wife, and carryings-on by

Bat and Nellie in a theater box at California Hall led to the Spencer-Masterson clash and the later dustup with Bagsby.

Although the Denver paper reported that Nellie had filed for divorce from Spencer and "eloped" with Bat, and six months later newspapers were still referring to the two as husband and wife,[29] the liaison between them was short-lived. Nellie did not divorce Spencer (if she ever legally married him in the first place), and she certainly never married Masterson.

The Palace Theater, already branded an infamous resort by social reformers, came into greater disrepute when two murders were committed there within the space of a few weeks in the fall of 1888. Responding to a public outcry, the city aldermen revoked the Palace's license, but, after a quick change of management and a change of name to "The Mascot," business continued there.[30]

With the problems at the Palace, Emma Moulton took her act to another Denver variety house, Laura LeClair's Central Theater, but troubles with Ed continued to plague her. In March 1889 Denver police took Ed into custody as a con-game artist, a charge he later beat, but in the story of his arrest the *Rocky Mountain News* mentioned that Emma Moulton had run off to Los Angeles with Ed. H. Sheehan, a minstrel show comedian, and Moulton had to go there and bring his wife back. (If this tale was true, Emma, by cavorting with Sheehan, was risking serious retaliation from Sheehan's violence-prone wife, Ada Hulmes, who once tried to kill him and later shot and killed another lover in Silver City, New Mexico.)[31] But whether or not Emma was seeing other men, her marriage to Ed Moulton was falling apart, and, according to notices in the theatrical journals the Moultons appeared from this point on to have traveled separate paths. While Emma stayed close to Denver, Ed was recorded in many cities of the Midwest and in late 1889 went to England in company with a young sprinter with whom he had teamed, and did not return until March 1890.[32]

Meanwhile the Palace owners, Chase and Gaylord, had convinced the Denver city aldermen, probably by a cash transaction, that the license for their enterprise should be renewed, and in March 1889 the place reopened with W. B. Masterson as the new manager. In a notice he had published in the vaudeville trade papers Bat made it clear that he would run a tight ship:

Performers writing to this house for an engagement will state the quality and quantity of their wardrobes and amount of salary they will work for, not what they want, for we make all the allowances for a performer's gall. We care nothing about how they "split 'em up the back at Grand Rapids," or "How we knocked 'em silly on the coast."

Variety ladies with more than three husbands need not write to this house for a date.

The proprietor doesn't care whether the performers worked one or thirty seasons with Tony Pastor, all he expects of you is to please the hoboes of Blake Street.[33]

When the Palace, remodeled and with Masterson as manager, again opened its doors in April, Emma Moulton was one of the featured performers, and her engagement continued through the spring and summer months of 1889. It was during this period that she and Bat became close, more than just boss and employee. Then in September Nellie McMahon, the beauty with the "sweet voice" who had once been a consort of Bat Masterson, joined the Palace performing company, thereby triggering a crisis as two attractive, strong-willed women vied for the affections of one man. Within days Emma departed in a huff, taking a job at the New Central Theater, and the same trade paper issue announcing her departure reported that Bat Masterson had given up his position as manager of the Palace.[34]

After a short engagement at an Ogden, Utah, theater, Emma returned to Denver in June 1890 to appear on the stage of the newly opened Elitch Gardens. Finding that Nellie McMahon was dying and no longer was her rival for Bat's affections, she renewed her amorous relationship with Bat. Nellie died in Denver on September 21 of that year, a victim of "paralysis of the heart." She was only twenty-five years old.[35]

Emma was still married to Ed Moulton, but she and Masterson began living as husband and wife at this time. It was in January 1891 that Emma traveled to New Orleans with Bat to see the middleweight title bout between Bob Fitzsimmons and Jack Dempsey, and in her determined effort to witness the bout got herself arrested in her male jockey's costume.

Although, according to Tom Masterson, Bat and Emma were married in November of that year, Emma was still married to Ed Moulton in 1891. Bat and Emma may have exchanged private vows on that date and told relatives and friends that was the day of their betrothal, but Emma, quite wisely, was unwilling to have a formal marriage and risk a charge of bigamy.

In 1892 Emma accompanied Bat and his boxing protégé Billy Woods to Creede, a new boom camp in the Colorado Rockies, where Bat oversaw the gambling in the Denver Exchange and arranged boxing matches for Woods. At the first wedding held in the new camp Bat and Emma stood up for a couple who were married on March 7.[36]

Emma filed for divorce from Ed Moulton on June 29, 1893, claiming willful desertion and failure of support for more than a year. Moulton could not be found, and on November 9, 1893, the marriage was dissolved in the Arapahoe County Court.[37]

When enumerated in the 1910 U.S. Census, Bat and Emma said they had been married for seventeen years, indicating they had been joined in wedlock about 1893, or the year of Emma's divorce. If they were indeed married on November 21, the date specified by brother Tom, it has been suggested that the year he gave was wrong or misreported, and Bat and Emma were actually legally married, not in 1891, but in 1893, within two weeks of the divorce decree. We know that Bat entrained for the East in the late fall of 1893 to help prepare Charlie Mitchell for his January 1894 title bout with Jim Corbett at Jacksonville, Florida, and that Emma accompanied him. Perhaps she and Bat tied the knot that November somewhere in the eastern states, but, if so, to date no researcher has turned up that record.

About this time a writer for the *Kansas City Times* penned a detailed description of the man with whom Emma had chosen to spend the rest of her life. Bat Masterson, "the Denver sport," was, said the newsman,

> a man probably 38 years of age, although looking two or three years younger; about five feet nine inches tall and weighing, say, 165 pounds; his hair dark and cropped closely to a well-shaped but rather round head; eyes gray, large and full; complexion dark and inclined to be florid, evidently from dissipation; moustache dark brown, nearly black, and trimmed almost to the corners of his mouth; feet and hands small and well-shaped. He wore a black derby hat and a spring suit of clothes, light in color and beautifully made. He was not flashy in any respect and yet he

looked like a gambler or sporting man. He is extremely polite in manners, talks well and easily and uses good English, and neither more nor less slang than would be expected. This is the man who is said to have killed as many men as any other of the noted border characters, and yet never a one by unfair advantage, and who has now a reputation as an authority on pugilism and a man who is willing to back his judgment as long as his money lasts.[38]

— 3 —

OTTO, REDDY, AND KI YI

They want to get a man killed for $2 and a $2 man is a dangerous man to do business with. I will say to you, Mr. Fred Bonfils and "Ki Yi" Tammen, be sure and get the right man when you hire one to do the job. I am on to your every curve, and if your man misses me I will not miss either of you.

W. B. "Bat" Masterson

In 1898 Bat Masterson turned forty-five, an age when men tend to think seriously about their life, where they have been, and where they are going. For fifteen years he had been a professional gambler, a precarious vocation at best. "I can't say that I have been prosperous, although I have not suffered much from adversity," he wrote a friend. "I came into the world without anything and have about held my own up to date. . . . In the gambling business [I] have experienced the vicissitudes [characterizing] the business. Some days—plenty, and more days—nothing."[1]

His employment as an officer of the law had been desultory. He had served a two-year term as sheriff of Ford County, Kansas, and a one-year stint as city marshal of Trinidad, Colorado, and had taken deputy sheriff appointments for brief periods in both Kansas and Colorado, usually to provide polling place security at election time, but had never really considered a career in law enforcement. In lean times he dealt cards, tended bar, or managed pool rooms, saloons, and hurdy-gurdy houses for wages. Landing a job was never a problem; saloon and gambling house proprietors welcomed his services because his gunfighting celebrity drew customers. When he accumulated a stake, he opened his own faro game or financed other gamblers; it was the way of the fraternity.

However depleted his bankroll, Masterson always looked prosperous. His vested suits were tailor-made and his button shoes polished. A gold watch chain draped his vest, and a diamond stickpin sparkled at his throat. Derby hats were stylish, and he favored a pearl gray model. He often carried a walking stick, part of the ensemble of the well-dressed gentleman of the period. Dodge City residents at their Fourth of July celebration in 1885 voted him the most popular man in town and presented him with a gold watch chain and a gold-headed cane.

Having reached his mid-forties, that age of introspection, with a wife to consider, Masterson knew he needed a more stable vocation than gambling. Whatever that new profession might be, he wanted it somehow to be connected to boxing, his paramount interest. He could sense a change of attitude and a wider acceptance by the general public of boxing as a legitimate sport. The passage of a new law in Colorado in the spring of 1899 legitimizing prizefights further confirmed his optimistic view. He was sure the game would grow in the future and those connected with it could prosper. Management of fighters and occasional refereeing jobs would not provide the steady source of income he sought, but promotion of boxing matches on a regular basis, he believed, offered great opportunity in this new era.

With that end in view, he entered into a partnership with Otto Floto, a rotund native of California who was also an avid devotee of the ring. Newspapermen Fred G. Bonfils and Harry H. Tammen, having recently acquired ownership of the *Denver Post*, were employing staff, and when Floto professed to have journalistic ability and ambitions, Tammen hired him as sports editor of the paper for no other reason, he later said, than his name was so beautiful.[2]

On April 8, 1899, Masterson and Floto established a fight club in Denver and called it the Colorado Athletic Association. John G. Morgan, a Denver stockbroker and Masterson friend who provided most of the finances for the venture, was named president. Floto assumed the office of vice president, Volney Haggert took office as secretary, and W. B. Masterson was made official referee. Others in the founding group were Nels Innes, another Masterson crony, and two pugilists, Patrick "Reddy" Gallagher and Norman Selby, who, under his ring name, "Kid McCoy," had recently won the welterweight title. Of course Masterson had not forgotten his difficulties with Gallagher nor forgiven him, and Gallagher was brought into the enterprise at Floto's insistence over Bat's strong objections. The disagreement set the tone for internal dissension and doomed the enterprise from the start. Within a week Floto secured the financial backing of Bonfils and Tammen of the *Post*, forced the others out, and took personal control of the club. Masterson, furious at what he called Floto's "dirty, underhanded work," met with the *Post* owners and argued his case to no avail.[3]

Thus began a Masterson-Floto feud that did not end until Bat's death twenty-two years later.

With characteristic quick and decisive action, Masterson struck back. Only days later he announced the formation of the Olympic Athletic Club to compete with Floto's venture. He installed himself as president and named John W. Gordon vice president, Gus Tuthill treasurer, and Nels Innes secretary. He leased an old building, formerly the Academy of Music, and began renovations to provide seating for 2,000. In press releases he announced that he would draw on his wide ring contacts to bring topflight fighters to Denver and provide stellar boxing programs for the enjoyment of the city's fight fans. He invited Selby and even Gallagher to join him in the enterprise. Selby decided the looming boxing war in Denver was not his kind of fight and left town to concentrate on his ring career. Gallagher initially joined the Masterson venture, but soon deserted to the Floto camp, thus confirming Bat's original doubts about his loyalty and trustworthiness. Reddy now joined Floto at the top of the Masterson hate list.

Bat poured all his angry energy into making a success of the Olympic Club. He was promoter, matchmaker, press agent, and referee of all bouts held there. By the fall of 1899 F. A. McClelland, sports editor of the *Denver Republican* and at that time a neutral observer of the Masterson-Floto war, noted that Bat controlled the fight game in the city. To compete in Denver, he said, fighters had to "crook the pregnant hinges of the knee to Bat before they [could] secure good matches."[4]

But it soon became evident that as sports editor of the *Post* Floto enjoyed a distinct advantage in the competition with Masterson, for he could use his columns to promote and advertise his ring offerings. Undaunted, Bat quickly found a means to retaliate. George D. Herbert, a former owner of the *Post*, was now publishing a Denver paper he called *George's Weekly*. He had no love for Bonfils and Tammen and ballyhooed Bat's Olympic Club from its inception. He printed lengthy "interviews" with the club's president that were obvious products of Masterson's own pen. All pretense was dropped on September 23, 1899, when the first regular sports column under Bat Masterson's byline appeared in the pages of *George's Weekly*. It contained, as its headline proclaimed, "Gilt Edged Opinions Concerning 'Pugs,' a Bouquet of Puffs, Criticisms, Jabs in the Slats and Other Things Too Numerous to Mention."

During the following year Masterson's columns, or letters, if he was out of town, appeared regularly in the paper. All dealt with boxing, local and national. Of course Bat lauded Olympic Club promotions while deprecating offerings of the rival Colorado Club. He also maintained a constant vituperative campaign against Floto, Gallagher, Bonfils, and Tammen.

One fine spring day in 1900 a Denver attorney named W. W. "Plug Hat" Anderson marched into the offices of the *Post* and shot and wounded both Bonfils and Tammen. It was said that Tammen, in mortal terror, cried out "Ki Yi!" during the attack. Masterson seized on the story to tag the *Post* owner with a deprecatory name, thereafter invariably referring to the man as "Ki Yi" Tammen. When he learned that Tammen had used the paper's popular female writer, Polly Pry, as a shield during the shooting, Bat wrote with obvious delight that "Ki Yi" showed "yellow cur blood" by hiding behind the lady's skirts. He went on to say that "a cornered rat will fight, and a trod-on worm will turn. But Tammen, without the courage of a rat, without the spirit of a worm, does a back-scuttle waltz with Polly Pry, trying to escape what had long been coming to him. What a spectacle!"[5]

Bat ripped rival Floto frequently, calling him "puddin-headed" and a "blatherskate," but he directed some of his most colorful invective at Pat Gallagher, for whom his favorite epithet was "pediculous," meaning lice-infested. When Gallagher began giving young students boxing instructions at the Colorado Club, Bat labeled him "Professor

Patrick Pediculous." Among other calumnies, he taunted Gallagher as an

> unreliable, chesty, swellheaded counterfeit fighter, [a] cleaner
> up of cuspidors . . . , the rankest quitter that ever put on a box-
> ing glove, the coarse and uncouth production of Goat alley in
> Shanty town, [one who] could neither read [n]or write [and] did
> not know a punctuation mark from a boiled Irish potato . . . , a
> sublime ignoramus . . . , a degenerate . . . lacking in every qual-
> ity that constitutes a man . . . , cowardly, miserly and untruthful,
> with no sense of honor or decency . . . , an evil-minded, tale-
> carrying mischief maker, a coarse-grained, self-opinionated
> buffoon, garrulous, treacherous, and venal.[6]

These were unmistakable fighting words, and many in Denver expected the boxing club war to erupt in violence. Given Bat's awesome gunfighting reputation, his enemies were unlikely to brace him with pistols, but fists were another matter. Bonfils and Tammen had shown they had no stomach for fighting, and the obese Floto gave Masterson little concern. Gallagher, however, was a professional prizefighter, albeit, in Masterson's opinion, a chicken-hearted one. He was eleven years younger than Bat and undoubtedly in much better physical condition. In anticipation of a fistic encounter with the redhead, Bat began to work out in the Olympic gym. He was in the best of health, but "fleshy," he wrote a friend. "I weigh 200 pounds and I find that a moderate amount of exercise will not reduce the adipose tissues as it used to do."[7]

The *Denver Times* took notice: "Bat Masterson, the dignified sheik of the Olympic Athletic club, is working up his muscle, [spending] an hour a day in the gymnasium of the club, dallying with the punching bag, the dumb bells and the pulley weights." Asked by boxer Jack Grace if he was preparing for a ring career, Bat replied: "Not on your kinetoscope. I am getting tired of hearing the bluffs of that redheaded fake. . . . When I get into shape, I propose to knock the block off one Professor Red Gallagher and put him out of the business forever."[8]

According to a story carried in the *Boston Police News* and other eastern publications, Bat and Gallagher came face to face in Bob Stockton's saloon in the early morning hours of February 4, 1900. Gallagher was said to have blasted Bat "with fluent vigor" even after

Masterson pulled a pistol and thrust it under the redhead's nose. Completely demoralized, "the killer of desperadoes" put his weapon away, went the story, and slunk off.[9]

Masterson vehemently denied the account, calling it a "miserably constructed fake," too ridiculous to be taken seriously. Publisher George Herbert rushed to Bat's defense, denouncing the story as a disgrace to Denver journalism. He charged the author of the piece, F. A. McClelland of the *Republican*, who was now supporting the Floto-Gallagher combine in its war with Masterson, with concocting the fable in an effort to "queer" Bat's eastern connections. Bat and Reddy had met, Herbert said, and "hot words" passed between them, but no weapons were drawn or blows struck. Unfortunately, he added, the story would spread, for Masterson was nationally known, and it would take a year for the truth to overtake the "infamous lie."[10]

There did seem to be a concerted effort to discredit Masterson during this period. Several false stories in which he was supposedly beaten, shot, or otherwise embarrassed appeared in newspapers around the country. A report in April 1900 that fighter Jim Hall had knocked him out cold in Chicago was immediately denied by Parson Davies in a letter to the *Chicago Tribune*. Bat Masterson, he said, was one of the finest men he ever met, "a prince of good fellows" who sought no quarrels, and Jim Hall, if asked, would agree.[11]

Three months later Denver newsmen heard that Bat had been shot and killed in Cheyenne, Wyoming. Unable to confirm the story with Cheyenne authorities, they wired Chicago sport Lou Houseman, at whose theater Bat had last been reported. The telegraphic response was purportedly from Masterson himself: "Houseman and I just had a drink. It hasn't killed me yet. Am still making books. Four to one on Doc Holliday. Six to one on Jim Allison. Seventeen to one on Morgan, Wyatt or Bill Earp." (Bat, who probably had more than one drink before sending this wire, was a notorious practical joker and was undoubtedly pulling the leg of the Denver reporter. The "books" mentioned were evidently odds on which famous gunfighters, other than Masterson, had recently been slain. Bat knew full well that Doc Holliday had been dead for thirteen years, Morgan Earp had been murdered eighteen years earlier, there never was a "Bill" Earp, and Jim Allison was a fictional western gunfighter Bat had invented to spoof gullible newsmen.)[12]

GUNFIGHTER IN GOTHAM

In August 1900 Masterson sued Gallagher for $120 he claimed Reddy misappropriated during the short time he was associated with the Olympic Club. It turned out Gallagher, without informing Bat, had given $40 to sportswriters for each of the three Denver papers to ballyhoo upcoming fights at the club. The explanation did little to mollify Masterson, who then, and until the end of his life, abhorred the practice of bribing reporters to gain favorable news coverage.

Although Bat's cannonades in *George's Weekly* were generally directed at Gallagher, he did not neglect Floto, Tammen, and Bonfils, a combine he called a "cheap and good-for-nothing gang of grafters."[13]

On Monday, July 30, 1900, Masterson and Floto engaged in a brief street altercation that future celebrated author Gene Fowler, then a cub reporter on the *Post*, witnessed and colorfully described. When the men he considered "America's foremost critics of pancratia" met, they did not "indulge in fancy steps, neat left hooks, graceful fiddling" as he expected, but "advanced like any charcoal burners of the Black Forest, and began kicking each other in the groin." They then "whaled away with roundhouse rights that stirred up more wind than the town had felt since the blizzard of 1883." Fowler confessed the incident was the beginning of his disillusionment. "Since that brawl I have questioned the infallibility of critics, pugilistic or otherwise."[14]

The fracas received extensive coverage in the Denver papers. Masterson attacked the corpulent Floto with a cane, according to the *Times* story, and when Floto ran, chased him down the street.

> "I used to think I was a pretty good runner," Bat was quoted, "but that fellow started to pull away from me on the jump, and before we had gone ten feet I saw . . . I could never catch him, so I just stopped and stamped my foot like you do when you scare a dog, and [he] let out another link and was knocking big chunks out of the time for a city block. . . . There are some fellows you can reason with and talk them into being decent, and there are others just like a stubborn mule that you have to beat to death to teach them. . . . I understand that my friend Floto is carrying a derringer. The next time I see him I am going to ask him to give it to me and I will soak [hock] it. The darn thing cost $8 and you can soak it for $5 easy."[15]

The *Rocky Mountain News* took a less insouciant view of the affair. Under the headline "Masterson's Ruffianism," it said Bat "assaulted" Floto in a "vicious" attack, striking him across the neck with his loaded leather stick so brutally that the steel rod doubled.[16]

Of course the *Post* gave the story the greatest coverage and most slanted treatment. In this version, based on Floto's recital of events, Masterson's attack, more than a simple assault, was a premeditated attempt by Bat and his "gang" to lure the paper's sports editor into a fight and then kill him. As he stepped into the street, Floto said, Masterson suddenly appeared out of the crowd and struck at him twice with his cane. He was able to deflect the blows with his arm, but, seeing Biddie Bishop and other known friends of Masterson nearby, Floto became "morally certain" that a trap had been set for him by the man reputed to have killed thirty men. "It is a well known fact that Masterson carries a gun at all times," he said. "If I had resisted his assault with the cane, he would have shot me, and his henchmen would have sworn that I attempted to shoot him, and would have placed a revolver at my side as I lay dead on the sidewalk." He fled the scene in order to save his life. He did not explain how Masterson and his "gang" proposed to carry out this assassination on a crowded city street in full view of many bystanders.[17]

In his *George's Weekly* column Masterson scoffed at the Floto account and expressed surprise that the press had made so much of what he called "a little street scrap." He derided Floto for cowardice and said the attempted assassination story was not only untrue, it was not even original. "Pediculous" Gallagher, he said, had previously told a very similar fable around town with himself as the intended victim.[18]

Bat seemed to take a lighthearted view of the situation, but actually the stage was set for deadly violence. In Denver were men who would kill him if given the opportunity. One was Corteze D. "Cort" Thompson, a one-time foot-racing champion who later degenerated into a drug-addicted tinhorn gambler and "solid man" of Denver's leading madam, Mattie Silks. When Thompson died from dissipation in 1900, George Herbert remarked in his paper that "every time 'Cort' got full of 'hop' he borrowed a gun and started out to kill Bat, fancying it would shed much glory upon him to kill a man of Masterson's worldwide reputation."[19]

GUNFIGHTER IN GOTHAM

A much more dangerous gunman stalked Bat that summer. Bat's enemies imported James L. Smith, veteran cattle inspector, railroad detective, and man-hunter, for the express purpose of killing him or running him out of town. When he learned of the plot, as Masterson later told the story, he sent a $100 bill to Gallagher, saying he could keep the money if Reddy and his gunfighter hireling would just meet him in front of Murphy's saloon. "Gallagher refused the money, and . . . Smith made haste to explain that his purpose in coming to Denver was wholly innocuous."[20]

The *Denver Post*, of course, told a different story. In this version, Smith followed Masterson from saloon to saloon, seeking a confrontation, but Bat kept avoiding him. Finally Smith sent a message that Masterson "had better leave Denver." Bat took the next train "and hasn't been back since."[21]

This account is incorrect in one respect at least. Bat did not leave Denver for good in 1900; he would maintain residence there for two more years. He did believe, however, that Bonfils and Tammen had contracted to get rid of him. In September 1900 he stated that clearly and issued an equally unambiguous warning:

> [They] have tried to hire someone to take a fall out of me, but so far have failed to find the right man. They won't pay the price, they are too rotten miserly. . . . They want to get a man killed for $2 and a $2 man is a dangerous man to do business with. I will say to you, Mr. Fred Bonfils and "Ki Yi" Tammen, be sure and get the right man when you hire one to do the job. I am onto your every curve, and if your man misses me I will not miss either of you. This is official, final and irrevocable.[22]

Bat was in and out of Denver all that year. In April he returned from a gambling sojourn in Hot Springs, Arkansas, "burdened with a goodly roll of the elongated green" and with ambitious plans for Olympic Club matches.[23]

A few weeks later he was off to New York City to referee a title fight between middleweights Tommy Ryan and Jack Root and to witness Jim Corbett's unsuccessful attempt to regain the heavyweight crown from Jim Jeffries, who had taken the title from Bob Fitzsimmons the year before. In the big city he stayed at the Delevan Hotel, owned and managed by his close friend Tom O'Rourke. There he was the featured guest at a banquet hosted by O'Rourke and described by Charlie Matheson of the *New York Morning Telegraph* as "a gathering of notable men of mark . . . , who know the mysteries of poker and other devices for the speedy transference of money better than any minister knows his theology." Matheson said he was impressed by Masterson, who in his youth had dispatched "considerably over a score" of gunfight victims and was now "one of the most distinguished patrons of the fighting game." He described the famous man as "somewhat grizzled and slightly short of hair on his head [but] still firm of foot and hand and could probably make as good a gun play as ever [if] called upon."[24]

Discussion that night focused on the future of boxing in America and in New York in particular. The Horton law, which had permitted boxing in New York, was scheduled for repeal in September, and no one knew what the future held. Masterson, Parson Davies, and others urged formation of a national organization to promote the sport and pressure politicians of New York and other states for favorable boxing legislation. Since the men in the group were basically gamblers and not political lobbyists, nothing ever came of the proposal.

The Ryan-Root fight was canceled when the contestants could not agree on terms, and Bat returned to Denver, where in a newspaper interview he extolled New York City and the quality of its fight promotions. He was convinced New York offered far better opportunity for the sporting man than Denver, a city he bitterly castigated upon his return as filled with "bluffers and hoodlums and robbers and fakirs" who did nothing on the square. Only his wife's health had kept him in Denver so long, he said.[25]

By that time he had disposed of the Olympic Athletic Club, selling it to Joe Gavin, a well-known sporting man with investments in Leadville, Cripple Creek, Seattle, and Denver. Bat publicly warned Gavin he would be strongly opposed in the operation of the club by the owners of the *Denver Post* and their minions, Otto Floto and Pat Gallagher, "the most unprincipled, sneaking, lying, cowardly set of yellow curs that the sun ever shone on."[26]

In a letter to Charlie Matheson a few months later, Bat explained with less passion why he bowed out of boxing club management in Denver. In his first promotions he had set admission prices at $1 to $3, amounts he figured would generate sufficient funds to enable him to attract first-rate ring talent, but his competition, Floto and company, offered inferior programs for 25 and 50 cents. By meeting these prices he found it impossible to bring in quality fighters, and the Denver boxing patrons, "educated to cheap prices," settled for second- and third-rate matches.[27]

His enemies in Denver no doubt rejoiced at Masterson's retirement from the local fight scene and imminent departure, but someone at the *Times* recognized that the city was about to lose one of its most colorful residents:

> Although [his] hair is beginning to turn a little gray around the edges and he is getting well along in life, he is still the same Bat Masterson who commanded respect from the thugs who at one time posed as the bullies of the West, and when the gray-tinged hair is rubbed the wrong way his gray eyes flash as they used to of old and the sparks commence to fly off in a threatening manner. Bat has by no means got to that stage of life where he is unable to take his own part, but he has grown a little more sedate.[28]

Masterson stuck around Denver long enough to referee the first national championship prizefight in the city's history, a match he had scheduled for the Olympic Club before turning over the reins to Joe Gavin. On October 2, 1900, Joe Gans and George McFadden met in a ten-round battle for a $1,000 purse and the lightweight title. The fight went the distance, and Masterson, consistent with his oft-expressed view that a boxer must beat his opponent decisively to be awarded the victory by a referee, called it a draw. The decision was strongly condemned by many who thought Gans dominated the action and should have been declared the winner. And so, not surprisingly, he departed the Denver fight scene on a controversial note.

During the next year and a half Bat spent most of his time in Hot Springs, Arkansas, the health mecca and gambling center. A dispatch to a Denver paper in January 1901 reported he was "a full-fledged citizen" of the town and was planning on purchasing property, building a home, and living there the rest of his life.[29] But clearly Masterson had not yet decided where he would settle and purchased no property in Hot Springs. He never owned a home. He had always rented his domicile in Denver and would do the same in the coming

New York City years. He traveled extensively, visiting racetracks during season and any city in the country where an important prizefight was scheduled.

Bat had not cut all ties to Denver; he still rented a home at 1825 Curtis Street, on the edge of the tenderloin district. Apparently he had kept the place for the express purpose of maintaining a legal residence so that he could vote in the district. In the spring of 1902 he came back to Denver to exercise that right. A municipal school board election was scheduled for May 5. Feminine activists led by Margaret T. True had succeeded in getting a slate of women on the school board ballot, a slate vigorously opposed by many men of the city. Campaigning had been heated, and activity was intense around the polling places on Election Day. The *Denver Times* called it "the most bitter fight that has ever occurred in Denver at a school election."[30]

That morning Bat strolled from his Curtis Street home to cast his vote. He later told a friend what happened when he arrived at the polling place:

> I lived in the same house in Denver for nine years. And then the women got to voting. On one election morning I went [down] to cast my ballot in the same old precinct, when a woman who was standing around the polls exclaimed: "I challenge that vote!"
>
> I was never so surprised in my life. I didn't know the woman, couldn't recall ever having seen her before, hadn't the faintest idea why anybody would want to prevent me from exercising the prerogative of a citizen, but I said as mildly as I could: "Madam . . . , why [do] you challenge my vote? I have lived in this city for fifteen years, and nine years in my present domicile."
>
> The only answer I got was a rap across the neck with her umbrella. That was enough for me. Yes, I decided . . . to dig out for Chicago.[31]

Denver newspaperman and western novelist William MacLeod Raine later spun a vivid tale of subsequent events. An enraged Masterson, he said, went on a drunken rampage of several days' duration, and law enforcement officers, daunted by his killer's reputation, were disinclined to arrest him. Finally the police chief sent for "Three-Fingered Jim" Marshall, an old Masterson friend and fellow gunman, who came in from Cripple Creek, "got the drop" on Bat, and ordered him out of town. The chastised Masterson caught an eastbound train and never returned. To explain why none of this ever appeared in the Denver papers, Raine said Marshall visited each in turn and requested the story not be printed.[32]

Although Raine claimed to have taken this story from an unpublished manuscript written by Harry Lindsey, then district attorney at Denver, no copy of this document has ever been found, and the account appears to be a product of Jim Marshall's affinity for spinning tall tales and novelist Raine's penchant for the melodramatic. Bat Masterson was never a heavy drinker, and no one ever remembered seeing him drunk. That any Denver newspaper, especially the Masterson-hating *Post*, would suppress such a sensational story is unbelievable.

An entirely different, even more humiliating, story of Bat's final departure from Denver was published fifty-six years later by a columnist for the *Post*, a newspaper that apparently still retained animosity toward Bat long after the turn-of-the-century feudists were dead and buried. Hero of this canard was Reddy Gallagher, who was said to have loudly announced in a saloon that if Masterson ever spoke to him he would spit in his eye. Told of the challenge, Bat appeared and in the barroom's sudden silence remarked that some redheaded Irishman had "run out of spit." Whereupon Gallagher ordered a double shot of Old Crow, rolled it around in his mouth for its flavor, and then hit Masterson square in the eye. "That was the night 'Bat' Masterson left Denver to turn up a sports writer in New York," according to this tale. Probably based upon the discredited Masterson-Gallagher confrontation of 1900, the account is laced with historical inaccuracies and lacks any credibility.[33]

Without fanfare or dramatics Bat Masterson left Denver for the last time in May 1902. He stayed in Chicago several weeks, and then continued on to New York, the city that had fascinated him ever since he "tumbled into a softest sort of soap," the George Gould bodyguard assignment seven years earlier. There, in the metropolis of the East, the man of the West would find a new home, a new career, a new life.

— 4 —

A BROADWAY GUY

Mr. Masterson was sawed-off and stumpy legged, with a snub nose and a tedious sniffle; wore a flat-topped derby, . . . and in doubtful weather carried an umbrella. He [looked like] a steam fitter's helper who has been dissipated but now is reformed.

Irvin S. Cobb

The arrival of Bat Masterson in the city that would be his home for the rest of his life might be termed spectacular; he certainly caught the attention of New Yorkers. Within twenty-four hours he was in jail, charged with swindling and carrying a concealed weapon. The city's papers carried front-page stories of the arrest of the famous pistol-packing western gunfighter on the streets of Gotham.[1]

Accompanied by Parson Davies, who had joined him in Chicago, Masterson arrived in the city on Thursday, June 5, 1902, and checked into Tom O'Rourke's Delevan Hotel. The two were on their way to England, where they planned to promote prizefights in connection with the coronation celebrations for the new king, Edward VII. They had booked passage on a steamer sailing from New York harbor on Saturday, June 7, but events would prevent Masterson from ever seeing England.

On Friday afternoon he was standing on the corner of Sixty-Ninth Street and Columbus Avenue, eating an orange he had purchased from a fruit peddler and having his shoes shined at a bootblack stand. Lounging nearby was a West Coast gambler named James A. Sullivan. Suddenly, two plain-clothes officers, Detective Sergeants Patrick

F. Gargan and John Tinker, appeared, flashed badges, and placed Masterson and Sullivan under arrest on suspicion of being members of a gang of crooked gamblers. A beat patrolman stood guard over the suspects while the two detectives went in search of other quarry. They raided a nearby house and returned in an hour with gambling paraphernalia and J. E. Sanders, a former Denver bookmaker, and Leopold Frank, a Chicago gambler, in tow. The officers then herded the four suspects into hansom cabs and took them to central police headquarters, where they booked them on charges of conspiring to fleece a victim in a crooked faro game.

George H. Snow of Salt Lake City, a Mormon elder and the son of the late president of the Church of Jesus Christ of Latter-day Saints, had filed the complaint. He claimed he had been swindled out of $16,000 and reportedly named the four men as members of a crooked gambling combine that had fleeced victims from Hot Springs to New York. Masterson, "white with anger," vehemently denied these allegations. Although Snow failed to recognize Masterson at the station, he refused to withdraw the charge, and Bat was held. At some point officers removed what newspapers called a "huge revolver" from Bat's hip pocket and filed an additional concealed weapons charge against him.[2]

Infuriated by what he always claimed were unfounded charges and the confiscation of his pistol, Masterson was further incensed when Detective Bureau chief George Titus made him submit to Bertillon measurements and photographic "mug shots."[3] Bat strenuously objected, and he and Titus exchanged "vicious language." The arrival of Bat's bondsmen "saved him from further humiliation."[4]

Coming to his aid were Tom O'Rourke; John Bittner, O'Rourke's partner in the operation of the Delevan Hotel; and George Considine, manager of the Hotel Metropole. After stewing several hours in a jail cell Masterson was arraigned in police court on a charge of "aiding and abetting in gambling games and inducing men to go to their rooms to play games of chance." The judge scheduled a hearing for the following Monday and set bail at $2,500, which Bat's friends quickly provided.

Police reporters jumped on the story of the arrest of the legendary western gunfighter. Typical was the story in the *New York World* wherein Masterson was described as "well-built and vigorous looking," a man "noted for his quiet and affable manners," whose record of twenty-eight killings was "more or less accurate."[5]

While all the papers focused on Masterson's man-killer notoriety, some expressed surprise that his honesty was in question as he had always been considered "square" by the gambling fraternity. Interviewed in Chicago, William A. Pinkerton of the famous detective agency said that he had known Bat for twenty years and had "never heard the faintest whisper from any quarter to indicate he was not absolutely honest."[6]

At the hearing before Magistrate Leroy B. Crane on Monday, June 9, Elder Snow failed to appear and press his charges. Detective Sergeant Gargan, obviously disconcerted, requested a postponement so that he might find Snow. Crane denied the request and asked if Gargan would care to make the complaint. The officer declined, and the magistrate then dismissed the case. On the secondary concealed weapon charge Bat pleaded guilty and was fined $10.

Never one to remain long on the defensive, Masterson soon moved to the attack. He brought suit against Snow, claiming false arrest and "injury to his good name." He estimated the allegation that he was not a square gambler had damaged his reputation to the tune of $10,000.[7] In a panic, Snow demanded signed affidavits from Detectives Gargan and Tinker exonerating him from all responsibility in the affair. In turn he provided Masterson his own affidavit in which he stated that he had never accused Bat of being mixed up in the scheme to fleece him, and the suit was settled out of court.

The New York police force in general and Detective Sergeant Gargan in particular became targets of Bat's wrath. It took him eleven years, but he finally got a crack at Gargan. In another Masterson civil suit in 1913, the officer testified about the 1902 arrest. After the case was resolved, Bat filed a complaint with the police commission, charging Gargan with having committed perjury on the witness stand in an attempt to blacken Masterson's character. Gargan, a thirty-three-year veteran of the force who had risen by 1913 to the rank of captain, was about to retire. The commissioners took the case under advisement, and the matter ended there.

Masterson had missed his sailing because of the Elder Snow affair. Despite New York's rude welcome, he was still fascinated by the huge city, whose population by the turn of the century had reached three and a half million people, and decided to remain right there. His wife joined him from Philadelphia, and together they moved into rooms in the Delevan Hotel, located on the corner of West Fortieth Street and Broadway. Later they would take an apartment at 243 West Forty-Third Street, between Broadway and Eighth Avenue, and still later another apartment only a few doors away at 257 West Forty-Third. All these locations were within easy walking distance of Longacre (later Times) Square at the intersection of Broadway, Seventh Avenue, and Forty-Second Street, the heart of the sporting and theatrical district, and the center of New York nightlife. It was an environment as foreign to the plains of Kansas and the dusty streets of Dodge City where Bat had come of age as could be imagined, but the aging westerner fit into this new milieu as confidently as he donned a new tailor-made suit.

In a 1903 interview, a year after Bat's arrival, a reporter described him as a modest, quiet "sport about town." Asked if he didn't miss the excitement he had experienced in the Wild West, Bat replied that at the age of fifty he was "different." He was now, he said, "a Broadway guy."[8]

The street that would later be called the Great White Way was undergoing major changes around the turn of the century, with a continual relocation of hotels and theaters from lower Manhattan up Broadway to the Longacre Square district. In the five years following Masterson's arrival, nine theaters were built in the area, many on Forty-Second Street. In 1904 a new subway line went into operation, and the New York Times moved to Longacre Square. The name was officially changed to Times Square, although many Broadwayites, including Masterson, continued to call the area Longacre Square for years.

With the influx of theaters came restaurants and cabarets, many of which, celebrated in song and story by their patrons, have since become legendary. Churchill's, at Broadway and Forty-Eighth, was for many years one of the premier restaurants of the city, as was Delmonico's at Fifth and Forty-Fourth. The Astor Hotel Bar at Broadway and Forty-Fourth Street was renowned for a powerful drink concocted from grape juice and Swedish rum and called "Astor Hotel No. 1." Jack Dunstan's restaurant at Sixth Avenue and Forty-Third, much frequented by newspapermen and writers, was open twenty-four hours a day and seemed always to be packed. Jack's was "famous for its Irish bacon and its flying wedge of waiters who ejected obstreperous customers with a minimum of motion and a maximum of efficiency."[9] At Broadway and Forty-Fourth was Rector's celebrated restaurant and cabaret, and two blocks south was the Knickerbocker Hotel Bar, across Broadway from Considine's Café, a favorite resort of the sporting crowd, where many contracts for important prizefights were signed. Between Forty-Second and Forty-Third Streets on Broadway was Redpath's Café, noted for Ramoz fizzes and Sazerac cocktails. Beyond Considine's was the Opera Café, and farther south between Thirty-Ninth and Thirty-Eighth Streets were Bustanoby's, the Café Maxim, and Kid McCoy's Normandie Rathskeller.

Favorite hangouts for Bat Masterson before 1910 were Shanley's original restaurant and the old Metropole on Longacre Square. The Considine brothers, George and Jim, in partnership with Big Tim Sullivan, political boss of the Bowery, owned and operated the Metropole. The Considines were nephews of Seattle gambler and theater impresario John W. Considine, an old Masterson friend. In a contest conducted by the *New York Morning Telegraph* in 1910 to determine the nation's most popular sportsman, George Considine won easily, beating his closest rival, Jack Skelly, by more than 60,000 votes. The old Metropole was renowned for a round table frequented by Masterson and other raconteurs. Jim Considine called them "the jolly knights of the theatrical and sporting world" and claimed they had King Arthur's knights "skinned forty ways from the jack for imagination and versatility."[10] The Considine brothers closed the old Metropole in May 1909 and in December of the following year opened their new Metropole Hotel, a narrow, six-story building on the north side of Forty-Third Street, about fifty yards from Broadway. The new place was as successful as its predecessor, but became infamous after the notorious assassination of gambler Herman Rosenthal on its doorstep in July 1912.

A new Shanley's Restaurant opened the same month as the Metropole. A huge establishment, Shanley's extended along Broadway from Forty-Third to Forty-Fourth. Entry was available from the Longacre Building or through either street doorway. The maître d' supervised a staff of ten assistants and seventy-five waiters in the main dining room, where 800 patrons could be seated comfortably. This was a gorgeous room with a twenty-seven-foot ceiling supported by twelve columns of exquisitely carved English oak. Fifteen hundred yards of bronze Wilton velvet carpet covered the floor. From a lofty balcony musicians provided instrumental and vocal entertainment. In a "cabaret extraordinaire" as many as twenty different vaudeville acts performed during the evening hours. There was a men's grill on the Forty-Third Street side near the taproom, and "waiting and retiring rooms" for women at the other entrance. Chefs prepared food in an enormous kitchen, 150 feet long and 100 feet wide.

Lunch at Shanley's could be purchased for 75 cents, and evening meals were equally inexpensive. Prices spiraled upward during the world war years, the price of a regular luncheon going to 90 cents and special luncheons on Saturdays and holidays to $1. After the war prices continued to rise, and Bat, who did not lack money but hated to be overcharged, grumbled in 1920 that an eight-ounce steak "with a little gravy thrown in" set him back $3 at Shanley's.[11]

The historian Herbert Asbury remarked on the excellent quality of Shanley's steaks, but said that for years the restaurant "possessed an even greater attraction—it was the favorite loafing place of the celebrated Bat Masterson. Every night the old-time gun fighter, resembling nothing so much as a huge spider, presided over a big steak in a corner of Shanley's grill, holding a crowd of admirers spellbound with tales which were about as wild and wooly as the West he was describing."[12]

Among those rapt listeners were some of the most colorful characters of the time. As the theatrical and entertainment center of the nation, the Broadway district was home to producers, directors, performers, musicians, and writers, all the leading drama and vaudeville folk. The foremost figures of the sports world, especially devotees of the racetrack—jockeys, horse trainers, and bookmakers—and the pugilistic crowd—fighters, managers, and promoters—were also its habitués. Newsmen from the fourteen New York City newspapers, notorious for their love of nightlife, were regular denizens of the district. Lawyers, politicians, and police officials mixed freely with gangsters, gamblers, racetrack touts, and confidence men. Bat Masterson joined this heterogeneous assemblage, and, although he became one of the journalistic crowd, he always held a unique position: there were no other legendary western gunfighters among the Longacre Square gathering.

Never before or since has there been such a concentration of notable newsmen in one place as in New York City during Masterson's years there. Those who achieved fame as journalists or went on to success in other literary fields included Arthur "Bugs" Baer, Arthur Brisbane, Heywood Broun, Bozeman "Boze" Bulger, Donald Henderson Clarke, Irvin S. Cobb, Thomas Aloysius "Tad" Dorgan, Bob Edgren, Nat Fleischer, Gene Fowler, Rube Goldberg, Hype Igoe, Will Irwin, Stuart N. Lake, brothers Alfred Henry and William E. Lewis, W. O. McGeehan, Charles F. Matheson, Frank Ward O'Malley, Grantland Rice, Robert L. Ripley, Damon Runyon, Herbert Bayard Swope, Jimmy Sinnott, Jimmy Swinnerton, Sam Taub, and Albert Payson Terhune.

Many of these men impacted Masterson's life. The Lewis brothers eulogized him in print and guided and abetted his newspaper career. Broun, Lake, and Taub worked with him on the *Morning Telegraph*. Runyon, Dorgan, Igoe, and Sinnott would be counted among his closest friends. Some would become enemies, and he would feud with one in particular—Bob Edgren—until he died.

Like Bat, Damon Runyon came to New York from Colorado. Born in 1880, he grew up listening to stories of Bat Masterson, Indian fighter, boomtown lawman, gunman, and fight promoter. As a young man Runyon worked on newspapers in Pueblo, Trinidad, Colorado Springs, and Denver, all former Masterson stomping grounds in Colorado. As a young reporter he probably knew Bat slightly in the West, but he did not become a close friend until, at the age of thirty, he came to the big city in 1910 to take a job as sportswriter for the *New York Morning American*, and began frequenting Bat's favorite Broadway resorts. Runyon had worked for Otto Floto on the *Denver Post* and had sometimes ghostwritten Floto's column for him, a fact that did not ingratiate him with the inveterate Floto-hater, but Bat liked the young man and forgave him for what he considered a young man's foolish indiscretions.

Soon after his arrival in New York Runyon began writing short stories, and some of his early tales were published in the Sunday magazine section of the *Morning Telegraph*, probably as a result of

Masterson's influence with the paper's editors. These stories, credited to "Alfred Damon Runyon," were written before the author developed the distinctive Broadway jargon style for which he later became famous.

Surprisingly, Runyon, a notoriously taciturn sort who did not make friends easily, and Masterson, who once described himself as a misanthrope who avoided meeting other humans because he did not trust them,[13] became close friends. As the years passed the bond between them strengthened, and the young writer became for Bat Masterson almost the son he never had. In his columns Bat expressed an affection for Runyon that was perhaps equaled only by his often-declared fondness for Charlie Mitchell.

To Runyon, the older man was "one of the most indomitable characters this land has ever seen . . . , a 100 per cent 22-karat real man," and an entertaining companion.[14] Bat was dead when these lines were written and could not respond, but after a similar Runyon accolade in 1916, he had thanked his friend publicly, saying that the "beautiful tribute" was appreciated "more than words can express."[15]

Bat liked Runyon because the young sportswriter followed his older friend's example and refused to accept money and serve as a press agent for mediocre fighters and shady matches. He also respected him for having smelled gun smoke. While still in his teens Runyon had volunteered for military service in the Philippines, helping to put down the Moro uprising. As a war correspondent in 1916 he covered the U.S. Army's campaign against Pancho Villa in Mexico. When the nation entered the world war he again left to report from the scenes of action. Bat called him "a splendid soldier, a fine gentleman and one of the most painstaking and energetic newspaper correspondents in all this broad land."[16]

Runyon and Masterson spent many hours together in the Grill Room at Shanley's or the Metropole barroom. Runyon would drink black coffee while Bat sipped a Tom Collins, his favorite drink. It was at one of these sessions, according to a Runyon biographer, that the young writer got an idea. Often as he listened to Bat spinning his

> marvelous stories that featured gambling and guns, the sound
> of a tuba rumbled through the barroom. Then a drum began
> to thump. Outside a Salvation Army woman . . . led a band

through the street of sinners. Runyon heard this so often over the years that finally he figured out what it meant: put together Bat Masterson, a.k.a. Sky Masterson, and the Salvation Army woman . . . , call her Sarah Brown, and have her fall in love with Sky. He titled the story "The Idyll of Miss Sarah Brown," . . . but it would be many years before he wrote it.[17]

This short story, one of Runyon's most popular tales of Broadway life, in later years was developed into the hugely successful musical and motion picture *Guys and Dolls*.

Another who listened in awe as Masterson recounted his tales of the Wild West was Irvin S. Cobb, a young reporter for the *World*. "In his contours," Cobb remembered,

> Bat didn't in the least answer to the formalistic image of those tall, spark-spitting regulators of the formerly untamed cattle capitals. He wasn't tall which was one of the disqualifying counts against him. . . . To come right out with the disillusioning details, Mr. Masterson was sawed-off and stumpy legged, with a snub nose and a tedious sniffle; wore a flat-topped derby similar to the one worn by that symbol of civic virtue, Mr. John D. Rockefeller, Sr., and in doubtful weather carried an umbrella. He was addicted to selzer [*sic*] lemonades and tongue sandwiches; and in general [looked like] a steam fitter's helper who has been dissipated but now is reformed.

To Cobb, only Masterson's eyes, "like smoothed ovals of gray schist with flecks of mica suddenly glittering in them if he were roused," gave a hint of the man who had cleaned up Dodge City "with a Colt forty-five for his broom."[18]

"Tad" Dorgan, the gifted boxing writer and cartoonist of the *American*, also frequented the Metropole and was a Masterson favorite. Dorgan is credited with inventing or popularizing many contributions to the American vernacular, including "the bum's rush," "the bunk," "23 skidoo," "dumbbell," "nobody home," "yes, we have no bananas," "hard-boiled egg," "fall guy," and "cheaters" (for spectacles).[19]

Masterson crony Hype Igoe, who covered boxing for William Randolph Hearst's afternoon *Journal*, managed Stanley Ketchel, the great boxer, until Ketchel brandished two six-guns and told Hype he had decided to take Wilson Mizner for his manager.[20]

Managing prizefighters was only one of Wilson Mizner's many talents. Another of Bat's special pals, Mizner was a raconteur par excellence, and a regular at the Broadway watering holes. A veteran of the Klondike gold rush, where he made his first large stake operating a combination saloon, gambling hall, and flophouse, Mizner went on to make a fortune with confidence games, Florida land speculation, and cardsharping on transatlantic liners. He wrote several Broadway plays as he guided the careers of some topflight prizefighters. He managed Ketchel until a cuckolded husband shot the tough middleweight dead in 1910. When he heard the news, Mizner reportedly exclaimed: "Start counting to ten over him; Stanley will get up at nine!"[21]

Masterson was one of Mizner's pantheon of personal heroes, which included Denver gambler and con artist Jefferson "Soapy" Smith, New York governor and presidential candidate Alfred E. Smith, celebrated writers H. L. Mencken and Ambrose Bierce, New York mayor and governor Jimmy Walker, and heavyweight boxing champion Jack Johnson. Seemingly a diverse lot, these men, according to Mizner biographer John Burke, shared a common quality: style, "and style was what Wilson admired and would endlessly seek to attain." When, years later, Mizner, in partnership with movie mogul Jack L. Warner and Herbert K. Somborn, opened the first of his famous Brown Derby restaurants in Hollywood, he chose the motif and name "in honor of the headgear worn by two men he admired, Bat Masterson and Governor Alfred E. Smith."[22]

Two other Broadway characters, Ben Harris and Jim Young, always amused Masterson. Harris, dubbed "Laughing Ben" by Bat, made a fortune with a theater on Young's Pier in Atlantic City. After retiring in 1910, he traveled extensively, including a trip to England the next year to see the coronation of George V. The affair was a big blowout, he told Bat on his return, but could not compare to Broadway on a presidential election night.[23] An avid fight fan, Harris was timekeeper for Jess Willard when he fought Jack Johnson for the heavyweight title in 1912. He returned to show business in 1914, opening the Savoy Theater in Atlantic City with a vaudeville program featuring Eva Tanguay, an actress greatly admired by Bat Masterson. In 1920 Harris made a spectacular return to New York after one of his junkets.

Flying in from New Orleans in a chartered airplane, he landed at Forty-Second Street and Fifth Avenue. He told reporters that he and Jim Young had been racing across the country, and he figured by using the airplane he had edged out his pal by at least three days.

The referenced Jim Young, a convivial drinking and eating buddy of both Harris and Masterson, was so closely identified with the Considine brothers' establishment he was known on Broadway as "the Bull Moose of the Metropole." A voracious eater, Young weighed more than 300 pounds during his days in New York, but later moved to Los Angeles, lost almost a third of that weight, and prospered in the hotel and restaurant business.

Henry Munro, scion of a publishing family's fortune, was another big eater who often accompanied Masterson on his nightly rounds. Bat described him as "Broadway's biggest, best-natured and best-loved man . . . , 5 feet 10 inches tall and 5 feet 10 inches wide. He weighs more than 300 pounds, every ounce of which is solid gold good fellowship."[24]

Those who tore into food, ignoring the consequences, fascinated Masterson, who also loved to eat and constantly contended with a weight problem. He often sat and watched in rapt admiration as famed Broadway gourmands Jim Villepigue, Otis Harlan, Jim Collins, and Jack Curley attacked their plates.

One of Bat's closest cronies was Valerian J. O'Farrell, a police detective who was only in his twenties when the two met shortly after Masterson's arrival in New York, but had already built an impressive record as a tenacious and clever man-hunter. O'Farrell probably reminded Bat of himself at the same age, and Bat took a fatherly interest in the young man as he did with Damon Runyon. O'Farrell left the force in 1911 after a bitter dispute over accusations of bribe taking. He opened a private detective agency that soon became the largest in New York. No less an authority that W. A. Pinkerton called him one of the best sleuths in the business. In 1915 O'Farrell wrote a series of articles dealing with New York City crime that Bat helped to get published in the *Morning Telegraph*. Through his contacts with Masterson and others, he landed lucrative boxing arena security contracts. During the world war his agency expanded to Philadelphia and Boston and did notable work in detecting and preventing riots planned by subversives at plants throughout the East.

To Bat Masterson, the diverse and unique characters of Broadway were so many ingredients in a spicy human stew that made life interesting. The Longacre Square district was the most exciting place he could imagine, and he never remained away from it long until his death in 1921. During those years he became something of a Broadway institution himself.

He was "a Broadway guy," never a New Yorker or even a Manhattanite. The Bronx, Brooklyn, Queens, and Staten Island were distant lands to be visited only for special events, like an important prizefight. Much of Manhattan itself was foreign to him, as evidenced by a comment in a 1911 column: "Over on the West Side somewhere there is a place called Greenwich Village. I can't tell when or how it got the name, but it's there nevertheless."[25] Greenwich Village was only a few blocks from the Great White Way, but for Bat Masterson it might as well have been in Nebraska.

— 5 —

THE LEWIS BROTHERS, THE *MORNING TELEGRAPH*, AND THE HAM REPORTER

Alfred Henry Lewis is a sort of human word-factory, the foremost coiner of unique words and bizarre phrases in the land and one of the best-liked and best-hated pen-wielders between the seas.

New York Morning Telegraph

Bat Masterson made many friends in his life—staunch and true friends who stood by him in times of difficulty—but none had a more profound effect upon the last third of his life than the brothers Alfred Henry and William Eugene Lewis.

Natives of Cleveland, Ohio, the Lewis brothers were descended from a line of professional writers, teachers, and preachers. Their father, Isaac Jefferson Lewis, was a successful contractor and architect; it was said that every city between Cleveland and Denver had at least one important building designed and erected by I. J. Lewis.[1]

Alfred, born in 1858, had a law degree by the age of twenty-one and within four years was prosecuting attorney in Cleveland. William, five years his junior, also studied law and was admitted to the bar in 1881. Both abandoned law careers in favor of journalism soon after moving to Kansas City in 1883, where they first met Bat Masterson.

Alfred wandered the West for several years. He cowboyed in Kansas, New Mexico, and Texas, and freighted, drove stagecoaches, and pitched manure and kept books for a Trinidad, Colorado, livery stable. In New Mexico he worked on several small newspapers and had an opportunity to utilize his facility with words and caustic wit.

When filling in for the editor of the *Las Vegas Optic*, he received a letter complaining about the paper that ended, "I read your paper only when I am drunk." Lewis printed it with the comment that at last he had discovered the identity of the letter writer signing himself "Constant Reader."

In his travels Lewis collected tales of the frontier—some of them true, many of them western windies, and many of them dealing with Bat Masterson—upon which he drew in his later literary career. He returned to Kansas City in 1885 and opened a law office. Within two years he was earning $20,000 annually, a huge income for the time. But his interest in the law waned, and his practice languished as he spent most of his waking hours in the lobby of the St. James Hotel, soaking up more stories of the pioneer West from the veteran ranchers who stopped there. In 1889, under the pen name "Dan Quin," he began writing these tales as fanciful interviews with imaginary cattlemen. Printed in the *Kansas City Times*, they proved to be instantly popular and were later picked up and reprinted in other publications. In 1891 Lewis took down his law shingle and began full-time work at the *Kansas City Star*, where brother William, who had already left the law for journalism, was an editor. Sent to Washington, D.C., to cover capital news, Alfred met and formed a lasting friendship with Theodore Roosevelt.

Several years later, Roosevelt, who had read and enjoyed Lewis's western stories, suggested the author gather them into a volume that he would edit and have illustrated by his artist friend Frederic Remington. The resulting book appeared in 1897 under the title *Wolfville*, and catapulted Alfred Henry Lewis into national prominence.

The following year Lewis began editing the *Verdict*, a humorous weekly founded by politically ambitious Oliver Hazard Perry Belmont, and published in New York City. The magazine died with Belmont's stunted political career, but during its short life Lewis learned a great deal about New York politics and formed ties with the powerful men of Tammany Hall.

A prolific writer, Lewis published eighteen fiction and nonfiction volumes over the next seventeen years. Most dealt with either the western frontier or the culture and politics of New York City. *Wolfville Days* and *Wolfville Nights*, both published in 1902, were his most popular works. Lewis also turned out many articles for periodicals and by

1912 was the highest paid magazine writer in the country. "A sort of human word-factory," one observer called him, "the foremost coiner of unique words and bizarre phrases in the land and one of the best-liked and best-hated pen-wielders between the seas."[2]

In many respects Alfred Henry Lewis, medium-sized, with a deep chest, square features, and a pugnacious chin, was a man out of the same mold as Bat Masterson. In 1902 Bat and Lewis renewed the acquaintance they had formed twenty years earlier in Kansas City. Lewis became Masterson's mentor and guide as Bat struggled to make the transition from western frontier sporting man to eastern metropolis newspaperman and ring commentator. He would immortalize Bat in print, support his journalistic career, and lobby the president of the United States for a Masterson sinecure.

Unquestionably Lewis was the major author of the Bat Masterson legend. Beginning in 1904 he began writing magazine articles about his friend. That year four of his stories based on Bat's western experiences appeared in popular periodicals of wide circulation.[3] In 1905 he published *The Sunset Trail*, a fictionalized account of Masterson's adventures in Kansas and Texas. Although Lewis wove actual incidents and real people from Bat's past into the narrative, imaginary events and characters so distorted the story that little historical accuracy remained. Writers, unknowing or uncaring, drew upon the Lewis novel to enhance the Masterson legend.

About this time the indefatigable Alfred Henry Lewis began editing a slick monthly magazine called *Human Life* and persuaded Masterson to contribute a series of articles on the famous gunfighters he had known in the West. Bat's first effort at biography, published in the January 1907 issue of the magazine, was a sketch of Ben Thompson, the Texas gambler he considered unequaled as a pistoleer. During that year articles on Wyatt Earp, Luke Short, Doc Holliday, and Bill Tilghman appeared under his byline. When his literary production fell off, Lewis leaped into the breech. Explaining that Masterson was too modest to write autobiography, he contributed a piece to the series entitled "The King of the Gun-Players: William Barclay Masterson." One more article authored by Masterson, a sketch of Buffalo Bill Cody, appeared in the March 1908 issue of *Human Life*.

Much of the credit for Masterson's success in New York could be credited to Alfred Henry Lewis, but it was younger brother William

Eugene who was primarily responsible for sponsoring Bat's journalistic career. After newspaper editorial stints at Kansas City and Chicago, W. E. Lewis worked as a political correspondent in Washington, D.C., where he developed a terse, trenchant writing style that some compared favorably with his brother. It was said that in political commentary Alfred Henry Lewis wielded a war club while his brother brandished a rapier.[4]

William Randolph Hearst employed both brothers as political experts. During the Spanish-American War W. E. Lewis commanded Hearst's dispatch boat system and saw service at sea and ashore. Later he edited the *Philadelphia North American*. In 1903 he moved to New York to become managing editor of the *Morning Telegraph*.

The third oldest daily newspaper in New York, the *Morning Telegraph*'s history dated back to 1836. When other Manhattan papers sold for two cents, the front page of the *Morning Telegraph* proudly proclaimed that it was the only five-cent daily in New York. The claim would be continued until World War I inflation forced the other dailies to increase their price to five cents. Immediately the *Telegraph* responded by raising its price to a dime and changing its boast to being the only ten-cent daily in New York. By the 1960s the paper sold for fifty cents and advertised itself as the most expensive newspaper in the world.

The Morning Telegraph Publishing Company, a corporation with William C. Whitney as major stockholder, acquired the paper in 1902, and the following year Finley Peter Dunne, author of the popular Dooley stories, became general manager, and W. E. Lewis took over as managing editor. One of Lewis's first moves was to hire Bat Masterson as a sportswriter specializing in boxing. Bat would be employed by the paper for eighteen years, from 1903 until 1921, a much longer period than he devoted to any other of his life's pursuits. It was at the *Morning Telegraph* that his restless nature found a home.

During those years W. E. Lewis gained increasing control of the paper. Following the death of Whitney in 1905, Edward R. Thomas purchased the parent company's controlling stock. He released Finley Peter Dunne and appointed Lewis as general manager. In 1911 he assumed the presidency of the Morning Telegraph Publishing Company and immediately named Masterson as vice president. Bat held this position until June 1918 when, for some unexplained reason,

Thomas replaced him as vice president. Two years later, in July 1920, Masterson was again appointed to corporate office, this time as secretary of the company. He still retained that position when he died the following year.

In 1903, the year that Lewis and Masterson joined the paper, the Morning Telegraph Publishing Company absorbed a sports tabloid called *Daily America*, an acquisition that contributed to the breezy style for which the *Telegraph* became famous. Also about this time the paper found a new home at Fiftieth Street and Eighth Avenue in what had been a stable for the horsecar railroad, since electrified.

In the first two decades of the century New York City supported a dozen or more newspapers, most of which were published on Park Row. The *Morning Telegraph*, headquartered in a former car barn blocks from the center of Manhattan journalism, was considered by many at the bottom of the city's newspaper scale. But the owners and editors of the paper gloried in what they considered their singular position on the New York journalistic scene. *The American Newspaper Directory* of 1904 echoed that view: "The *Morning Telegraph* is a unique publication in every respect—the only one of its kind in this country. Its circulation is particularly among the wealthy and persons interested in theatricals, racing, automobiling and the higher branches of sport. It has a clientele distinctly its own and is read . . . by persons [with] money to spend. . . . The paper is the brightest and breeziest published this side of Paris."

Major stories in the paper were heavily weighted to news of marriages, divorces, and deaths of prominent people. Scandal and suicide always received extensive coverage. A photograph of a beautiful woman, usually a showgirl, adorned every front page. Lead stories ranged from presidential elections to horse-race results. Politics, theatrical news, and sensational crime stories were featured, but sporting events also received a great deal of attention. Full pages were devoted to racetrack results and betting odds, financial reports, vaudeville, theater, and—in later years—motion picture news and advertisements, and sports, especially boxing, Masterson's forte. The *Morning Telegraph* was a combination of racing form, *Wall Street Journal*, *Variety*, *Sporting News*, *Billboard*, and *Silver Screen*, with a dash of *National Inquirer*. The daily edition ran to about twelve pages, the Sunday edition from thirty-five to forty.

The unique qualities of the *Telegraph* drew many colorful personalities to its editorial rooms. Charles F. Matheson came from Detroit to work on the paper and later wrote boxing news for several other New York papers. Matheson, W. O. McGeehan of the *New York Journal*, and Bat Masterson came to be regarded as the sages of ring lore. Matheson and Bat were never close friends, primarily due to differences regarding Tom O'Rourke, who was one of Bat's best pals and Matheson's worst enemy.

In 1908 Bat hired an office boy named Sam Taub, a twenty-one-year-old Jewish youngster from the Lower East Side who, in sportswriter Red Smith's colorful phrase, "never grew bigger than a growler of beer."[5] It was the start of Taub's career in the boxing game, which lasted until he was in his nineties. On the rare occasions when, due to illness, Bat could not turn out his column, Taub substituted for him under the byline, "The Understudy." In 1920 he began writing his own daily column in the *Telegraph*. Two years later he announced the first of some 7,500 radio broadcasts of prizefights he would do over the next twenty-five years.

Another Masterson office boy did not turn out so well. Frank Greenfelder augmented his weekly $8 salary with a scam that for a time produced income exceeding that of his boss. One of Bat's duties was supervision of a page of ads purchased by horse-race touts boasting of successful tips on the previous day's races. Greenfelder took money from the touts to alter the ads after the race was run, substituting actual winners for the losers chosen. It was Bat's practice to lock the ads in his rolltop desk when he went to lunch. Greenfelder would fish the slips of paper from the desk with a wire, change the selections, and return them. One day Bat returned early, caught the office boy in the act, and chased him out of the building and up Fiftieth Street. Needless to say, that ended Greenfelder's employment at the *Telegraph*.

A financial page contributor to the paper in 1913 was George Graham Rice, who has been called the "most audacious, plausible and successful swindler" in the nation's history.[6] Born Jacob Simon Herzig in the same Lower East Side Jewish district from which Sam Taub sprang, he served time in prison for larceny and forgery before adopting the name George Graham Rice. He made and dissipated a million-dollar fortune with a horse-race tipping service before going west in 1904. Spectacular plunges in the mining camps of Nevada netted him a second fortune that he also blew. Convicted of mail fraud in 1910, he served another prison term. His confessional book, *My Adventures with Your Money*, was published in 1913, the same year he worked at the *Telegraph*.

Masterson never commented in his column about Rice and his shenanigans, but he had plenty to say about Fred Wenck, onetime sports editor of the *Telegraph*. Wenck brought down the Masterson wrath by having the temerity to edit Bat's columns and was forced to leave the paper. He later became chairman of the New York Boxing Commission and was the target of a constant barrage of Masterson criticism.

An ambitious young woman named Louella O. Parsons joined the *Telegraph* staff in 1918 and soon was writing a column devoted to news of the fast-growing motion picture industry. Later she went on to become the foremost commentator on the movie world and its denizens, and a powerful Hollywood figure. In her memoirs she remembered Masterson, who had befriended and helped her in the early years, as "a kind-hearted old man, a grand newspaper crony."[7]

Stuart N. Lake was a twenty-one-year-old cub reporter when he worked briefly at the *Telegraph* before moving on to the *Herald* in 1911. By his own account, the Wild West stories he heard spun by Bat Masterson sowed the seeds for Lake's very popular biography of Wyatt Earp published twenty years later.[8]

A caricaturist on the *Telegraph* for a time was John Barrymore, a young man from a celebrated theatrical family who, together with his brother Lionel and sister Ethel, was destined to achieve fame as a stage and screen actor.

Another who began on the *Telegraph* and went on to national prominence was Heywood Broun, a highly respected journalist of the 1920s and 1930s, and the first president of the American Newspaper Guild. After a lifetime in journalism, he recalled with nostalgic pleasure his days at the old *Telegraph*. There he saw his first words in print as contributions to the paper's front page "Beau Broadway" column. By 1910 his name was bylined in a baseball column running next to Masterson's boxing column. Broun, always a free spirit, adapted easily to the casual atmosphere at the paper, where strange people drifted in and out. "Very often," he remembered, "you couldn't get to your desk because there would be a couple of chorus girls sitting there waiting for a friend who was finishing an editorial." Everybody wrote editorials; the paper's only consistent position was an abhorrence of reformers. Broun never regretted having learned his trade at "a car barn instead of a school of journalism."[9]

The boxing columns authored by Bat Masterson began appearing on the sports page of the *Telegraph* in 1903. Lengthy, 1,700-word, double-column commentaries, they appeared three times a week, in the Tuesday, Thursday, and Sunday editions. Bat maintained that routine for eighteen years with few lapses. In the early years the column featured his photo under a headline and two subheads. On November 15, 1914, a regular column title, "Masterson's Views on Sport Topics," appeared. Since it was evident that Bat's comments were not limited to sports, on February 7, 1915, the title changed to "Masterson's Views on Timely Topics" and so remained until he wrote his last column in 1921.

The columns were not distinguished by great writing. An account of a club fight in 1911 between Sailor Burke and Jim Maher, claimant to the middleweight championship of Ireland, laced with slang and jargon, was typical of the Masterson style. At the bell, said Bat, Burke found Maher "a fine piece of cheese" who "punctured the atmosphere" with wild swings. After the Irish "mug" threw a haymaker that "put a crack in the air," Burke planted a left "into the Irishman's potato pit [and] cracked the Mick alongside the head with another left. . . . It was curtains for Erin's representative" when the sailor landed a hard right that caused his opponent "to curl up on the floor like a drunken Mexican."[10]

Masterson was given to excess verbiage, repetition, and the use of the clumsy first-person plural pronoun. He delighted in the unusual word, preferably polysyllabic. A voracious reader, he tried to add two new words to his vocabulary every day. He fell in love with some of the oddities he exhumed from *Webster's*, and obscure words like "troglodyte" and "Senegambian" made frequent appearances in his columns. Once, after referring to referee Charlie White as an "enigma," he admitted that he could have said "puzzle" or "mystery," but "enigma," he thought, "sounded more classical."[11] After opining that promoter Tex Rickard was "not overly burdened with perspicacity," he suggested facetiously that for a definition of "perspicacity" his readers might consult a Broadway character called "Kid Broad," notorious for his illiteracy.[12] (Masterson shared his passion for big words with his old Denver enemy, Otto Floto, who also kept a thesaurus on his desk and "harbored a stubborn belief that polysyllabic words were trumps.")[13]

Occasionally Masterson came up with quaint aphorisms and maxims, some of which may have been original:

"There are more ways to kill a dog than by choking him to death with a piece of custard pie."[14]

"Any man who will commit a prison offense for a friend is indeed a good pal."[15]

"There must be a difference of opinion to make life worthwhile."[16]

"Every dog, we are told, has his day, unless there are more dogs than days."[17]

"When a man is at the racetrack he roars longer and louder over the twenty-five cents he loses through the holes in the bottom of his pocket than he does over the $25 he loses through the hole in the top of his pocket."[18]

"There are those who argue that everything breaks even in this old dump of a world or ours. I suppose these ginks who argue that way hold that because the rich man gets ice in the summer and the poor man gets it in the winter things are breaking even for both. Maybe so, but I'll swear I can't see it that way."[19]

What distinguished the Masterson columns were his passion for the sport of boxing, his deeply held beliefs, and his willingness to express those beliefs honestly and with utter fearlessness. "I dare and double dare any sports writer of today to say some of the things about managers and boxers that old Bat Masterson used to say in almost every column he produced," Damon Runyon wrote in 1933. "Bat had no literary style but he had plenty of moxie."[20]

Sam Taub was most impressed by Masterson's incorruptibility: "Bat's honesty was the thing I remember best about him. In those days the boxing matches weren't always honest and Bat exposed a lot of phony fights." Masterson railed constantly against boxing writers who accepted money to tout certain fighters and matches. Taub said that in the thirteen years he worked with Bat he saw him lose his temper only once. A publicity man came into the office one day to promote a certain boxer. Bat accepted a box of cigars he brought, but when the man pulled out an envelope filled with gold coins, he ordered him out. "Do not ever come into this office again," he roared. "If you do, I'll throw you out this window!"[21]

Because he pulled no punches in expressing his opinions, Masterson often received critical mail. He responded in his columns with courtesy if the writer identified himself, but with billingsgate if the correspondent hid behind anonymity. To him, the anonymous letter writer was a "breed of vermin," a "troglodyte," a "mental pervert," too "craven-hearted" to sign his own name.[22]

He was proud of his experience in fistic matters and openly boasted that no one had officiated more matches or been longer in the game. This was not "self-laudation," he insisted, "but merely a statement of fact."[23]

His celebrity as a ring critic grew, and his comments were quoted by sportswriters in this country and in newspapers as distant as England and Australia. Bat perused many sports publications and was pleased to be quoted when proper recognition was given, but took umbrage if his material was used without credit. A writer who would use another columnist's remarks without crediting the source, he said testily, was a "pirate" whose only talent was with "a pair of shears and a paste pot."[24]

Although Alfred Henry Lewis and others had called him modest, Masterson unabashedly reprinted laudatory comments about himself he found in other newspapers. In one column he repeated fulsome remarks by his old Denver friend Biddy Bishop, taken from the *Tacoma Daily News*, where Bishop was sports editor. In ring matters, Bishop gushed, Bat's opinions were "gospel." His word was his bond and his judgment the best. "A whole-souled fellow and generous to a fault," Bat would forfeit his life before stooping to anything crooked. A staunch defender of friends, he was "more aggressive even than the devil" in attacking enemies.[25]

This was exactly the way Masterson viewed himself.

He took pride in his reputation as a watchdog of the boxing game. Harsh in his criticisms of those he thought were detrimental to the sport, he knew that some called him a "knocker," but cared not a whit.

He had been called all manner of vile names in his time, he said, but that had not deterred him in the least, and he was "still on the bridge and keeping a close watch."[26]

Refusing to embellish his accounts of ring battles with fanciful and verbose imagery as did some other writers, Masterson noted that "the fight reviewer who lacks the knack of drawing imaginary pictures and incidents that did not exist and tossing them into the story of a fracas is promptly set down by the reading public as a ham reporter." "I am," he said, "a ham of the most pronounced type."[27]

— 6 —

A BADGE FOR "OUR HOMICIDAL FRIEND"

*I want you not only to be a vigilant, courteous and efficient officer,
always on hand, always polite to every one, always ready for any duty
that comes up, but I also want you to carry yourself so that no one can
find in any action of yours cause for scandal or complaint.*

*You must be careful not to gamble or do anything while you are a
public officer which might afford opportunity to your enemies and my
critics to say that your appointment was improper.*

President Theodore Roosevelt

In January 1904 the president of the United States invited Bat Masterson to visit him in the White House.

Theodore Roosevelt, who had ascended to the presidency following the assassination of William McKinley in September 1901, was fascinated by western men of action. In the 1880s Roosevelt had gone west, "sickly, foppish, and racked with personal despair; during his time there he had built a massive body [and] repaired his soul."[1] The frontier attributes of rugged individualism, physical courage, strength of character, optimism, resourcefulness, loyalty, and determination were prized by Roosevelt, and he always believed his experience in the West honed those qualities within him and made it possible for him to rise to the highest office in the land. He particularly admired the "two-gun man" who had exercised "the right of private war under primitive western conditions."[2]

During his years in the White House Roosevelt entertained a number of noted gunfighting frontier lawmen, including Pat Garrett,

Ben Daniels, Seth Bullock, Bill Tilghman, Chris Madsen, and Jack Abernathy, several of whom were subsequently rewarded with federal appointments by the president.

As a New Yorker who had become a westerner, Roosevelt had a special interest in Bat Masterson, the westerner who had become a New Yorker. The president and the gunfighter turned sportswriter shared another bond: love of the prize ring. During Bat's visit to the White House in 1904, statesmen waited while Roosevelt quizzed his guest on such puzzles as how he ever managed to get Denver Ed Smith to whip Joe Goddard.[3] Interviewed by a reporter later, Masterson said he had long admired the president and just wanted to shake his hand. "And a right down, good, hearty, manly handshake I got, too. I guess the President was glad to see me, knowing that I had no politics to talk about and no favors to ask. . . . We talked over old times in the West . . . and I was able to tell him what has become of a good many of his old friends."[4]

At this meeting Roosevelt offered Bat appointment as U.S. marshal for the Western District of Arkansas (Indian Territory), a position carrying a $4,000 annual salary and authority to name twenty-two deputies. According to Alfred Henry Lewis, Masterson respectfully declined, saying that because of his "peculiar reputation," it wouldn't work. "Some kid who was born after I took my guns off would get drunk and look me over; and the longer he looked the less he'd be able to see where my reputation came from. . . . He'd crawl round to a gun play and I'd have to send him over the jump." Others could do the job without trouble, he said, but not himself. "My record would prove a never-failing bait to the dime-novel reading youngsters, locoed to distinguish themselves and make a fire-eating reputation, and I'd have to bump 'em off." Having gotten out of that zone of fire, he assured the president he had no wish to return.[5] Newspapers reported a more prosaic excuse: Bat said he declined the offer simply because he liked to live in New York City.[6]

Although Bat had turned down one federal law enforcement job, Alfred Henry Lewis continued to lobby the president for an appointment for his friend. If Masterson wanted to stay in New York, so be it. There were U.S. marshals all over the country; why not a New York position? When Roosevelt questioned Bat's level of schooling, Lewis assured him "that the education of our homicidal friend has not been neglected," and, as evidence of Masterson's erudition, gave the president a note Bat had written.[7]

Roosevelt was hesitant, having already come under severe criticism for his appointments of other western gunfighters to federal office. He had named Pat Garrett, celebrated slayer of Billy the Kid, as collector of customs at El Paso, Texas, and had later suffered political embarrassment when Garrett and another customs employee engaged in a common street brawl. His political enemies also made hay at his expense when he bestowed the office of U.S. marshal for Arizona on Ben Daniels, an old Masterson crony at Dodge City and a Rough Rider with Roosevelt in Cuba, and it was later disclosed that the appointee once served a prison term for stealing government mules.

Knowing that appointment of another controversial frontier figure would open the door for more rebuke, Roosevelt waited until after the 1904 general election, which he won handily, to deal with the Masterson question. Early in 1905 he suggested to Attorney General William H. Moody that a place be found for Masterson in New York City. Moody contacted William Henkel, U.S. marshal for the Southern District of New York, who promptly responded with a formal request for authority to hire an additional deputy. The new appointee, to be paid "a salary not exceeding $2000 per annum," was to be assigned to the office of the U.S. attorney with security responsibility in the grand jury room when that body was in session. His recommendation for the position was "W. B. Masterson, a resident of this city, most highly endorsed and in every way worthy to fill this office in a most creditable manner."[8]

Henkel's letter was dated January 26, 1905. Since everyone from the attorney general on down knew the appointment came on the president's personal recommendation, the bureaucratic wheels spun quickly, and the request was approved within a week. On February 2 Roosevelt wrote a remarkable letter to Masterson, notifying him of the appointment and cautioning him regarding his behavior:

Dear Bat:
It was a pleasure to get you the appointment as Deputy Marshal. Now you have doubtless seen that there has been a good deal of hostile comment upon it in the press. I do not care a

snap of my fingers for this; but I do care very much that you shall not by any act of yours seem to justify this criticism.

I want you not only to be a vigilant, courteous and efficient officer, always on hand, always polite to every one, always ready for any duty that comes up, but I also want you to carry yourself so that no one can find in any action of yours cause for scandal or complaint.

You must be careful not to gamble or do anything while you are a public officer which might afford opportunity to your enemies and my critics to say that your appointment was improper.

I wish you would show this letter to Alfred Henry Lewis and go over the matter with him.

> Sincerely yours,
> Theodore Roosevelt[9]

The appointment, announced on February 7, 1905, drew wide attention in the press. The *New York Times* of that date headlined its story:

ROOSEVELT GETS JOB FOR BAT MASTERSON.
GOOD BAD-MAN APPOINTED A DEPUTY MARSHAL HERE.
PERSONAL REQUEST DID IT.
WESTERNER HAS LONG RECORD AS DEAD SHOT AND KILLER
OF SURE-THING GAMBLERS.

The story contained the usual recital of Masterson's fabled bloodletting record in the West. Other New York papers reported the appointment in a similar vein, and the story, complete with legendary gunfighting embellishments, was spread nationally by the *National Police Gazette*, which said that Masterson had killed twenty-eight white men, but his record of "Greasers and Indians" was incomplete, since he deemed them "of no consequence."[10]

When the appointment was announced, Bat was in Hot Springs, Arkansas, and seemed in no rush to assume his new duties. The bestowal of a lucrative sinecure by the president of the United States apparently did not excite him enough to precipitate an early departure from a pleasant sojourn at his favorite spa. He and his wife remained in Hot Springs through February and most of March. They returned to New York City on March 27 and were immediately besieged by a horde of newspapermen. Bat, forewarned by friends that newsmen would meet his train, telegraphed that he would come in by the Pennsylvania and then changed railroads to arrive at Grand Central Station. The ploy did not work, and reporters and cameramen were waiting in force.

Masterson did not appreciate all the press attention. "You would have thought that I had been appointed to an Ambassadorship abroad," he growled. "They met me by the hundreds. By the hundreds!"[11] When pressed by the reporters about his blood-and-thunder adventures and man-killing record, he responded that the stories were simply tommyrot. He said he was "just an ordinary, two-legged man," and wished the wild, blood-curdling yarns would diminish.[12]

The next afternoon Bat walked into Marshal Henkel's rooms in the Post Office Building and took the oath of office. He would hold his deputy marshal commission for the next four years and four months, an enjoyable and lucrative period for him. It soon became clear that the duties and responsibilities of the job were virtually nonexistent. Assigned to the office of U.S. District Attorney Henry L. Burnett, Bat saw his immediate superior, Marshal Henkel, only when he showed up on payday. In no way did the job interfere with his work on the *Morning Telegraph*, nor did it prevent him from taking his annual month-long vacations in Hot Springs and Saratoga. And all the while he knocked down $2,000 a year in federal pay during a period when the average American worker, toiling twelve hours a day, six days a week, was earning only $523 a year. Of Marshal Henkel's twenty-seven office deputies, only two, the chief and his assistant, were paid more than Masterson. The average annual salary for the twenty-five office deputies was $964, compared to Bat's $2,000.[13]

In March 1905, while the Masterson appointment was still a hot news item, Ben Daniels was in the East, quietly lobbying Roosevelt for reappointment to the Arizona marshalship. He stopped in New York City but missed seeing Masterson, who had not as yet returned from Hot Springs. When Bat got back he wrote Daniels: "Isn't President Roosevelt about the best ever? After you once get acquainted with him you can readily understand why he is so popular. There is no red tape about that man. He thinks well of you and there is no mistake but what you will get what you want if he can give it to you."[14]

Later that year Roosevelt reappointed Daniels as Arizona marshal, but the action met opposition in Congress, and the Senate delayed confirmation. In December Masterson was in Washington, D.C., and, at the request of the president, tested the political waters by discussing the Daniels appointment with several congressmen of his acquaintance. In a report to Roosevelt he identified Senator Henry Moore Teller of Colorado as the principal stumbling block in the way of a Daniels confirmation. Bat thought Teller's motive was simply "a desire on his part to take a slap at the President," but several congressmen, friendly to the administration, were working on the "senile statesman from the Rockies" to induce him to drop his opposition. "I imagine," Bat said, "Ben is not anxious to have that penitentiary matter exploited again in the press as well as an executive session of the Senate."[15]

In a letter to artist Frederic Remington several months later Roosevelt voiced his frustration with the opposition to his appointments of the western frontier characters he so admired: "You know I have appointed to office in the West, and in the case of Bat Masterson, in the East, a number of the very men whose types you have permanently preserved with pencil and pen. . . . I have a good deal of difficulty to get the Senate to take the proper view about some of these men, notably Ben Daniels, who is really a first-class fellow."[16]

Typical of the protests against Roosevelt's controversial appointments was a letter to the president from a physician who objected to the appointments of Daniels and Masterson, both of whom he accused of murder. He claimed to have known them in Dodge City, where Masterson had filled twenty-six graves, and where Daniels, "cowardly and sneakily," shot a man in the back. The appointments, he said, blackened an "otherwise brilliant administration."[17]

Despite the objections, Roosevelt continued to push for the confirmation of Ben Daniels. In April 1906 he had Bat to lunch in Washington and announced that he finally had convinced influential senators to support the nomination, and Daniels would be confirmed. The following spring Bat was back at the White House, where he had the pleasure of meeting with the president and his old friend Daniels, newly installed U.S. marshal for Arizona.

Later that year, when Oklahoma achieved statehood, the national press reported that Bat Masterson's name led the list of candidates for appointment as U.S. marshal for the new state. It was a name that "has come thundering down the ages," said one hyperbolic account.

GUNFIGHTER IN GOTHAM

Masterson, with "the old Dodge City gleam" in his eye, would bring to the job a hand that could manipulate "the new-fashioned hammerless gun" as steadily and swiftly "as the one that cut the notches on the sawed off Colt's in the old Kansas days." Masterson was much better fitted, in this writer's opinion, to lead "the wild free life of the west" than "idling on Broadway, serving subpoenas on wicked trust magnates and writing dilettante articles for the sporting journals."[18]

If Roosevelt ever made a formal offer of the appointment to Masterson, Bat turned it down; he had no desire to relocate in Oklahoma, but the thought of a full New York marshalship was appealing. Deciding to take a shot at his boss's job, Bat wrote Roosevelt in July 1908, suggesting that Marshal Henkel might be reassigned to New Mexico, thus opening up for Bat the marshal's position in southern New York. The president's response was not encouraging. Henkel, he believed, wanted to remain in his present position and, in addition, reaction in New Mexico might be extremely negative if an "outsider" was given this important post.[19]

Roosevelt chose not to run for reelection in 1908. His personally selected successor was his secretary of war, William Howard Taft, who was duly nominated by the Republicans and elected in November. Soon after Taft assumed office in March 1909 it became apparent that he and members of his administration did not share Roosevelt's affinity for colorful western characters. In June Henry A. Wise, newly appointed U.S. district attorney in New York, wrote his boss, Attorney General George W. Wickersham, reporting that a deputy marshal, "one W. B. Masterson, commonly known as 'Bat' Masterson," was assigned to his office but apparently had no duties. In his several months on the job, Wise had not seen Masterson or been aware of any service he performed. He asked to be relieved of any responsibility for this deputy's actions (or inactions).[20]

This letter set the bureaucratic termination proceedings in motion. Within a week Wickersham brought the matter of Bat's no-show sinecure to the attention of President Taft. He pointed out the disparity of deputy salaries, and suggested that the position was wholly unnecessary and the service would be improved by Masterson's separation from it.[21]

Taft's response was prompt and unambiguous: "With respect to 'Bat' Masterson . . . , I don't see that there is any course possible for you to pursue [other] than to discharge him from the government employ."[22]

Wickersham gave Henkel one last chance to justify Bat's job. On June 30 he wrote the marshal, advising that U.S. Attorney Wise had no use for the deputy's services and asked Henkel to define what other duties, if any, Masterson performed. Henkel's reply contained a short summation of how Masterson got the job "at the personal request of Theodore Roosevelt, then President of the United States," and his assignment to the district attorney's office. Since that office indicated his services were not required, Henkel suggested a reassignment of the deputy to his direct control.[23]

The day after Henkel's letter was posted Alfred Henry Lewis got wind of the official correspondence between New York and Washington over the matter of Masterson's job retention and dashed off a letter to Taft, expressing his concern. Bat's appointment, he reminded the president, had been at the "personal suggestion" of Theodore Roosevelt, and it had been the wish of the former occupant of the White House that Bat be retained. For that reason alone he believed it would be "publicly and politically better" for the administration if Masterson were kept on. The matter, no doubt minor for the president, was nevertheless "grave" for Masterson. While admitting he was in a poor position to request the reappointment as a personal favor as he enjoyed no "nearness" with the new president, Lewis did exactly that.[24]

His pleas fell on deaf ears. The matter was referred to Chief of the Division of Accounts J. J. Glover, who noted that Henkel had not indicated an actual need or justification for the deputy's services, and added his recommendation that Masterson be terminated. That same day, July 12, Wickersham wrote Henkel asking for an official termination request. The marshal promptly provided the request, and on July 15 Wickersham authorized the issuance of formal notice to Masterson that his commission would be terminated as of August 1.

Bat shrugged off the dismissal with the nonchalance of the seasoned gambler. The deputy's job had been a sweet arrangement, a real soft touch, but, as a gambler, he knew that no run of luck lasts forever, and when it was over, you simply pocketed your winnings and moved on.

— 7 —

BLUNDERBUSSES AND BADGES

Some of the New York papers express surprise that at the time of his arrest Bat Masterson, late of Denver, did a great deal of fiery talking, but showed no disposition to pull his gun. Those esteemed papers seem to be ignorant of the fact that Bat's most effective weapon is his mouth.

Denver Post

The public image of Bat Masterson as a western gunfighter faded somewhat as he became more closely identified with the newspaper profession and more widely recognized as a prize ring authority. But the legend of Masterson, pistol-wielder and man-killer, was firmly established, and his name would always be associated with handguns and their usage.

At his arrest in 1902, according to press reports, he had seemed more concerned that his pistol had been taken than that he had been charged with swindling. He was quoted as saying it was like losing his best friend, for that pistol had often saved his life. He vowed to get the gun back if it cost him "many stacks of blues" to do it. Prodded by reporters to identify the weapon as the instrument with which he had dispatched twenty-eight men, he would only say that he had owned it since 1877.[1] After payment of his concealed weapons fine, the pistol was returned to him.

He told a *World* reporter that all the newspaper attention about his pistol would cause him to be "jollied from one end of the country to the other." This was ridiculous, he said, because there were at

87

least 40,000 "fakers" in New York carrying bigger guns than "that old shooter the fly cops took from me." Asked why he carried a gun, Bat explained that he often carried "bunches of money" at late hours, and if anyone tried to hold him up, he had "the old gun ready to make a bluff with."[2]

In another interview he protested that he was wearied by all the stories of the many men he had killed and the notches on his gun. Nothing published about him, he said, came within "gunshot of the truth."[3]

In later years readers of his column sometimes made snide references to his reputed affinity for firearms. In a vitriolic letter to Bat, someone signing himself "Claudius Hespro" as late as 1919 compared victims of the columnist's "typewriter shooting" to those who once fell before his murderous "blunderbuss." Responding in his column, Bat snorted: "Claudius, we have never used a blunderbuss or any other sort of lethal weapon on such as you. We have always been able to dispose of your sort of cattle with a dash or two of insect powder."[4]

The pistol he was carrying when arrested in 1902 was one of many .45 caliber single-action Colt's revolvers he had purchased over the years. Letters he wrote to the Colt Firearms Company indicate he ordered at least eight of these weapons, either for his own use or for friends. He was very particular about his pistols, specifying barrel length, front sight thickness, material and decoration of the handle, and always, "very easy on the trigger."[5]

Zoe Anderson Norris, feature writer for the *New York Times*, interviewed Masterson in his home at the time of his deputy marshal appointment. Anxious to disprove the stories that his pistol was notched for the men he had killed, Bat brought out two six-shooters, one he said was his personal weapon, and another he identified as belonging to a friend in Alabama. His own gun, he pointed out, was free of marks, but Norris noted that the other was nicked with "eighteen or more" notches.[6]

According to Emma Masterson, Bat kept two pistols in his home and took them with him when he traveled. She was certain neither of these weapons was notched because she had practiced with them herself when she and her husband were in Hot Springs. Both pistols were given away, she said, after he died.[7] If these were the same two guns Bat showed Zoe Norris, the notches the *Times* reporter thought she saw are unexplained.

Only a month after Norris said she saw "eighteen or more" nicks on one of Bat's guns, he was quoted as saying that he had never seen a gun with notched handles and never heard of anyone who did. He dismissed all New York writers as not knowing "a gun from the hind leg of a mule."[8] In a *New York Herald* interview five years later he repeated his contempt for eastern reporters who wrote "trash" about events of which they knew nothing. He was particularly irked because they insisted on repeating the fable that "a peaceable man" like himself owned a gun with twenty-seven notches.[9]

Stories of Masterson six-shooters with notched handles persisted throughout Bat's lifetime and beyond. An oft-repeated tale is that he picked up an old six-gun in a Manhattan pawnshop, nicked the handle, and palmed it off to a gullible collector as his "favorite" six-shooter, the sidearm he had carried in the West. Stuart Lake, in his semifictional biography of Wyatt Earp, attributed this story to Earp. "Bat's sense of humor was responsible, and he didn't dream of the consequences," Wyatt supposedly explained.[10]

This specious story clearly originated in a book published after Bat's death, but four years before Lake's panegyric to Wyatt Earp. In his 1927 book, *Hands Up!*, Fred Sutton claimed to have visited Masterson in New York and been given a six-shooter with twenty-two notches, or "credits."

"You killed twenty-two men with this gun?" Sutton asked.

"And I didn't count greasers or Indians," was the enigmatic reply.[11]

Bat's brother Tom called this story ridiculous. "Bat never gave him his old six-shooter with 22 notches, had a gun with notches, and had no respect for anyone who had."[12]

The apocryphal story, expanded to include lucrative sales of phony notch-handled pistols by Bat to many awestruck and gullible admirers, has become part of the Masterson legend.[13]

Although Bat was always identified with the Colt's .45 caliber single-action revolver, about 1909 he lent his considerable prestige as a handgun expert to the promotion of a new pistol being introduced to the market. The Savage Arms Company had developed a light, .32 caliber, ten-shot automatic and commissioned Masterson to write an article extolling its virtues. Bat turned out a piece called "The

Tenderfoot's Turn," which was part treatise on western frontier gun-fighting and its practitioners, part analysis of the benefits and drawbacks of single- and double-action revolvers, and finally, in the last paragraphs, a testimonial to the efficiency of the Savage automatic and its superiority over what he called the old "crude six-shooter with its walking stick handle." He assured prospective pistol buyers that "a tenderfoot, with a Savage Automatic and the nerve to stand his ground, could have run the worst six-shooter men the West ever saw right off the range."[14]

Owners of any kind of handgun in the state of New York were dealt a severe blow shortly after Savage introduced its new pistol. On September 1, 1911, a stringent "dangerous weapon" statute, called the "Sullivan law" after its author, State Senator Timothy D. Sullivan, went into effect. It prohibited the carrying or keeping of handguns in homes or business places, with heavy penalties for violators. It was then, and remains today, one of the nation's strictest gun control laws. Broad enough to include as dangerous weapons "blackjacks, bludgeons, sandbags, sandclubs, billies, slungshots and metal knuckles," the law made it a felony to own or sell any of these items.[15]

Masterson had long known and socialized with Tim Sullivan, political boss of the Bowery and partner of the Considine brothers, but that did not deter him from attacking the measure as one that would only be welcomed by criminals. Under this "obnoxious" law, Bat fumed, law-abiding citizens who owned a weapon could be convicted and sent to prison, while criminals would no longer fear effective resistance from victims defending their lives and property. His arguments can be heard today, almost a century later, from opponents of gun control legislation.

Bat called on politicians to come to their senses and rescind the "abomination." He knew Tim Sullivan well, he said, and spoke from firsthand knowledge when he charged him with being almost "in a state of mental collapse" when he introduced his gun bill. Shortly thereafter Sullivan did have a mental breakdown and died under peculiar circumstances, but the law remained on the books. Long after its author was gone, Bat was still railing against the gun ban.[16]

Of course the law did not deter Masterson from the ownership of handguns, although he may have obtained a permit through his influential cronies. Over the years he owned several unusual specimens, which he gave away to friends. Damon Runyon had a .44 caliber Smith & Wesson revolver and a sword cane given to him by Masterson. Runyon said the cane was more than a curiosity; Bat used to carry it on his strolls through the streets of New York.[17]

William E. Lewis also acquired several Masterson items, including an odd revolver, a D. Moore .32 caliber rim-fire seven-shooter, and a 14-karat gold badge with blue enamel marked "Deputy Chief, Bureau of Special Service, Police Department, New York." According to Lewis family tradition, the items were found in Bat's desk after his death.

Masterson was given another badge when a group of his friends gathered in the café of the Delevan Hotel on May 6, 1905, to celebrate his deputy marshal's appointment.

Tom O'Rourke and others made speeches, and W. E. Lewis made the presentation. The badge was formed of solid 14-karat gold, studded with four large diamonds, and was valued at $1,000, almost twice the annual earnings of an average American worker in 1905. With its historical significance added to the vastly increased value of its gold and precious stones, this badge, were it to surface today, would be worth many tens of thousands of dollars. What happened to it is unknown.

Bat Masterson and prizefighter Charlie Mitchell at Minnehaha Falls, Minnesota, in 1886. (Courtesy Western History Department, Denver Public Library)

In 1894 the *Illustrated Sporting West* called Masterson "one of the best judges of pugilists in America." (Courtesy Western History Department, Denver Public Library)

Sketch from *Logansport Journal*
August 17, 1895

Mrs. "Bat" Masterson, née Emma Walter Moulton, as she was depicted in an artist's drawing in the *Logansport Journal* of August 17, 1895. (Courtesy Chris Penn)

Otto Floto, one-time partner with Masterson in a Denver fight club, became a bitter enemy. (Courtesy Western History Department, Denver Public Library)

Bat Masterson in 1899. (Courtesy Kansas State Historical Society, Topeka)

Masterson lent his prestige as an expert wielder of handguns to this 1909 ad for the new Savage automatic pistol. It is the only known photo of Bat with weapon in hand. (Author's collection)

— 8 —

GOTHAM FEUDS

The element that I resented more than anything else was the fact that I was charged with shooting drunken Indians and drunken Mexicans when nothing of the kind ever happened. It wouldn't make any difference, shooting them in the back or in the stomach.

W. B. "Bat" Masterson

Bat Masterson was seldom without a dragon to slay. In Dodge City he had jousted with his political opponents, and in Denver he had warred fiercely with Floto, Gallagher, and Tammen. His natural belligerence was easily aroused, and he attacked his enemies with a vengeance, especially when he thought his honor was being challenged.

In New York these assaults mostly took the form of written harangues, but some led to physical clashes. On at least two occasions while wearing his deputy U.S. marshal's badge, he forgot Teddy Roosevelt's admonition to behave himself and engaged in common brawls.

One of these altercations was with Richard D. Plunkett, whom Bat had known as an officer at Creede, Colorado, where Plunkett gained some frontier prominence by arresting Ed O'Kelley, the man who killed Bob Ford, slayer of Jesse James. A big man, weighing 238 pounds, Plunkett got into the ring game in Oklahoma as a prizefighter, promoter, and official. He also was reputed to be a gunfighter who packed a revolver with "enough notches to make a good nutmeg grater."[1]

In 1906 Plunkett came to New York accompanied by a Texas newspaperman with the unlikely name "Dinklesheets," and toured the Broadway watering holes. In each he denounced Bat Masterson, the city's famous western gunfighter, as a fraud and a phony. It did not take long for this calumny to reach Bat.

On the evening of June 22 Plunkett and Dinklesheets were in the café of the staid Waldorf-Astoria Hotel when "the dreaded Bat gathered himself into the café with blood in his eye." Confronting Plunkett, Bat growled, "Let's go outside." He grabbed the big man's coat and pulled him toward the door. Plunkett did not resist, but Dinklesheets, very inebriated, intervened. He swung clumsily at Masterson, missed him, but knocked over a table, shattering glassware. Bat retaliated with a right-hand punch that landed flush on the jaw of the Texan and knocked him out cold. Masterson then thrust his hand into a side pocket and shoved "something hard" against Plunkett's stomach. "Look out! Bat's going to flash Betsy!" someone yelled. There was a general rush for the exits to the clatter of more overturned tables and broken glasses. House detective Joe Smith appeared, separated the men, and ordered them out of the establishment. The combatants exited by separate doorways. Once Bat had left, Plunkett roared that he could wipe up the floor with anyone "who would offer himself as a mop." Dinklesheets, regaining consciousness, also became loud and boisterous before Waldorf-Astoria employees escorted him to a cab.[2]

A reporter cornered Masterson later that evening and asked to see the gun that had panicked the Waldorf-Astoria patrons. Bat smiled and pulled a package of cigarettes from his pocket. When told that Plunkett was continuing his bombast against him in other bars, Bat shrugged and said: "He'll probably recover from the cigarettes I threatened him with."[3]

A year later Bat was in another fistic encounter, this time with Walter St. Denis, sports editor of the *New York Globe*. The two came to blows at the Belmont Race Track after a series of "mutual recriminations" in their respective columns. Witnesses to the fracas said that Masterson struck St. Denis three times. The *Globe* editor filed a complaint with the Belmont stewards, who tabled it, and there the affair ended. Having made his point, Bat studiously avoided references to

St. Denis in his columns thereafter. The *New York Herald* reported that "friends of Bat were inclined to treat the whole matter with levity."[4]

Not long after the St. Denis affray, Masterson began a long-running feud with sports columnist and cartoonist Bob Edgren of the *New York Evening World*. Edgren edited what a full-page banner daily proclaimed was "The Best Sporting Page in New York," a boast the Masterson found particularly irksome. After some fairly innocuous sparring in their respective columns, on December 10, 1909, Edgren accused Bat of writing falsehoods and performing "the unique feat of starting with nothing and evolving a whole column." Under the heading "Why Gun Fighters Fail as Referees," he then proceeded to rip Bat's record as a ring official. To buttress his argument, he added a lengthy account of Wyatt Earp's role as referee of the controversial Fitzsimmons-Sharkey fight of 1896. Edgren, a twenty-two-year-old fledgling reporter on William Randolph Heart's *San Francisco Examiner* at the time, remembered Earp as a broken-down gambler whose shabby Prince Albert "hung on his gaunt frame with a wrinkled seedy air of poverty." Edgren said Earp, who had been hired by the paper's editor as a bodyguard, was hanging around the editorial rooms when the young reporter asked to see the famous gunman's pistol, and Earp pulled out a six-shooter and proudly pointed to a row of nicks on the handle. "There were twelve, if I remember right," said Edgren. Shortly thereafter came the disputed fight that Earp awarded to Sharkey on a foul. It was clear from the Edgren account that he believed Earp had been bought off by the gamblers.[5]

Bat sent a copy of Edgren's column to Earp, then living in Parker, Arizona, and requested a written response. On December 24, 1909, Wyatt obliged with a letter Masterson quoted in his column. Earp began by saying that he had always tried to ignore what was written about him in the newspapers, as much of it was untrue and his friends knew that. "So long as I retain the esteem and good opinion of my friends," he said, "what others think of me does not in the least disturb my mind." (This attitude was in sharp contrast to that of Masterson, who reacted quickly to adverse press.)

Earp called Edgren's representations "absolute falsehoods." He had hardly been poverty-stricken in 1896, he said, for he owned and raced a stable of thoroughbreds at that time, lived in a suite of rooms at the Baldwin Hotel, and wore personally tailored clothes. He had never been employed as bodyguard for a newspaper editor, nor had he ever owned a notch-handled pistol. But if he had carried such a weapon, he would never have shown it to "a callow youth" like Edgren. Earp called Edgren's remarks "both cowardly and reprehensible," and said he would like "to put twelve neatly carved notches on Edgren's tongue."[6]

Bat was sure he knew why Edgren had chosen this particular moment to bring up Wyatt Earp and the controversial prizefight of thirteen years earlier. In early 1910 the *Morning Telegraph* was running a contest to determine its candidate for selection as referee of the upcoming and long-awaited heavyweight title fight between Jack Johnson and Jim Jeffries. Edgren and Masterson had both been nominated, as were a host of other sporting men, former fighters, and boxing commentators. Although the winner would not necessarily be chosen to referee the fight, his influence and prestige among ring enthusiasts would be enhanced. Not surprisingly, readers of the *Telegraph* quickly voted Masterson into a commanding lead. Edgren's column, "Why Gun Fighters Fail as Referees," was an obvious attempt to deprecate the honesty and ability of his rival.

As far away as California, boxing writers followed the *Morning Telegraph* contest and the Edgren-Masterson competition. Eddie Smith of the *Oakland Tribune* opined that Edgren's attack was unfair to Masterson, who was regarded in the West as "one of the gamest men who ever pulled a high-heeled boot over his foot."[7]

Bat later withdrew his name from the contest, assuring his readers that Edgren's slander had not influenced his decision, but that he had no desire to referee the big fight. Edgren, who never had a chance in a contest sponsored by Masterson's paper, also dropped out. Another contestant who was no friend of Masterson, Walter St. Denis of the *Globe*, received only 501 votes. The winner, announced in March, was Michael "One-Eyed Buck" Connelly, Bat's old pal of bare-knuckle days, who received 60,000 of some 300,000 votes cast.

Bat never forgave Edgren for his disparaging remarks and often took shots at him in his column, seldom deigning to call him by name, but referring to him sarcastically as "the editor of the best sporting page in New York." He accused Edgren of duplicity, saying he would "shake your hand and beam on you in the most sycophantic way, and then stab you in the back." Bat concluded that the man was "a fit subject for an observation ward in some sanitarium."[8]

Edgren had come to New York from San Francisco to take a job on the *Evening Journal* as a political cartoonist. Sent to Cuba during the Spanish-American War, he was acclaimed for his "Sketches of Death," graphic artistic depictions of war atrocities. Captured by the Spaniards, he escaped to Key West. After he became sports editor of the *Evening World* in 1904, his cartoons and writings were widely syndicated.

In college Edgren had gained some renown as a track and field athlete, and had competed in the Olympic games as a hammer-thrower. Bat sneered at Edgren's hammer-throwing ability, saying all he could throw expertly was the "bull con."[9]

Bob Edgren had a younger brother, Leonard, also a cartoonist and journalist, who played a key role in one of the most explosive controversies of Masterson's newspaper career. The story began in 1911 during the "White Hope" period when obscure Caucasian heavyweights jousted for the honor of taking on black champion Jack Johnson and restoring the title to the white race. One of these untested fighters was Carl Morris, managed and promoted by wealthy Oklahoma oilman Frank B. Ufer. In the summer of 1911 Ufer mounted a campaign to match Morris with old warhorse Jim Flynn, at Madison Square Garden in New York. He touted Morris, 235 pounds of bone and muscle, as "a sure thing" to beat Flynn.

It was such a sure thing that Bat smelled a frame-up. In a column he called the match "a piece of Limburger," with the oilman's money guaranteeing a Flynn dive, and unsuccessfully called on the boxing commission to put a stop to the affair.[10] Cornering Flynn in the Metropole Hotel, he demanded to know what he had been offered to take a dive. Sputtering, Flynn confessed that he had been promised $7,500, but now that Bat had exposed the "fix," he intended to double-cross Ufer and knock out Morris if he could.

As Masterson predicted, with the "fix" off, Morris proved to be no match for the veteran Flynn, who hammered him terribly for ten rounds. Morris bled so profusely that referee Charlie White had to change shirts midway in the bout.

Not everyone accepted Bat's claim that he had single-handedly prevented a flagrant frame-up from being perpetrated on New York's

GUNFIGHTER IN GOTHAM

fight fans. Bob Edgren and others ridiculed his story. He received many anonymous letters calling him what he said were "the vilest names imaginable" and containing "the foulest abuse that a degenerate mind could conceive." Bat struck back at Edgren and those he termed "we boys," sportswriters who took money from promoters to boost setups, saying it would be impossible to pull off fake contests without their support. His detractors never challenged the veracity of his assertions, he said, but simply vilified him as a "knocker."[11]

Frank Ufer, thwarted in his planned build-up of Carl Morris leading to a title match, sought revenge by mounting a smear campaign against Masterson. Aware of the enmity already existing between Bat and Bob Edgren, he enlisted the aid of Edgren's brother Leonard in that effort. Assuring Leonard that Masterson's record in the West was deplorable, that he had built that record by shooting "drunken cowboys and Indians in the back," he gave the young man a prepared typewritten statement of this accusation and said he was distributing it to all the New York papers.[12] If Ufer did pass copies to writers at other papers, no one except Leonard Edgren chose to print his allegations.

In addition to his regular job at the *Evening World*, Leonard Edgren wrote occasional boxing pieces for the *New York Globe and Advertiser*. He turned over Ufer's screed to reporter James E. MacBride of the *Globe*, who quoted it in an article that appeared on page one of the September 15, 1911, issue under Leonard Edgren's byline. Ufer was quoted as calling Masterson "an alleged bad man and gun fighter who made his reputation by shooting drunken Mexicans and Indians in the back." Somehow in the transmission, Ufer's original phrase "drunken cowboys and Indians" had become "drunken Mexicans and Indians."

Outraged, Bat Masterson quickly retaliated. Within a week he brought separate court actions against Ufer and the Commercial Advertiser Association, publishers of the *Globe*. In the Ufer suit he charged the defendant with two causes, maliciously uttering "false and defamatory words" regarding the plaintiff "in the presence and hearing of a number of persons," and maliciously composing and publishing the same "false and defamatory matter," thereby injuring and damaging the plaintiff's reputation. Damages were figured at $5,000 on each cause. The plaintiff demanded judgment against the defendant in the sum of $10,000, plus costs of the action. Benjamin Patterson, attorney for Masterson, filed the suit on September 22, 1911.[13]

On the same day Patterson filed another action against the publishers of the *Globe*, charging that the same "false and defamatory matter" had been "maliciously composed and published" in the paper, thereby injuring the plaintiff's reputation. Damages were reckoned at $25,000.[14]

The Ufer suit, scheduled for hearing on Monday, February 5, 1912, was postponed when the defendant's attorney reported to the court that his client was not in the state. A series of postponements followed until lawyers representing the two sides meeting in Oklahoma on October 22, 1913, agreed on an undisclosed settlement, and the suit was dropped from the docket.

After several postponements, the case against the *Globe* came to trial before a jury on May 20, 1913. Justice John Ford presided, Benjamin Patterson represented Masterson, and Benjamin N. Cardozo, later a justice of the U.S. Supreme Court, represented the defendant.

In his formal answer to the complaint, Cardozo said:

> The plaintiff has been for a great many years well known throughout the United States as a promiscuous carrier of and user of fire arms and as having shot a number of men, including Indians, some of whom died as a result of said shooting, and he did on divers occasions become involved in conflicts in which he shot, wounded and killed a number of men, including Indians, and that his reputation at the time of the publication was due to such alleged exploits.

Cardozo also claimed that Masterson had long been known as a "sporting man," and that Ufer's comment was simply "the remark of one sporting man concerning another sporting man, and [was meant] to be humorous and jocular."[15]

During the trial both attorneys and Judge Ford questioned Masterson closely and at length regarding his experiences in the West and the basis for his reputation as a gunfighter. Since Bat never wrote an autobiography, his answers, given under oath, provide a fascinating and unique insight into how he viewed the violent episodes in his career and the notoriety they engendered.

He vehemently denied the allegation that he shot Mexicans, Indians, or anyone else in the back. He told of his participation in the Battle of Adobe Walls and his service as a scout in the Red River War. When asked how many Indians he had shot, he said he wasn't sure, but he had done his best to shoot them and it wasn't his fault if he didn't hit any. He could not say whether any of the Indians he shot were drunk. Having never had a personal altercation with a Mexican, he denied ever shooting one, drunk or sober, in the back or in the front.

Cardozo wanted to know exactly how many men he had shot and killed in his life. Masterson thought "about three," whom he identified as a soldier in Texas who had shot him first (Corporal King), a Texas cowboy in Dodge City who had just fatally wounded his brother (Jack Wagner), and another Texan, a wanted murderer, in 1879 (Jim Kenedy). He didn't think he had killed any others.[16]

Cardozo was incredulous. "You are not sure?"

"Well, let me see—I shot another man. I don't know whether I killed him or not; I think he got well. I shot him about two years later, in about 1881, in Dodge City, Kansas." (Here he referred to Al Updegraff, wounded severely in an April 1881 gun battle with Masterson at Dodge City. Updegraff survived this fight to die of smallpox two years later.)

Bat could think of no other shooting scrapes in which he took part. When asked about firing his pistol in a Denver polling place and inflicting a minor wound on a citizen, he made light of the affair. A policeman pulled a gun on him, and he had to shoot the weapon out of his hand. "That was all there was to it. I would not call it a fight. I certainly did not hurt him." He admitted having "one or two" fistfights, including the one with Otto Floto on the Denver street. A question from Cardozo prompted this exchange:

"Now, do you think of any other fights that you ever had?"

"Well, I am not thinking; I suppose you are doing the thinking. I do not know of any other fights that I ever had; I have never had very many fights."

"You don't think you have been a fighting man at all?"

"No, indeed; I never had any one accuse me of it."

"How many fights have you had?"

"Well, I am fifty-nine years old, and I have been—I can't tell you. I told you all about the serious troubles. The fist-fights . . . I couldn't tell you anything about that. . . . I would not like to say positively that I have not had some more; I couldn't think of any more."

"And you would not like to say positively that you had not shot some more men, would you?"

"Yes sir; I state that most positively . . . "

"I don't mean men you have killed, but men you have shot at. Have you fired any shots at any other men?"

"No, sir."

Later Cardozo asked Masterson if it wasn't true that he was proud of his record as a man-killer.

"Oh, I don't think about being proud about it. I feel perfectly justified," Bat responded. "The mere fact that I was charged with killing a man standing by itself I have never considered an attack upon my reputation."

"Well, then, was the element in this publication which you resented the fact that you were charged with shooting them in the back?"

"The element that I resented more than anything else was the fact that I was charged with shooting drunken Indians and drunken Mexicans when nothing of the kind ever happened. It wouldn't make any difference, shooting them in the back or in the stomach."

"Then you didn't like the idea of shooting Indians or Mexicans, was that it?"

"I didn't like the idea of being accused of something I wasn't guilty of. I had endeavored to shoot a great many Indians. I was in the war; I was serving my country. I resented the charge that I had been shooting Indians, because I was charged with shooting drunken Indians in the back."[17]

William E. Lewis and John Coulter of the *Morning Telegraph*, both of whom had known Masterson years before in Kansas, were the only witnesses for the plaintiff. Generals Frank Baldwin and Nelson A. Miles did not appear as witnesses as has been reported.[18]

The defense called Leonard Edgren and James MacBride of the *Globe*; Patrick F. Gargan, the policeman who had arrested Bat back in 1902; and Charles S. Whitman, New York County district attorney and future governor of the state.

Masterson's New York reputation, Whitman said, was "for peace and good order," but he was renowned for getting any man he went after. He was famous as "a dead shot" who had killed a number of men.

Cardozo: "Do you remember it was as many as twenty-eight?"

Whitman: "I should say it was more."

Gargan's testimony regarding Bat's arrest in 1902 so infuriated Masterson that he later filed a complaint with the Police Commission, charging the officer with perjury.

The jury agreed with Bat's claim that he had been defamed, and awarded damages of $3,500 plus $129.25 in court costs. W. E. Lewis personally wrote the story of the trial for the *Morning Telegraph*, delightedly reporting that Masterson had been vindicated and the *Globe* was being punished "for baseless and maliciously careless assaults on the character of a square man."[19]

Although the offending phrase had appeared under Leonard Edgren's byline, Bat had not named the humble young sportswriter in his suits, targeting instead those with abundant assets, millionaire oilman Ufer and the large publishing house. He may have also considered Leonard simply a pawn in a campaign hatched by Bob Edgren and Ufer to vilify him. The affair further hardened his animosity toward Bob Edgren, and he sniped at him at every opportunity. The editor of "the best sporting page in New York" was, he assured his readers, "as wild as a March hare,"[20] "an awful joke,"[21] whose opinions should be ignored unless verified by a reliable authority, someone like Masterson.[22]

Edgren left the *World* in 1918 to take a newspaper position in California. In noting his departure, Bat conceded that Edgren "meant well and tried to the best of his ability to make the page all he claimed it to be," but he was a dreamer who confused his nightmares with facts.[23] In another column Bat suggested that Edgren's "dreams" stemmed from drug use, and he never forgave the man.[24] Like Otto Floto and Reddy Gallagher, Bob Edgren remained a target of his spleen until Bat wrote his last column in 1921.[25]

While exchanging barbs with his New York foes, Masterson never forgot his Denver enemies, often firing long-distance salvoes at Floto and Gallagher. As with Edgren, he seldom referred to them by name. After he heard that Gallagher had "several dashes of Negro blood in his make-up" the redheaded boxer became the "Memphis Coon" in the Masterson lexicon. Always ambivalent in his racist remarks, Bat obviously attached the appellation to Gallagher in scornful deprecation while at the same time he heaped praise on Christy Williams, a black boxer fighting under the ring name "Memphis Coon," for his talent and courage.

In 1916 Otto Floto, usually referred to by Bat as "a certain bloviating kidney-footed sporting writer," refereed a lightweight title match between Ad Wolgast and Freddie Welsh in Denver and nearly triggered a riot when he awarded the fight to Welsh on a foul in the eleventh round. Wolgast later complained bitterly to Bat that he was "deliberately robbed" by Floto. Not having seen the fight, Bat declined to comment on whether there was a foul blow or not, but agreed that the referee didn't know the difference "between a contest waged according to Queensberry rules and a catch-as-catch-can wrestling match."[26]

When he learned a month later that Floto had been selected to referee an important bout in Tulsa, Oklahoma, Bat advised all those "speculatively inclined" to avoid the match if "the gazook sporting writer of Denver" was involved, and reminded them that decisions in previous bouts Floto had refereed had been so outrageous that he became "the target of all manner of missiles, including decayed eggs" and had to be "escorted to the depot by the local gendarmes."[27]

Gene Fowler, who was working for Floto on the *Denver Post* during this period, refereed some bouts promoted by the paper and its sports editor, including one in which he also had to be escorted from the arena by police to protect him from angry fans. This, of course, delighted Masterson, who reported the affair in all its sordid detail.

In 1917 Fowler followed his friend Damon Runyon to New York to work on the *American*. When he introduced himself to Bat Masterson and announced he was from Denver, he received a less than cordial reception. Bat, no doubt recalling the young man's association with Floto, gave him the cold eye and snapped: "Denver can go to hell!" Fowler had the distinct impression that the damnation applied to him as well, and the two never became friendly.[28]

Masterson also viewed the spectacular rise of another Coloradan with a jaundiced eye. Not only was heavyweight boxer Jack Dempsey, soon to become famous as "the Manassa Mauler," loudly touted by the likes of Bob Edgren, but Otto Floto had guided the fighter's early ring career in Colorado and, it was said, retained a financial interest in him. Personal dislike and disdain for both Edgren and Floto tainted Masterson's judgment, leading him to underestimate badly Dempsey's remarkable ring ability.

Bat even disparaged a racehorse that had the misfortune, in his view, of being saddled with the name Otto Floto. "How could a horse win any kind of a race with that sort of a name wished on him?" he asked his readers. He thought it shameful that anyone would handicap a poor defenseless horse with such a "moniker."[29]

This horse name business cut both ways. About this time a horse named Bat Masterson was racing on tracks around the country. When he dropped dead in the back stretch one day, Otto Floto entitled a column "Poetic Justice" and opined that even an elephant could not bear the weight of both a jockey and a bad name.[30]

— 9 —

THE CURMUDGEON OF THE CLUBS

*Bat was one of the most out-spoken, don't-give-a-damn-for-conse-
quences commentators that ever roasted a faking scrapper or took a
fall out of a crooked promoter.*

Nat Fleischer

Bat Masterson was drawn to New York City originally because the
big city at the turn of the century was a center of boxing activity.
At the Seaside Athletic Club, the original Madison Square Garden,
and the Westchester Club he had seen some of the greatest fighters
of the era perform—champions like Dal Hawkins, Kid Lavigne, Joe
Gans, Joe Walcott, Kid McCoy, Jim Jeffries, Bob Fitzsimmons, and
Jim Corbett. The bouts had been refereed by some of the most famous arbiters of the period: Sam Austin, Charlie White, Dick Roche,
Johnny White, George Sisler, and Masterson himself. The Horton
law, then in effect in New York, permitted "boxing bouts" of a pro-
scribed number of rounds to be fought under Marquess of Queensberry rules, with a referee's decision if the match went the limit. But
the Horton law was repealed in 1900 after an apparently fraudulent
match between Jim Corbett and Kid McCoy. During most of the
years Bat lived in New York, the sport was shackled by a series of
restrictive statutes administered by political hacks. To his dismay, this
led to matches (often rigged) between mediocre fighters and staged
by unscrupulous managers and promoters.

About the time Bat settled in New York, the Lewis law replaced the
Horton statute. Under its provisions prizefights were essentially out-

lawed, but "fistic exhibitions" were permitted if presented at private boxing clubs for the entertainment of members only. This led to the era of "fight clubs" and "club fighters."

Bat's old friend Tom O'Rourke opened one of the first of the clubs, the National Sporting Club of America located in Amsterdam Hall on West Forty-Fourth Street, near Ninth Avenue. Later the place was given over to new management and the name changed to the Pioneer Athletic Club. Eventually as many as three-dozen fight clubs were operating in Greater New York.

The Frawley Boxing Bill of 1911, limiting bouts to ten rounds and prohibiting referee decisions, had a chilling effect on prizefighting in New York, and many of the clubs closed their doors. Masterson, a vociferous opponent of the law, noted a few months after its enactment that only Madison Square Garden and the St. Nicholas Arena were operating at a profit. By mid-1912 he could count only fourteen clubs still in operation: five in Manhattan, four in Brooklyn, four in Queens, and one in the Bronx.

Masterson had no financial interest in any of these clubs, nor did he promote bouts, manage boxers, or officiate ring contests after going to work on the *Morning Telegraph*. He last worked as a referee in 1903 when he was the third man in the ring at a historic match held in Detroit. Jack Root and Kid McCoy were matched in the first title fight of the newly formed light heavyweight division. At the end of ten furiously fought rounds referee Masterson raised the hand of Root, the first light heavyweight champion. Masterson's name was proposed as referee for several big fights in later years, including the much-ballyhooed Johnson-Jeffries heavyweight title fight of 1910, and he was invited to referee several military benefit bouts during the world war, but he declined all further officiating proposals.

In his columns Bat unabashedly touted the fight cards offered by Tom O'Rourke, and went to some lengths to help his friend succeed. When police threatened to shut down O'Rourke's club for presenting prizefights rather than "fistic entertainments," Masterson personally called on Mayor William Jay Gaynor to protest what he called gross discrimination. Gaynor talked to his police commissioner, and O'Rourke had no further problem. Bat's critics alleged he supported the O'Rourke club for personal gain, but he angrily denied the charge.

Generally Masterson did not use his column to promote matches or individuals, but chose instead to defend the fight game by exposing its seamy side. He saw himself as the guardian of the sport and constantly attacked those he thought brought discredit to it. In the words of ring historian Nat Fleischer, he was "one of the most outspoken, don't-give-a-damn-for-consequences commentators that ever roasted a faking scrapper or took a fall out of a crooked promoter. . . . He never pulled his punches, and wrote, just as he used to shoot, with deadly accuracy. He was dogmatic in his judgments, but never unfair, and went after the boxing crooks with a persistency of a bloodhound on the trail."[1]

He spared no one. Prizefighters, managers, referees, promoters, boxing commissioners, club proprietors, boxing writers, even the fans came under his critical eye, and when they strayed from what he considered the path of pugilistic virtue he skewered them with his barbed pen. He held the general run of club fighters in low regard, believing them pale imitations of earlier pugilists. They mainly suffered, he said, from poor breeding. "A fighter who isn't bred right can't fight a whit better than a horse can run which has a cold streak in his make-up. It takes a thoroughbred, whether man or horse, to achieve success."[2] In column after column he accused the era's pugilists of being ungrateful, greedy, vain, stupid, corrupt, cowardly, arrogant, and untruthful.

He sometimes directed his barbs at particular boxers for whom he had a personal antipathy. From his first meeting with lightweight champion Ad Wolgast in 1911 he disliked the man, describing him in his column as "an offensive upstart, the sublimation of egotism and self-esteem."[3] Leach Cross, a notoriously dirty fighter, was a frequent target of Masterson opprobrium. Bat found Cross's methods "contemptible," doubted if there was "a drop of sporting blood in his veins," and said the pug combined "the natural characteristics of a rattlesnake and prairie coyote."[4] Heavyweight Jim Savage could take a dive, he said, as gracefully as Annette Kellerman and suggested he change his name to "Jim Sausage" as he was "a sausage both inside and outside."[5] Masterson had always liked the personable Porky Flynn, but after a particularly dismal performance by the heavyweight, he blasted him as well. In his time, Bat said, he had seen plenty of wild-swinging saloon fighters, but for "awkwardness and downright stupidity" Flynn outdid them all.[6]

Utterly hopeless club fighters became "bohunks" in the Masterson lexicon. Bat called Al Reich, known in New York ring circles as the "diving Adonis" of the heavyweight division,[7] "the champion bohunk, a big piece of Gorgonzola who could hold all offices in the poltroon society without a dissenting vote."[8] Pugs like Reich were "never-wuzzers," several degrees below "has beens," who might once have amounted to something.[9]

He roasted managers and promoters who brought these "bohunks," "has beens," and "never-wuzzers" before the public. He had a low opinion of fight managers as a class, saying they were generally "a low conniving set of unprincipled cheats." Among the worst was manager John Reisler, who, because of his sharp practices, had been tagged by someone "John the Barber." Bat preferred to call him "John the Razor," or simply "the Razor." In addition to managing fighters, Reisler ran several clubs. In 1916 he signed a hungry young fighter from Colorado named Jack Dempsey to a contract and matched him in a ten-rounder at his Harlem Club with John Lester Johnson, the veteran black heavyweight. Johnson broke three of his opponent's ribs in the second round and beat him severely. Dempsey went the distance, but later said he was never hurt so badly in his long career. The treacherous Reisler kept $400 of Dempsey's $500 purse and left him to figure a way to mend his injuries. Disgusted with New York, Dempsey returned to the West. A few years later, after Dempsey hit the big time, Reisler unsuccessfully sought an injunction to prevent him from fighting under the management of anyone other than himself. "John the Razor," Bat scoffed, was a "bull peddler" in a class by himself.[10]

Masterson also ripped the New York City fight fans who supported with their dollars the poor fare offered in the clubs. They were, he said, "sapheads" and "boobs" for patronizing the "jug-handled affairs" offered by scoundrels who would "make Black Bart, the California road agent, turn over in his grave and sigh bitterly for being such a piker."[11] He deplored the loutish behavior of many of the club patrons, "leather-lunged, unwashed hoodlums," who often started fights in the galleries, but grudgingly admitted some of those battles proved more interesting to watch than the featured bout. When a spectator and a security guard put on what Bat called "a real nifty slugfest" one night in St. Nick's, he ignored the pugs pawing each other in the ring, and in his column the next day gave a blow-by-blow account of the amateur event.

Notorious for its rowdy clientele, the 135th Street Sporting Club was also frequented by the city's criminal class. The place was packed, Bat said, with "gunmen, Jack the Rippers, house-burners, horse poisoners and pickpockets." Gangs of pickpockets worked crowds in many of the clubs. Their work became so raw in a club one night a chaotic stampede resulted. "It was," Bat said disgustedly, "a gala old night for the Arverne Sporting Club."[12]

John Reisler's Harlem Sporting Club was another hangout for criminals and rowdies. During a riot there in 1916 someone threw a heavy wooden chair that landed squarely on Reisler's bald head. The chair shattered in pieces, but the Razor seemed unfazed. This was enough for Bat; he never went back to Reisler's club.

Masterson called for strong action by the club operators to control the rowdies. Perhaps remembering his cane-wielding days in the West, he recommended "the generous use of a hardwood stick in the hands of a healthy and determined man" to halt riotous behavior. After another disturbance at the Empire Athletic Club in which several inoffensive spectators were injured by missiles, he urged all club owners to employ special officers to maintain order. He advocated the forced closing of those clubs that failed to root out the hoodlums, saying that the "guerrilla element," if left uncontrolled, would destroy the sport.[13]

There were sporadic attempts to bring some sense of order and decorum to the clubs. In a 1912 match referee Young Corbett wore a tuxedo and officiated from a high chair outside the ring in the English style. Joe Jeannette and Battling Jim Johnson, the combatants, paid little attention to his shouted orders and clinched most of the time. Corbett finally had to climb in the ring and pry the men apart. The experiment in civility was deemed a failure.

In commenting on the New York boxing scene, Masterson directed most of his heavy salvos at what he considered onerous state laws regulating boxing, the politicians who enacted the laws, the commissioners appointed to administer them, and the sportswriters he accused of using those laws for personal gain. He attacked the Frawley law even before its passage, calling it "a piece of political bunk . . . , a transparent scheme to provide a few political hacks with jobs."[14] In his estimation the bill's only redeeming feature was a clause requiring those engaged in boxing to be of good moral character, but he cautioned that if the provision was designed to keep politicians out of boxing, it would fail miserably.

Since the law banned referee decisions, the practice began of having prominent boxing writers announce the winners of important fights that went the distance. The appointee of the *Morning Telegraph* was Bat Masterson, of course. In announcing Masterson's selection, editor Charles J. Meegan said the responsibility was important because many wagers were made on the outcome of these contests, and Bat's cool, unbiased judgment and long experience made him eminently qualified to render the decisions. Bat reluctantly accepted the assignment. "It has never been one of the ambitions of my life to decide sporting events, although it has often fallen to my lot to do so," he said. Well aware that the job was often thankless and opened wide the door to criticism, he warned his readers that those looking for "a closely scientific reading" in his decisions would be disappointed. He believed a fighter had to defeat his opponent decisively to be awarded a victory. When a match ended with both men erect, fully able to continue, he would not announce a winner based on mere technical out-pointing of one by the other, but would declare the bout a draw.[15]

Boosting of certain boxers by sportswriters, often for kickbacks from promoters or managers, had long been commonplace in boxing. Fixed and faked fights were also nothing new, having been a blight on the game since its beginnings. But with the innovation of fight decisions by newspaper columnists, Bat could see an even darker form of collusion developing. Now disreputable fighters, managers, promoters, and sportswriters could set up a "jug-handled" match and hype it through the writer's columns, ensuring a large turnout of "sapheads" and "boobs." After a phony pawing and clinching exhibition in which neither boxer suffered damage, an agreed-upon decision could then be rendered by the accommodating writer, thus guaranteeing all parties winnings on wagers they had made on the outcome. It was a tidy arrangement Masterson found to be absolutely despicable, and he harangued against it constantly.

He had long accepted the fact that, with few exceptions, those involved in the ring game—fighters, managers, and promoters—were driven by venality, but he was now particularly outraged that members of the journalistic profession were entering into the crooked deals, and he focused most of his attacks on his fellow sportswriters. Staging rigged fights on a regular basis would be impossible, he maintained, without the participation of the newsmen. By helping promote fake matches for money, they were killing the game. The writers were most censurable, he contended, for they made it possible for the others to pull off their fakes. Had newsmen exposed them, crooked fighters, managers, and promoters would have been driven from the game long before. If it were in his power, Bat vowed, he would jail everyone involved in the sorry mess, especially the "ballyhoo experts" of journalism.

These charges were almost impossible to prove, of course, and Bat, well aware of the slander and libel laws, generally confined his attacks to the general group of unscrupulous writers he termed the "we boys," and seldom mentioned individuals by name. (An exception was Bob Edgren, whom he often singled out for particular billingsgate.)

Of course Masterson did not ingratiate himself among many of his professional brethren with his constant attacks. This bothered him not in the least as he relished the role of the lone defender of honesty in the corrupt world of the ring. He was not a member of the Sporting Writers' Association of Greater New York and proudly proclaimed that fact.

In a January 1914 column Masterson accused promoter and manager Danny Morgan of contributing generously to the "we boys" for favorable press notices and assurance of arranged decisions. "It is those who pay who get the verdict, and Morgan pays," he said.[16] Morgan vehemently denied the allegation, but Bat, claiming he knew the beneficiaries, the amount of money received, and when and where the transactions were made, answered: "I'll neither qualify or retract. I know what I'm talking about." He added that the payoffs taken by certain greedy sportswriters exceeded their newspaper salaries.[17]

The Masterson charges stirred up a storm. Edgren and other boxing writers demanded that Bat be hauled before the boxing commission and compelled to substantiate his statements or be banned from all bouts. Bat responded that he would welcome an inquiry; he reminded his readers that for years he had pushed for an investigation into the evils of boxing. Since passage of the Frawley statute he had made several visits to Albany; voiced his opposition to the law to two New York governors, New York state senator James J. Frawley, and other legislators; and filed formal requests for a full review of boxing conditions. But he rejected the idea that the boxing commission was a proper tribunal to review his charges. The chairman of the committee was Frank O'Neil, a man Bat had long suspected of using the office for his personal financial benefit and had said as much in print. He knew he was unlikely to get a fair hearing before O'Neil.

The boxing commissioners evinced no desire to air the controversy and declined to hold hearings on the matter. Bat was not surprised. "Investigations are precisely what the boxing commission doesn't want," he said, and stood firmly behind his charges.

Throughout the years of the Frawley law Masterson hammered away at the "bunk" statute and the boxing commission, at one point declaring in frustration that he would prefer to see boxing abolished entirely than have it continue under a law that he believed was destroying the sport he loved. He thought the law, in addition to being a vehicle for graft, was politically motivated. The measure, he said, provided employment for at least 500 Democratic voters in New York City and perhaps as many more in other parts of the state. He thought it significant that in the city no fighter, manager, club proprietor, or their employees voted the Republican ticket.

Special targets of Masterson vitriol during these years were the boxing commission chairmen. Initially, he gave the first chairman, Frank O'Neil, appointed in 1911, his strong support, praising him as "fearless and independent," impervious to "sordid or political" influences.[18] But after O'Neil reneged on a promise made to Bat personally and revoked Tom O'Rourke's boxing club license, Masterson accused him of "a plain case of double-cross," and declared war on the man he now said had "displayed the cloven hoof."[19]

Typically, he opened an immediate offensive. He filed charges against O'Neil with the governor, alleging that O'Neil and his assistant, Charles Harvey, had a financial interest in Madison Square Garden and were squeezing out all competing promoters to line their own pockets. He said he could prove every allegation made and a number of others yet to be made.

As Bat waited for the governor's office to respond, O'Neil tried to launch a counterattack. In a brazen attempt to sully Masterson's reputation, he wired Otto Floto at Denver, asking for any dirt he could use against Masterson. However Floto felt about his old adversary, he chose not to be a party to such an underhanded maneuver. Instead of answering O'Neil, he sent the telegram to Bat with a note saying he did not approve of this sort of work. Masterson was obviously amazed. By treating O'Neil's clumsy smear effort with contempt, Floto had demonstrated class and integrity Bat never believed he possessed. "About twelve years ago Mr. Floto and I had a run-in and have not spoken to each other since," he told his readers. It was therefore "a very generous act on Mr. Floto's part to treat me in such a chivalrous manner and I appreciate it very much."[20]

Frank O'Neil remained chairman of the boxing commission as months, then years, went by. New York governors came and went. (This was a period of turmoil for the New York executive branch, with four men occupying the governor's chair in as many years.) As he waited impatiently for a response from Albany to his charges, Bat kept up his attack on O'Neil. When he somehow came into possession of an O'Neil check that had bounced, Bat began using the epithet "check kiter" with every reference to the commissioner.

Finally, in 1915, the state legislature responded to mounting criticism led by Masterson and held hearings on possible revision of the Frawley law. Bat was quick with suggestions. He wanted to see referee decisions restored, fifteen-round bouts permitted, and the three-member boxing commission replaced by a single appointee. His recommendation for the post was his old pal Billy Madden. Bat disagreed with one suggested reform proposal—that managers be eliminated—because, he said, the typical prizefighter lacked the mental capacity to find the arena where he was to appear without the aid of his manager.

The Malone bill, eventually enacted by the legislature, was little more than a weak amendment to the old Frawley law. It provided for none of the changes Bat proposed. Its major provisions called for the abolition of the O'Neil commission with replacement by a new three-member board, and an increase in the tax on gross receipts of boxing clubs. Bat acidly suggested that club managers offset this additional expense by reducing payments to the "we-boys" for publicity and fake write-ups. He knew that his proposal would bring "a howl from the write-up artists," but he cared not.[21]

The new measure did little to cure the ills afflicting New York boxing. The sport, in rapid decline, became little more than "a corrupt racket" over the next few years according to ring historian Nat Fleischer.[22]

But Frank O'Neil was gone, to Bat's great satisfaction. The newly appointed commission chairman was Fred Wenck, a former Masterson colleague in the sports department of the *Morning Telegraph*. At first Masterson viewed the changes optimistically and hailed the appointment, saying that Wenck was well qualified for the job and could be expected to lift the fight game in New York out of the mire into which it had fallen under the O'Neil regime. But within a few months Masterson, disappointed by what he called Wenck's "officious and undignified manner" and "dictatorial attitude," began a campaign to remove him from office. He alleged that the commission chairman was guilty of attempted extortion and complicity in fixed fights. When hearings into the charges were finally held, Wenck was cleared of any criminal offense, but was relieved of his position. Bat hailed the departure of the man he said would "no longer besmirch the boxing game with his greed and mendacity."[23]

Masterson could now claim credit for driving both Frank O'Neil and Fred Wenck from office. He boasted that he was the only sportswriter in New York with the guts to take on powerful boxing officials. Other sportswriters, the "we boys," had called him a "knocker" and defended these deceitful chairmen, he said, but, persevering, he had succeeded in getting not one but two scofflaws thrown out of office. He assured his readers that despite the best efforts of the "we boys" he would continue to fight to see that the boxing game was conducted honestly.

Bill Farnsworth, the highly regarded ring columnist of the *New York Evening Journal*, in 1918 proposed Masterson's appointment as boxing commissioner, saying he was the man to straighten out the sport's problems. Bat publicly thanked Farnsworth for the compliment, but said were the job to be offered, he would not accept. He preferred the position he held, where he "could hand out the slams when they were deserved." He didn't want to be "hog-tied in such a way that [he] would have to submit to the knocks without being able to reply in kind."[24]

In 1919 new boxing bills were introduced in the New York legislature. Senator Leonard Gibbs, the author of one, sought Masterson's help in pushing for its passage and invited him to Albany to testify before the Judiciary Committee. When Bat learned a delegation of New York sportswriters was going, he respectfully declined, saying that the "we boys" would not be apt to mention their complicity in creating the cesspool that boxing had become in Gotham. He thought that crowd would do better by staying home to begin their own reform.

The following year Senator James J. Walker sponsored a boxing reform bill that the legislature passed and Governor Alfred E. Smith signed into law. Many of the provisions Masterson had long advocated, including fifteen-round matches and referee decisions, were in the bill. Although his years of tirades had at last paid off, Bat regretted that one of his proposals had not been enacted. He had wanted a provision making it a felony for a sportswriter to take money, directly or indirectly, from ring figures.

When the Walker bill went into effect in 1921, Governor Smith appointed a new board of commissioners, headed by Walter Hooke. Bat disapproved of Hooke and in a column attacked him as being "wholly incompetent" and unqualified for the position. Hooke, of course, resented Masterson's comments and a few days later tried to provoke him into a fight. Bat was at Madison Square Garden, seated in his usual ringside seat next to Jack Skelly, boxing columnist for the *Yonkers Herald*. Hooke approached and, speaking to Skelly—but in a voice sufficiently loud that all around could hear—berated Masterson in sulfurous language. In relating the incident in his column later, Bat said, "Some [may] wonder why I didn't get up and resent the insult. I've wondered myself . . . why I let the foul-mouthed vulgarian get away unchallenged with his blackguardism." He did not react physically to Hooke's verbal attack, he said, because he was in Madison Square Garden among patrons who had come to see fighting in the ring and not outside it, and that a ringside brawl might redound to the discredit of his friend, Garden manager Tex Rickard, and boxing in general. For these reasons, he said, he controlled his temper and "allowed the blackguard commissioner to get away with his vulgarity."[25]

The explanation may have been less than forthright. The Bat Masterson of earlier years, when insulted and his character assailed, would have cared nothing for such considerations. His reaction would have been immediate and violent. But at the age of sixty-seven, Masterson no longer vented his anger in battle; he was too old, too tired, and also too wise. He retaliated instead with his pen. In his next column he called the governor's attention to the matter and demanded Hooke's immediate resignation. "If gentlemen cannot be found to supervise boxing," he said, "it would be better to have the manly art of self-defense dumped into the sewer than have it controlled by blackguards like Walter Hooke, who evidently prefers a rough-and-tumble battle outside the roped enclosure than one inside it."[26]

His remarks did not go unheeded. Soon thereafter he was gratified to see his third boxing commission adversary deposed. Governor Nathan L. Miller gave Hooke the hook, and appointed as chairman William Muldoon, an acknowledged boxing expert and an old Masterson friend. To Bat's further delight, Muldoon named Tom O'Rourke, another longtime Masterson crony, his deputy. After years of haranguing, Masterson had finally won his battle for a New York boxing commission to his liking.

— IO —

THE SNAKES OF NEW YORK: THE TRAIL OF THE SERPENT

The trail of the serpent is here and it will take a long time before it is completely effaced.

W. B. "Bat" Masterson

Since first serving as an officer of the law at the age of twenty-two, Bat Masterson had maintained an interest in crime and its suppression. William E. Lewis may have had this in mind when he assigned Bat, in December 1906, to cover a sensational murder trial in upstate New York.

Chester Gillette, a young man working at a skirt factory in Cortland, New York, was charged with the murder of Grace Brown, a fellow shop employee. An autopsy revealed that the dead woman had been pregnant, presumably as a result of an affair with Gillette, who had ambitions to marry another young woman of wealth and social standing. According to prosecutors, on July 11, 1906, Gillette took Brown boating on Big Moose Lake in the Adirondacks, beat her to death with a tennis racket, and threw her body overboard. When arrested, he confessed to the crime, but later recanted, claiming that the woman committed suicide. A cause célèbre of the day, the Gillette trial at Herkimer was followed closely by newspaper readers across the country, including a budding young writer named Theodore Dreiser, who, almost twenty years later, would immortalize the story in his acclaimed novel *An American Tragedy*. After a lengthy trial, Gillette was convicted, sentenced to death, and eventually executed in the electric chair at Sing Sing.

Bat Masterson did not agree with the jury and, in his usual outspoken, pull-no-punches style said so plainly. His story appeared on the front page of the *Morning Telegraph* under the headline: NEW STYLE OF LYNCH LAW IN NORTHERN NEW YORK. Bat called the trial "a flagrant travesty of justice" and "an inexcusable insult to the intelligence and civilization of New York." With inflammatory references to "lynch law" and "mob rule," he characterized the proceedings as "a subversion of law and order and a disgraceful mockery of justice" perpetrated by "Herkimer County bushmen."[1]

Outraged, Herkimer County Judge Irving R. Devendorf issued a warrant charging Masterson, *Morning Telegraph* publisher Henry N. Carey, and editor William E. Lewis with criminal contempt of court for publishing "false and grossly inaccurate" descriptions of the trial.

"I've been through a great deal out west," Bat grumbled, "lived in Dodge City when it was the toughest town on the cattle trail, ran a vaudeville house, enlisted as scout under General Miles against the Comanches. And here in my sober fifty-second year [*sic*: fifty-fourth] I get into trouble for writing something in the paper. If that isn't a funny trick of fate I don't know of one."[2]

Attorney Clarence J. Shearn represented Masterson and Carey at an arraignment before Judge Devendorf on December 17; Lewis was excused because of illness. The trial began immediately, and Shearn entered guilty pleas for both defendants, who faced possible six-month jail sentences and fines of $500 each. Judge Devendorf was clearly angry about the matter. "If the people who read newspapers demand such stories," he stormed, "why don't they write them without any pretense of them being true? Why don't they have the President assassinated every day?" Perhaps, he suggested sarcastically, certain papers should be licensed to publish untruths so that people who read them would know they were not to be believed.[3] He released the defendants on bail of $2,000 each pending his penalty decision. Later, after calming down somewhat, he imposed fines of $50 apiece.

The Chester Gillette murder trial came right on the heels of the first "Crime of the Century," a sensational murder committed in the roof café of Madison Square Garden on June 25, 1906. That evening

Harry K. Thaw, the wastrel heir of a Pittsburgh railroad baron, sauntered up to the dinner table of nationally renowned architect Stanford White, drew a gun, and shot White dead before a stunned crowd of people. Thaw explained that White had despoiled his wife, the beauteous showgirl and model Evelyn Nesbit. Stories of the murder and Thaw's subsequent prosecution dominated headlines for years. The high social standing of the principals and lurid sexual details emerging in the testimony enthralled the public. Thaw's first trial ended in a hung jury. Acquitted on the grounds of insanity at a second trial, he was committed to a mental institution. It was the quintessential story for the *Morning Telegraph*, and for years its front page was filled with news of Thaw's legal battle and adorned with photographs of the comely Evelyn Nesbit.

Other shootings involving well-known New Yorkers during these years received much press attention. On June 10, 1910, J. J. Gallagher, a discharged city employee, attempted to assassinate William Jay Gaynor, the city's mayor. Gaynor survived; Gallagher was committed to a lunatic asylum.

Gaynor was more fortunate than David Graham Phillips, a friend of Masterson who a few months later met a violent death at the hands of another mentally deranged man. Phillips, a former reporter, had become one of the most popular novelists in the country with his realistic stories of life in Hell's Kitchen. On the night of January 22, 1911, he had dinner in Shanley's Restaurant with Masterson and Alfred Henry Lewis. The following morning a demented musician named Fitzhugh Goldsborough, who believed Phillips's books defamed American womanhood in general and his sister in particular, accosted Phillips on the street, pulled a pistol, and pumped six bullets into the novelist. Phillips died the next day.

Sensational murder cases such as these tended to relegate to the back pages stories of the mundane street crime that had plagued New York City for decades. In 1905 interviews Masterson was quoted as saying he believed more concealed weapons were being carried in New York City than anywhere in the West, but he viewed with disdain the "cheap sports with guns twisted up in their hip pockets [who] couldn't get 'em out in an hour." New York City had it all over the West for gunplay, but Gotham shootings were cowardly "sneaking" crimes, committed by gun-packing "one-horse" hoodlums, he said. They were "ten times worse than a real, sure enough gun fracas."[4]

Bat may have made these comments after an excursion into Manhattan's infamous tenderloin district, the haunts of Paul Kelly, Monk Eastman, and other notorious New York gang-lords. At the request of Alfred Henry Lewis, who was doing basic research on the city's gangs for a book he later published under the title *The Apaches of New York*, Bat sometimes accompanied the author into the depths of that domain, bellying up to the bar in the criminal dives.

For some fifteen years following the turn of the century that portion of Manhattan south of Longacre Square was divided into gang-controlled sections, with boundaries as well recognized and tightly guarded as the frontiers of civilized nations. The Five Points Gang, led by Paul Kelly and claiming 1,500 members, ruled Hell's Kitchen. It was constantly warring with Monk Eastman's gang, 1,200 strong, and lesser bands, the Gas House Gang, the Hudson Dusters, and the Gophers.

One New York street-gang historian has suggested that in entering the lairs of the tenderloin toughs Lewis drew his courage from the company of Bat Masterson:

> The toughs of the West Side knew all about Bat Masterson.... Then a bald and dumpy middle-aged man, with "killer-gray" eyes visible under the brim of his black derby, Masterson commanded respect whenever he strolled into a Hell's Kitchen saloon with Lewis at his side. A *New York Sun* writer described how a barroom full of young thugs, noisy with brag and bluster, would become still as a church when the retired gunfighter, who was still known to carry his old Dodge City equalizer on occasion, made his way to the brass rail.[5]

The legend of Bat Masterson, deadly gunslinger and man-killer, was alive and well, even among the illiterates of New York's tenement canyons. Some may wonder how Masterson, then in his fifties, balding and overweight, wearing a tailored suit, and looking like anything but the popular conception of a leathery western gunfighter, could possibly, by merely appearing, have intimidated the toughs of Hell's Kitchen. The answer is that Bat, even in his younger days, had never presented an imposing physical presence, but he had "the eye." Wyatt Earp, who himself had intimidated many with a single glance, said that Bat's "wide, round eyes expressed the alert pugnacity of a blooded bull-terrier. . . . They were well-nigh unendurable in conflict—so bold, so bright, so unmitigable was their gaze."[6] As another westerner put it: "The face does not count. Bat Masterson had a round, jolly face, but he had the eye."[7] A St. Louis newspaper reporter in 1886 found "nothing particularly striking about 'Bat' save his eye, [which in action] gleams with a fierce and deadly light."[8] And Irvin S. Cobb was impressed by Masterson's eyes, "like smoothed ovals of gray schist with flecks of mica suddenly glittering in them if he were roused."[9]

Occasionally Masterson commented in his column on the criminality rampant on the streets of the city. The gang members, he said, were "half-witted boys" with no conception of law and order, right or wrong. Fearing neither prison nor electric chair, they would commit murder for pay or simply on impulse. Crime flourished in what he called, after consulting his thesaurus, the "maelstrom of heterogeneous elements" on the East Side. "The trail of the serpent is here and it will take a long time before it is completely effaced."[10]

If the district in which Bat Masterson lived, worked, and played was the heart of New York's theatrical district, it was also the gambling and prostitution center of the city. The area extending between Fortieth and Fiftieth Streets and Fifth and Eighth Avenues came to be known as "the Roaring Forties," where gambling houses could be found on almost every street. Among the better known were the establishments of Honest John Kelly, William Busteed, Sam Emery, Davey Johnson, Dinky Davis, and John Daly, while across town, at No. 5 East Forty-Fourth Street, next door to Delmonico's Restaurant, was Richard Canfield's famous Casino. The Broadway nightlife attracted prostitutes as well as gamblers. As early as 1901 a commission investigating vice in the district identified 132 different buildings in which prostitution was offered in the immediate thirty-three-block area surrounding Longacre Square. There were sixty-three out-and-out brothels, and prostitutes operated out of sixty-one tenements, eight apartments, and ten hotels. "Broadway from West Twenty-seventh to Sixty-eighth Street was a two-mile parade of prurient commerce."[11]

GUNFIGHTER IN GOTHAM

The staid *New York Times* observed in 1907 that "the glittering splendor of 'the Great White Way' does not symbolize the best spirit of the people of New York."[12]

The Masterson home was right in the center of this prostitution activity, as Bat frankly admitted in a 1913 column.[13] The Delevan Hotel, on the corner of Broadway and West Fortieth, where the Mastersons resided for four years, was just down the street from the German Village, at 147 West Fortieth Street, and the Denver Hotel at 209 West Fortieth, two notorious assignation houses owned and operated by Archibald Hadden, a power in Tammany Hall. The Delevan itself was a subdivided row house that from the outside resembled a parlor house, and prostitutes openly brought clients into its rooms. West Forty-Third Street, to which the Mastersons moved in 1906, was called Soubrette Row because of the many streetwalkers to be seen there.

Despite periodic clamor for reform, collusion between purveyors of vice and the New York City police had been going on for decades. Police corruption was as old and as firmly entrenched in the city as Tammany Hall. Theodore Roosevelt, who served as New York City police commissioner from 1895 to 1897, saw firsthand the workings of "the System," as it was called. "The New York police force was utterly demoralized by the gangrene," he later wrote. "Venality and blackmail went hand-in-hand with the basest forms of low ward politics. . . . The policeman, the ward politician, the liquor seller, and the criminal alternately preyed on one another and helped one another prey on the general public."[14] Roosevelt led a campaign to clean up the city's police force and succeeded in chilling the System for a time, but by 1911 it was well and operating smoothly again.

That year a crackdown on gambling houses was heralded by a series of spectacular police raids ordered by Mayor Gaynor and carried out under the direction of Police Commissioner John Cropsey. Bat Masterson, who had gambled professionally in the West for twenty years and still saw no sin in making a wager now and then, had little sympathy for the program. He thought it ridiculous to so assiduously pursue gamblers, whose offense was, after all, a mere misdemeanor, punishable by a fine, while much more serious crime was rampant in the city. He pointed out that police raids in the Broadway district were invariably pulled off when theater crowds filled the streets, accused

Cropsey of grandstanding, and called for his dismissal. He got his wish two months later when Mayor Gaynor replaced Cropsey with a dynamic young man carrying the unlikely name of Rhinelander Waldo. The raids continued under Waldo, and the gamblers, increasingly nervous, began to lash out at each other.

The Mastersons and other residents of the Longacre Square district were rudely awakened shortly after five o'clock on the morning of May 17, 1911. A bomb had exploded outside the gambling establishment of Sigmund "Beansey" Rosenfeld on West Forty-Fourth Street, only a block from the Masterson home. Large crowds quickly formed on the scene. Theatrical people from the area's hotels, including George M. Cohan, Wilson Mizner, William Collier, Douglas Fairbanks, James Montgomery, and Wallace Eddington, many still in sleeping garments, filled the street. No one was injured in the explosion, and damage was minor to Rosenfeld's place. The gambler was soon back in business, only to be shut down again by a police raid a month later.

There were more bombings as the gamblers warred with each other. Raids continued, most of them led by police lieutenant Charles Becker, head of one of the department's special "strong-arm" squads. Becker was a tough cop who had developed a lucrative protection racket, shaking down vice operators in the tenderloin. While earning only $2,150 annually, he had bank accounts totaling over $100,000. Under orders from Rhinelander Waldo to continue the raids, Becker smashed furniture and fixtures in the houses of gamblers who were slow in their payoffs to him, but employed less destructive methods in the places of those who were more cooperative. One of the houses he avoided entirely for months was a three-story brownstone at 104 West Forty-Fifth Street, the home and gambling rooms of Herman Rosenthal, with whom Becker was a silent business partner. Finally, on April 15, 1912, under a direct order from Waldo to close up the place and keep it closed, Becker and his squad raided the Rosenthal house. Rosenthal was not at home, but Becker padlocked the building and put uniformed officers at the door to prevent reopening. The place remained closed until July, when an exasperated Rosenthal spilled his story to the *New York World*, saying he had been double-crossed by a high-ranking member of the police department who was involved in his gambling business. The next day in an affidavit signed in the office of District Attorney Charles Whitman he repeated his story, named Charles Becker as the corrupt cop, and agreed to recite his tale before a grand jury.

Bombs had been going off in Manhattan during the gamblers' war, but for real shock effect, they were like firecrackers compared to the bombshell exploded by Rosenthal's revelations. Whitman, politically ambitious, knew that here was testimony, if properly exploited, that could finally bring down the System, launch him into the governor's chair, and perhaps even the White House. He should have guarded the loquacious gambler like a priceless jewel.

But he did not, and in the early morning hours of July 16 gunmen shot Rosenthal to death as he stepped out of the Hotel Metropole. According to sworn testimony by eyewitnesses, the killers, four young men, jumped into a gray Packard touring car parked at the curb, and sped off.

The gambler's revelations had created a furor in New York; his murder raised the level of sensationalism another notch. Because of Rosenthal's charges, Lieutenant Charles Becker was immediately suspected of being behind the killing, but evidence was lacking. Finally, under intense pressure by Whitman, several sordid members of the criminal community, Bald Jack Rose (Jacob Rosenzweig), Harry Vallon (Harry Vallinsky), and Bridgey Webber, all claiming to have detailed knowledge of the murder, its planning and execution, agreed to testify in exchange for prosecution immunity. They told investigators that Becker had ordered and paid for the Rosenthal assassination and named the triggermen: Louis "Lefty Louie" Rosenberg," Jacob "Whitey Lewis" Seidenschmer, Harry "Gyp the Blood" Horowitz, and Frank "Dago Frank" Cirofici, all members of Big Jack Zelig's gang. A possible fourth informer, Sam Schepps, fled to Hot Springs, Arkansas, where officers arrested him when he attempted to post a letter to Jack Rose. Becker's lead attorney, John W. Hart, aware that Bat Masterson had been a frequent visitor to Hot Springs and was well acquainted with people of importance there, hired Bat as a special investigator to accompany him to the Arkansas resort to interrogate Schepps.[15]

Soon after his arrival in Arkansas Bat issued a statement in which he denied press reports that he had a personal interest in the case because he and Charles Becker were friends. His only purpose in visiting Hot Springs was to interview Schepps, he said. He acknowledged acquaintanceship with Jack Rose and Bridgey Webber, but said he had never met Lieutenant Becker.

Bat interrogated Schepps, and concluded he was "as miserable a creature as the sun ever shone on" and completely unreliable. He did not think it possible that a jury would convict a man of first-degree murder on the testimony of characters as unsavory as Rose, Webber, and Vallon, with corroboration only by an "unmitigated scoundrel" and "consummate liar" like Sam Schepps.[16]

Such a jury was found, however. On October 24, 1912, Becker was convicted of arranging the murder of Rosenthal and a week later was sentenced to death in the electric chair. The trial of the four gunmen was almost anticlimactic, but they, too, were quickly convicted and given the death penalty.

Bat continued to castigate the men whose testimony had brought about those verdicts. Schepps had been warned to stay out of Hot Springs, he said. Many a man-killer had been welcomed at the spa, Bat said, but not a "mental pervert" of the Schepps ilk, who belonged in New York where he was born and bred. He contended that the criminal East Side should not be allowed to "dump its leprous output" across the country and that New York City, having "raised the snakes," should keep them. He said he was convinced that "degenerate, conscienceless and brazen" Jack Rose and his confederates, Webber, Vallon, and Schepps, were all conspirators in the Rosenthal murder and deserved the death penalty.[17]

A few days after the Rosenthal murder A. L. "Butch" Witte, an old gambler friend from the West, told Masterson a story that conflicted greatly with other eyewitness accounts. Witte said he had been standing in front of the Metropole when the shooting took place and that two men, neither of whom was one of those tried and convicted, gunned down Rosenthal. After the shooting, one of the gunmen ran across the street to the George M. Cohan Theatre. The other walked backward about thirty feet toward Sixth Avenue, then ran to an automobile. Witte took Bat to the Metropole and pointed out a bullet hole in the wall of the hotel near the spot where he had been standing that night. Although advised by Masterson to tell his story to the authorities, Witte declined, saying he had no interest in the case one way or another, seeing it as just a fight between a gang of gunmen and police and not wanting to get involved.

Following the conviction of Becker and the four Zelig gangsters, Bat related Witte's account to Charles F. G. Wahle, attorney for the gunmen. The Reverend James B. Curry, rector of St. James Catholic Church and chaplain of the Tombs prison, was also present. Father Curry told Bat he agreed with him that Becker and the others were innocent and were framed by those guilty of the Rosenthal murder. Under urging by attorney Wahle, the district attorney deposed Butch Witte, but the gambler recanted much of his story, and he was never called to testify in court. Masterson, Father Curry, and others always believed his original tale was true.

Charles Becker, with abundant funds amassed from his years of graft, employed lawyers who managed a series of execution post-ponements and finally got his conviction set aside. A new trial was ordered. On April 13, 1914, Lefty Louie, Whitey Lewis, Gyp the Blood, and Dago Frank were electrocuted. At his second trial a month later Becker was again convicted and sentenced to death. After his lawyers exhausted all legal appeals he was executed on July 31, 1915.

Prosecution of the highly publicized Rosenthal-Becker case vaulted Charles Whitman into the governor's office as he had hoped. He served two terms, but in 1918 was defeated by Alfred E. Smith, the Democratic candidate. When Whitman remarked that he might challenge the election results because of suspected vote fraud in certain New York City precincts, Bat, still bitter over the Rosenthal case, commented that Whitman had little hope of success without the assistance of Rose, Webber, Vallon, and Schepps, the "unalloyed criminals" responsible for getting him elected in the first place. Since the statute of limitations for perjury had expired and Rose and company no longer feared prosecution on that charge, Bat concluded that the foursome would be unlikely to contribute further to Whitman's political success and a recount attempt would be futile.

After the Becker trial Bat Masterson was not involved, even peripherally, in any high-profile criminal case, but from time to time he commented in his column on New York crime. Shortly after America's entry into the great European conflict in 1917 he opined that the country would benefit if corner-idling pimps living off the earnings of prostitutes were rounded up and sent to the trenches where military discipline might straighten them out. If it did not, he suggested malevolently, their bodies could be used like sandbags. "Make the breastworks thick and high and spread them all along the line. . . . Now is the time to rid the city of this pestiferous and vicious element."[18]

Of course the federal government did not follow Bat's advice and conscript all the undesirables, but the New York state legislature did enact an antiloafing law a few months later. Bat commented that if the law helped to get the parasitic pimps off the street, it would accomplish great good. He could feel some grudging admiration for pickpockets, burglars, and stickup men, who had the backbone to take some chances to achieve their evil ends, he said, but pimps, the lowest of criminals, deserved only contempt and loathing.

In another column he turned his attention to what he called "the slattern element of women," which included, but was not limited to, the harlots working for the pimps. He pressed the police to clamp down on the females "burlesquing around with soldiers and sailors." They were, he clucked, a "menace to decency and good order," and their behavior was "nothing short of scandalous."[19] Bat was sixty-four years old when he wrote this. He had apparently forgotten the days of his own youth when he lived with a concubine in Dodge City, engaged in a public brawl over the favors of an actress in Denver, and managed a disreputable variety theater in that city.

He occasionally tossed his barbs at judges and juries in unusual cases that caught his attention, and often inveighed against the prosecution of women in capital cases. When the trial of a woman in West Virginia ended in a hung jury, he noted that the lone man who held out for conviction was "one of those detestable specimens of biped vulgarity called a cad." Only a cad would vote to convict a woman in a capital crime, and cads, he said, should be hunted down and killed like mad dogs.[20] He believed it to be a "diabolical crime against nature" to condemn a woman to death.[21]

On the overall issue of capital punishment he evidenced rare inconsistency. The man who advocated the killing of cads like mad dogs thought that capital punishment should be abolished. Murderers, he believed, were degenerates born with cruel and criminal natures. The imposition of the death sentence held no terror for them and therefore was not a deterrent. His arguments are echoed by death penalty opponents today, almost a century later.

As a former lawman, Masterson was usually supportive of the New York City police and law enforcement in general, but liked to poke fun at what he considered nonsensical bureaucratic regulations, like the 1917 departmental directive to clamp down on sidewalk spitters. Those with excess saliva, he observed, would now be required to carry cuspidors with them or "use their coat pockets as a depository."[22] A greater threat to public safety, he thought, were those who walked their dogs on the sidewalk, for these canines posed a real hazard to anyone like himself with eyesight "a little on the blink." He would rather take his chances with a spitter, he said, than with undisciplined dogs "enjoying themselves" on the sidewalk, and added that some of the dog owners showed little evidence of having been properly housebroken themselves.[23]

As the city's crime rate increased, Masterson noted that a few judges were hinting at a need for a return to vigilance committees and lynch law, and he vehemently rejected any such notion. He had personally witnessed vigilantism at work on the frontier, he said, and strongly condemned the custom and its practitioners. Western committees of vigilance were largely composed of criminals who organized for self-protection. Law-abiding citizens did not join these organizations and held no respect for those who did. Vigilantes, in his opinion, committed more cold-blooded crimes than all the road agents, horse thieves, and professional man-killers combined.

— 11 —

JACK JOHNSON:
WHITE HOPES AND WHITE SLAVERY

I haven't got any race prejudice.

W. B. "Bat" Masterson

In March 1905, the month that Bat Masterson pinned on his deputy U.S. marshal badge in New York City, James J. Jeffries announced his retirement as heavyweight champion of America. After knocking out Bob Fitzsimmons in the eleventh round at Coney Island, New York, on June 9, 1899, to take the crown, Jeffries had successfully defended the title seven times, KO'ing all of his challengers except Tom Sharkey, who went the twenty-five-round distance but was so battered that he had to be hospitalized with a mangled face and two broken ribs. Hailed as the "Iron Man of the Roped Square," Jeffries had never been defeated. He lacked style and boxing finesse, but was big, was very strong, and packed a devastating punch. His chin and body seemed impervious to the blows of opponents.

With the retirement of Jeffries, Noah Brusso, a clever, hard-punching Canadian boxing under the name Tommy Burns, claimed the title until John Arthur "Jack" Johnson, a black fighter, met him in a match at Sydney, Australia, on December 26, 1908. Twenty pounds lighter and several inches shorter than Johnson, Burns fought gamely against his stronger and more skillful opponent but was so badly beaten that police stepped in after fourteen rounds to prevent further mayhem.

Johnson returned to the States to great acclaim by people of his race, but to sullen disdain by most white ring devotees, who seemed to believe that the heavyweight title, the crown jewel of boxing, should be held in perpetuity as the exclusive property of their race. From boxing's earliest days in America whites who controlled the sport had tolerated black champions in other divisions, but had excluded Peter Jackson and other great black heavyweights from championship competition.

Almost immediately after Johnson's victory the cry went up in ring circles for a "White Hope," a paladin who could whip the black man and return the heavyweight championship belt to the white race where, they claimed, it rightfully belonged. Johnson would hold the title for seven years, 1908–15, and the period would forever be remembered as the era of the "Great White Hope." At its height the craze reached ridiculous levels, as when manager Walter "Good-Time Charlie" Friedman, unable to find a suitable Caucasian opponent to pit against the black champion, went to China in search of a White Hope among the Chinese peasants.

Johnson's flamboyant personality and freewheeling lifestyle contributed to the animosity whites felt toward him. Proud, arrogant, obstinate, and articulate, he personified the "uppity nigger" many whites in early-twentieth-century America feared and despised. When it became evident that he preferred the company of white women, Johnson became the most hated man in America; miscegenation was anathema to most whites and condemned by most African Americans.

On the subject of race Bat Masterson was ambivalent. After using the word "nigger" in a 1904 interview, he quickly added: "I haven't got any race prejudice." He thought it ironic that those most biased against blacks were southerners who had been nursed as babies by black "mammies."[1] In his columns he used ethnic epithets frequently and was fond of racially denigrating clichés like "nigger in the woodpile," which he sometimes expanded to a "big woolly-headed Senegambian concealed in the woodpile." He used the term "coon" derisively, as in his references to Reddy Gallagher as "the Memphis Coon." He called Joe Walcott the "star of Coondom" and Harry Wills the "new coon in town." Black fighters were "dusky sons of Ham," and Jack Johnson was "the Big Smoke." When two black fighters met in the ring he predicted "the fur, or rather the wool" would fly.

His ethnic slurs were not confined to blacks. To him Italians were "dagos" or "wops," Mexicans were "pisanos" or "greasers," Jews were "kikes," and Chinese were "chinks." It should be remembered, however, that racial and ethnic epithets were in common usage at the time, even by minority members. Thus Sam Langford billed himself as "the Boston Tar Baby," a black boxer fought as "Darkey" Griffin, Christy Williams was the original "Memphis Coon," and others were "Black Bill," "Little Chocolate," "Black Demon," and "Muldoon's Pickaninny."

Despite the use of language that today would bring down on the head of a columnist the wrath of the watchdogs of political correctness and destroy his career, Bat was unusually liberal in his racial views for the time. He strongly disagreed with people like lightweight champ Jack McAuliffe, who argued that blacks were as "out of place" in pugilism as they were in baseball and that "nothing should be permitted to happen to affect the dominance of the white race," a view that was undoubtedly held by most fight fans of the period. Masterson held the more enlightened view that color should never keep a man from demonstrating his ability in the ring.[2] He had always criticized John L. Sullivan for "drawing the color line" and refusing to fight Peter Jackson, although he strongly suspected Sullivan's reluctance was based less on scorn for Jackson's race than fear of his ring ability.

When the New York Boxing Commission banned matches between whites and blacks, Masterson decried the action and endorsed the comment of black newspaperman Lester A. Watson that the prohibition made no more sense than requiring horses of different colors to race together. "The Negro is entitled to the same rights under the law as the white man," declared Bat in 1913, "and it isn't within the province of any man or set of men to make a rule that deprives him of his rights."[3] The "obnoxious rule," as he called it, was rescinded in 1916.

During the period of the White Hope nonsense white supremacists had to accept the fact that not only did a black man hold the heavyweight title, but the three next best boxers in the division—Sam Langford, Joe Jeannette, and Sam McVey—were also black. Although black heavyweights were clearly the class of the ring at this time, matches pitting them against each other did not draw well. Bat blamed fight fans of both races for failure to support matches between blacks. Whites avoided the bouts out of obvious prejudice, but black ring patrons, who "whine about their race being discriminated against," he said, also were conspicuous by their absence at all-black bouts. "If they are not loyal enough to their own race," he concluded, "they should not feel peeved when the whites stay away."[4]

For years the top black heavyweight contenders tried to goad Jack Johnson into a match, but the champion steadfastly refused to meet any of them in a ring. "Who ever heard of two 'niggers' drawing a big amount of money in this country?" he asked with his usual wide, gold-toothed grin.[5]

Johnson defended his title against three white heavyweights: Victor McLaglen, who later became an Oscar-winning Hollywood actor; Philadelphia Jack O'Brien; and Al Kaufman—defeating them all easily. At Colma, California, in October 1909, he knocked out Stanley Ketchel, the middleweight champion, in the twelfth round.

As it became increasingly apparent that no active white contenders were capable of licking Johnson and restoring the championship to the white race, a clamor arose for the seemingly invincible Jim Jeffries to come out of retirement and whip this black upstart. When Johnson took the title in 1908, the celebrated author Jack London, covering the bout in Australia for the *New York Herald*, first issued the call: "Jim Jeffries must now emerge from his alfalfa farm and remove that golden smile from Jack Johnson's face. Jeff, it's up to you. The White Man must be rescued."[6]

Jeffries, out of shape and aging, was reluctant, but astute promoter George L. "Tex" Rickard, seeing an opportunity to stage a great event, employed his masterful persuasive powers and brought the former champion out of retirement by appealing to his racial loyalty. Jeffries signed, Johnson followed, and Rickard set a date of July 4, 1910, for what would become the first of his boxing promotions to capture national attention.

Long before the fight Masterson predicted Jeffries would defeat the champion. Johnson's bluster and braggadocio reminded him of the war cries of "near-bad men" on the frontier, he said. When one of these fellows got tanked up, "he would pull his six-shooter and loudly proclaim that he was a killer from Killersville and peace troubled his mind. Then somebody promptly shot him." He thought Johnson was, in effect, about to be shot by Jeffries.[7]

Powerful religious and political leaders still opposed to prizefighting threatened legal action to prevent the fight in many areas of the country, but Rickard finally found a congenial location in free-and-easy Nevada and late in June announced that the fight would be held in Reno. Bat quickly caught a westbound train. From June 28 until July 6 he wrote a daily report that appeared on page one of the *Telegraph* under his byline and photograph. Other special correspondents gathering for the big event included Alfred Henry Lewis, who would cover the fight for the *New York American*, and novelists Rex Beach and Jack London, employed by the Adams Newspaper Service of Chicago.

Fight fans from as far away as England, France, Australia, India, and China descended on Reno. Senator Tim Sullivan, who would hold the purse, led a large contingent from New York City. Upward of 8,000 fans were expected from San Francisco. Lou Houseman brought in 200 Chicagoans on a special train. Bat met western men he had not seen in years, including his old compadre Wyatt Earp.

He wrote amusingly of the cheap crooks also flocking into Reno, men who "could not ask the captain what time the ship left if tickets around the world were a dime a smash." Among this crowd he spotted the Two-By-Six Kid, Bull Con Jack, and Oregon Jeff, who had "not won a bet since Soapy Smith dealt on the square."[8]

After watching Jeffries and Johnson work out in their respective camps, Masterson saw no reason to change his earlier prediction of the winner. Jeffries was thirty-five and had not fought in five years, but he appeared confident, determined, and in splendid shape, with muscles rippling like whipcord. Johnson, three years younger and about twenty pounds lighter, was also in fine condition. He clowned around in his inimitable style, playing to the gallery.

The fighters' purses, including gate receipts and motion picture shares, totaled a record-breaking $235,000. On July 4 the largest crowd ever to see a prizefight, 30,000 strong, surged into the large arena Tex Rickard had erected, while 15,000 others milled outside, unable to get in. Rickard resolved disagreement over referee selection by assuming the job himself. When announcer Billy Jordan introduced him to the crowd as "the greatest man in the world," the ovation lasted almost six minutes.

Scheduled for forty-five rounds, the bout lasted fifteen. In that final round Johnson sent Jeffries twice to the canvas for eight counts—

While in Europe the fighter told a correspondent for the *London Daily Times* that he hated the United States and in the event of war would not fight for the country. That broke it for Bat Masterson, who lost all respect for Johnson after this remark. His references to the black champion became increasingly strident, even threatening. Johnson was "a greedy egoist," a "disgrace to the game," a "big black beast" who had made himself obnoxious by "flaunting his debauchery with white women" and had driven one wife to suicide. "Something is going to happen to this big sensual brute before long. . . . Johnson is due to get his."[15]

During Johnson's European expatriation the White Hope frenzy grew even more intense in the United States. For several years white heavyweights met and flailed away at one another in the ring, but none emerged as an outstanding contender for the crown. When Tom O'Rourke held a White Hope tourney at his National Sporting Club a bruiser named Al Palzer was the winner. O'Rourke took over management of Palzer, and Bat Masterson lauded the fighter in his column. After sitting behind Palzer at Hammerstein's Victoria Roof theater one night, Bat penned an amusing column:

> I got an aisle seat in the third row and was delighted. It's not an easy matter to get an aisle seat in the third row at Hammerstein's on a Sunday night. [I] was congratulating myself on my good luck for having procured such a desirable seat [when] Al Palzer came in and took the aisle seat directly in front of me, and from that time on it was Palzer who saw the show and not me. I tried several times to get a peep at what was doing on the stage, but I didn't make much progress. I peeked around Palzer a few times, and once or twice I stood up and tried to look over his head, but the fellow behind me wouldn't stand for that, so I sat down. The grouch behind me looked almost as formidable as Palzer, [so] I sat down. . . . I was raised on a farm and therefore know something about the size of an ordinary barn door, but the ordinary barn door isn't a marker for Palzer's back. He is at least three axe handles across the shoulders and the top of my head was about even with his coat collar, so you can imagine what a beautiful view of the stage I had. One of Palzer's shoulders was half way out of the aisle and, crane and twist as I might, the only time I saw the performers was when they came on the stage. Hereafter when I go to a show I'll first inquire if Palzer is

to be there, and if he is, I'll find where he'll be seated and then I'll get my seat on the other side of the house. The only way to get an idea of Palzer's size is to get behind him. Compared with the ordinary man, Palzer looks like a Liverpool dray horse alongside a Shetland pony. He is the biggest man across the back and shoulders I ever saw.[16]

Tex Rickard shared Masterson's enthusiasm for Palzer and considered matching him with Johnson after the young fighter gained more experience. "If this country is ever going to develop a white man capable of restoring the championship to the white race," he told Bat, "this fellow Palzer looks to me to be the man."[17] But Palzer ran out on his contract with O'Rourke and, in so doing, lost Masterson's support and Rickard's interest.

Nat Fleischer has written that the White Hopes who contended between 1910 and 1915 were "a mighty impressive lot,"[18] but Masterson was not so sanguine. In 1912 he saw no white heavyweight anywhere he considered a fit opponent for the champion. Punching bag club fighters with White Hope aspirations quickly disappeared from the contest when they lost to old warhorses like Gunboat Smith, Jim Flynn, and Frank Moran. Carl Morris fell to the bottom of the White Hope heap when Flynn licked him decisively after Masterson exposed manager Frank Ufer's attempt at a frame-up. Jim Flynn, the "Pueblo Fireman," got a shot at the title when Johnson took him on at Las Vegas, New Mexico, in 1912 and battered him unmercifully for nine rounds before police stepped in to stop the slaughter. In 1914 Frank Moran met Johnson in a twenty-round match in Paris. Moran did not win, but went the distance and surprised Bat by giving a good account of himself. (The referee for this bout was a nineteen-year-old French boxer named Georges Carpentier, of whom the ring world would hear a great deal a few years later.)

Jess Willard, Kansas cowboy turned boxer, standing six and a half feet in height and weighing 220 pounds, first caught the attention of Masterson in July 1912. Bat kept a close eye on this fellow he called a "cornfed giant" and devoted columns to an analysis of his strengths and weaknesses. He thought Willard moved with considerable speed for a man his size, and struck his blows with skill and power, but seemed to lack "the fighting instinct" and had a lot to learn about in-fighting and protecting himself in the clinches. Despite reservations about his aggressiveness, by 1914 Masterson came to believe that the big cowboy had the tools to lick any man in the world, including Jack Johnson. The first boxing authority of national prominence to proclaim Willard the top white contender for the heavyweight crown, he began to beat the drums for a Johnson-Willard title match.

The campaign proved successful when promoter Jack Curley in early 1915 signed Johnson and Willard to a contract. Finding a suitable site for a title match presented a problem, however. Johnson could not enter the United States because of his fugitive status, and the outbreak of the European war had eliminated possibilities in France or England. Curley tried to arrange the affair in Juarez, Mexico, across the border from El Paso, but fear in some quarters that the insurrectionist bandit Pancho Villa would disrupt the proceedings stymied that plan. Curley finally settled on Havana, Cuba, and set a date of April 5 for the match.

Most ring authorities favored Johnson, and the champion was a heavy favorite in the early betting, with odds quoted as high as ten to one, but Masterson rather guardedly gave the challenger an even chance to win.

In late March Bat left for Havana. When his train arrived at Key West, Florida, he faced an ocean trip to Cuba, a voyage he viewed with some apprehension, he confessed, for he was a poor sailor, as he had learned from his stomach's distress when he went by boat between San Francisco and Sausalito back in 1891. But he assured his readers that he was one who didn't mind traveling several thousand miles to see a title match and wouldn't be stopped by a little seasickness. As it happened, the seas were calm, and he made the seven-hour trip to Cuba without undue suffering.

In the succeeding days Masterson sent daily cable dispatches to his paper, reporting on prefight events. The battle would be staged at the Oriental racetrack, on the outskirts of Havana and easily reached by trolley. Attendance was anticipated at 10,000, and gate receipts were expected to top $150,000. Fight day was to be an official holiday, with operations of the Cuban Congress suspended and major shops and businesses shutting down at ten in the morning. The promoters presented President Mario Menocal with a ringside box of eighteen seats, and every notable on the island was expected to attend the fight.

Bat visited the camps of the fighters and talked to a confident Johnson, "smiling and jovial," a very serious Willard, "all business," and Jack Welch, who would referee.

Betting was desultory, with Johnson the early five-to-two favorite. The odds dropped as more Willard backers arrived; by the first of April Johnson was favored at two to one, two days later at eight to five, and by fight time the outcome was an even bet.[19]

Motion picture cameramen recorded scenes of the fighters preparing for battle, and one of them turned his lens on Bat Masterson. A brief ten-second strip of film reveals Bat with a tight-lipped half-smile, well dressed as always with a dark suit and tie, and light-colored vest, doffing his fedora for the camera. Other than glimpses of Bat at ringside in motion pictures of big fights, the strip of film taken at Havana is the only known movie film of the man.

On the eve of the big day, Bat cabled from Havana that while nations changed hands and dynasties toppled in Europe, the attention of many around the world was focused on the outcome of the title fight in Cuba. The sporting world, he reminded readers, had long awaited a gladiator who would defeat Johnson and return the title belt to "the descendants of Caucasus."[20]

Banner headlines above Bat's story on the front page of the following morning's *Telegraph* announced that the White Hope era was over:

WILLARD WRESTS WORLD'S TITLE FROM JACK JOHNSON. HUMAN DREADNOUGHT FROM KANSAS SENDS NEGRO TO THE MAT SENSELESS IN THE TWENTY-SIXTH ROUND OF THEIR SCHEDULED FORTY-FIVE ROUND BOUT AT HAVANA, CUBA. THE VICTORY PROVES POPULAR.

On Tuesday, April 6, Bat began the journey home. He sailed to Key West on the steamship *Olivette* with 260 other returning Americans and forty racehorses bound for the Bowie racetrack in Maryland. Struck this time with a bout of seasickness, he later grumbled about the voyage, complaining that sailing was two hours late, another hour was lost in debarking at Key West, and the customs officers were impolite. He did, however, praise a Dr. Light, the ship's physician, who rendered him "much valuable assistance" in the relief of Bat's dreaded mal-de-mar.

It did not take long for a story to circulate that the fight was fixed and that Johnson took the count per agreement. Bat first heard it on the return train trip. He was sitting in his drawing room with Damon Runyon and Ben Harris when a boy peddling newspapers stopped by and mentioned that black heavyweight Sam McVey was saying Johnson took a dive. Bat demanded to know to whom McVey made that statement.

"He said it to me," the newsy replied.

"I'll bet a hundred dollars against one that he didn't say anything of the kind to you," Masterson snapped.

The newsboy declined the challenge, thereby saving Bat a hundred, as he later had to admit. Runyon left to interview McVey, who, to Bat's surprise, confirmed the allegation. Soon McVey's story was on all the wires and appeared in New York papers even before the train carrying the fight attendees arrived back in the city.

Masterson castigated McVey for spreading the story "without one scintilla of evidence" to support a claim he said could only have been made to detract from Willard's victory. He hoped Willard would learn a lesson from the smear and never give "Negroes or foreigners" a shot at his title.[21]

Johnson would later claim that he threw the fight for $50,000 and permission granted by federal authorities to return to the United States. He said he was "shading his eyes" in a much-publicized photograph of the knockout, showing him flat on his back with one arm raised. Little credence can be given to his story, however, because he was evidently broke and peddling his "confession" to newspapers within a year, and he remained out of the country for five more years and went to prison after his return. Ring historians still debate the facts of this controversial fight.[22]

Until his dying day Bat Masterson never doubted that the fight was on the level and assured his readers any story to the contrary was "an unmitigated falsehood."[23]

He was still of two minds, however, with regard to the controversial former champion, and tried to explain his views in a number of columns. When Johnson was quoted as saying it was not easy for a black man to be champion of the world, Bat reminded him that he was the architect of much of his own trouble, that his popularity among both whites and blacks had plummeted after he flaunted his fondness for white women and he was criminally charged in Chicago, and that most Americans found very offensive his public renunciation of his native country while in exile. Masterson made it clear that he concurred in the prevailing national view that interracial marriage and cohabitation were abhorrent. He said Johnson had brought shame and humiliation to his race and deserved "to be ostracized by both Negroes and whites because of his immoralities, his flagrant and brazen defiance of decency and convention."

Although Johnson's ill-considered remarks about his country angered Bat, he took issue with those who criticized the black fighter for not taking up arms in the war then ravaging Europe. He pointed out that Johnson was not a European, or even a white man, and it was a white man's war. "The white man has not been particularly considerate of Johnson [and] he can hardly be expected to fight the white man's battles."

Bat defended Johnson in the violation of the Mann Act controversy. Having followed the case closely, he believed Johnson had been wrongly convicted solely on the unreliable, unsubstantiated testimony of Belle Schreiber, "a woman scorned," and had been forced to flee the country to avoid imprisonment on the trumped-up charge. Because he was black, he had not received equal treatment under the law. However reprehensible his conduct, Johnson was still an American citizen, and his rights were as important "as the best and bravest among us." America and its institutions, Masterson argued, were as much on trial in the case as Johnson himself.[24]

In an editorial *Collyer's What*, a Chicago publication, called Masterson's comments "one of the most remarkable expressions which has come within our ken. . . . Masterson disclaims holding any brief for the Negro and we know enough of Masterson to know that he would accept none, but in cold type he said what no other sporting writer in the United States has dared to say in Johnson's behalf and . . . he has told nothing but the absolute truth."[25]

Over the next several years Bat repeated his defense of the exiled fighter. When President Wilson in 1917 extended full amnesty to a number of felons convicted in federal courts, Masterson called on him to include Johnson, whose trial and conviction had been "a gross travesty of justice." Of greater concern than Johnson, he said, was "the good name of the courts, where everyone, regardless of race, creed or color, is presumed to be dealt with in a fair and impartial manner and to receive even-handed justice under any and all circumstances."[26] Wilson, probably not a reader of the Masterson column, did not include Johnson on his amnesty list. When in 1919 Johnson petitioned the government for a pardon, Masterson once again rose to his defense and launched a vitriolic attack on Belle Schreiber, whom he described as "a characterless, discarded street walker . . . as low as it would be possible for a woman to be."[27]

Masterson's arguments on his behalf were not lost on Johnson, who was in Mexico and reading the American papers. In an April 1920 letter to Bat he thanked him for his support and complained of "gross fabrications" about him that had appeared in other papers.[28] On July 20, 1920, after eight years as an expatriated fugitive, Johnson surrendered to federal officers at San Diego, California, and was escorted to Fort Leavenworth prison, where he would serve all but a few days of his sentence. "The only fault any one could find with Jack Johnson was his seemingly uncontrollable infatuation for white women," Bat mused. "That is what brought about his undoing. Had he let white women alone he would have been a most popular champion, for in all other respects he was a first-class good fellow."[29]

— 12 —

TEDDY ROOSEVELT AND POLITICS:
COPPERHEADS AND BULL MOOSES

I ain't going to attend any reception. Am headed east.
                                        W. B. "Bat" Masterson

Bat Masterson had been a Republican most of his life. He ran as a Republican for sheriff of Ford County, Kansas, and a Republican mayor appointed him city marshal of Trinidad, Colorado. He was a delegate at county and state Republican conventions in both states in the 1880s and 1890s. And yet there was always a strong strain of populism in his political outlook, quite evident in the *Vox Populi*, his first journalistic effort back in Dodge City. His vitriolic diatribes in that paper had skewered all those with whom he differed, including most of the Republican leaders of Ford County. He supported Republican presidential candidates throughout the latter years of the nineteenth century and, despite his differences with the GOP, stood steadfast against the onslaught of the People's Party and the arguments of William Jennings Bryan.

When Theodore Roosevelt moved into the White House in 1901, Bat had a leader he could admire and respect for his personal qualities as well as his political ideas. Roosevelt's brand of charisma and charm appealed particularly to men and most especially to men of action like Bat Masterson, who came away from his initial meeting with the president in Washington, D.C., singing his praises. The *Morning Telegraph* quoted him as saying TR was the "real thing," the "hottest President we ever had," and "a cinch" for reelection.[1]

Beyond his fascination with "two-gun men" of the West, Roosevelt enjoyed talking to Masterson because of their shared interest in prizefighting. Another frequent guest of the president was former boxer and trainer Mike Donovan, who sparred with Roosevelt in the White House gym and boxed ten brisk rounds with him the night before the March 1905 inauguration. Donovan was convinced that had Roosevelt entered the prize ring instead of the political arena he would have been successful. "The man is a born fighter," he said. "It's in his blood."[2]

Masterson's meeting with Roosevelt in 1904 was the first of many between the two men over the next fifteen years. During his occupancy of the White House Roosevelt invited Bat down from New York to see him at least once a year. A visit in December 1905 led to a wire service report that Masterson would become a bodyguard to the president and make his home in the White House. Bat quickly assured his New York readers the story had no basis in fact.

During the last year of Roosevelt's second term, Bat called on the president and urged him to run again. In a *New York Times* interview Roosevelt confessed that he was suffering from an attack of "third termitis" in its most virulent form.[3] But he held true to a promise he had made in 1904 not to seek a third term. In the campaign of 1908 he threw his support behind William Howard Taft, who was elected handily in November.

In February 1909 Bat, back in Washington to visit Roosevelt a last time at the White House before the Taft inaugural, met Ben Daniels, in from Arizona. As they strolled down Pennsylvania Avenue, talking over old times, they ran into Bill Tilghman, another former Dodge City peace officer who had moved on to Oklahoma Territory. Together with two other Oklahoma lawmen, Jack Abernathy and Chris Madsen, Tilghman was in town to promote some Wild West motion pictures he had produced. After viewing the films at the White House, Roosevelt invited the three Oklahomans to the last formal function of his administration, an army and navy reception.

Bat knew all about the reception. Reluctantly, he had already accepted an invitation to attend. The affair would be formal, and proper attire was a concern of the westerners. Since the reception was to honor the military, the Oklahoma lawmen concluded that guns would be in evidence and had polished up their six-shooters and purchased shoestring ties to match their flannel shirts. But Masterson quickly advised them that full formal dress would be required. To be admitted they would have to "shuck them duds" and get into "a claw-hammer coat and a stovepipe hat." The Oklahomans "turned pale at the thought," but, accompanied by Masterson and Daniels went to a shop and rented tuxedos.

Bat and Daniels "laughed until tears streamed down their cheeks" at the sight of Tilghman and Madsen in their finery. "Madsen had the most trouble with his shirt, the sides of the front flaring up from beneath his vest like a tent wall in a cow camp on a windy night," while Tilghman was most uncomfortable in a standup collar that called to his mind hempen necktie parties of frontier vigilante days. "The remembrance made him gasp for breath."[4]

Bat had borrowed a tuxedo from a friend, but the sight of Tilghman and Madsen convinced him that soup-and-fish was not for him. The friend, waiting for him in the hotel restaurant that evening, was handed a telegram dated at Baltimore an hour earlier and signed by Masterson. It read: "I ain't going to attend any reception. Am headed east."[5]

After leaving office Teddy Roosevelt embarked on an African safari and European tour. Returning a year later, the popular ex-President was greeted in New York with the biggest parade the city had seen up to that time.

Roosevelt partisans were disappointed with Taft, who failed to follow the progressive policies of his predecessor. To Masterson, Taft was "a joke" who seemed only to appear in public at "a big feed or a waltz," and he wondered if the portly president ever did anything other than eat and dance.[6] Bat's abrupt dismissal as deputy marshal when Taft took office may have contributed to his jaundiced view, but others whose political opinion he respected shared his displeasure with the chief executive.

Mike Sutton, who as county attorney had worked closely with Sheriff Bat Masterson in Ford County, Kansas, thirty years earlier, went on to become prominent in state Republican Party circles. After a falling-out in the 1880s, Bat and Sutton had reconciled their differences and once again became close friends. They kept up a correspondence and saw each other frequently at Hot Springs, the Arkansas spa they both enjoyed. Sutton's views regarding Taft mirrored

Masterson's. A staunch supporter of the Roosevelt policies, Sutton had supported Taft in the belief that he would continue those policies, but had been disappointed and admitted now to Bat that he was an out-and-out party insurgent.

Taft's speeches, Masterson maintained, were classics of verbosity and emptiness of message, a great oratorical descent from Roosevelt, who, Bat said, could pack more into one paragraph of a speech than Taft did in an entire address.

While critical of Taft, Bat was always quick to defend Roosevelt against all calumny. In 1910 he devoted an entire Sunday column to a fierce attack on the enemies of the former president. He likened them to the Civil War–era copperheads, "seditious malcontents" too cowardly to fight on either side of the great conflict, whose "only ambition was to raise a disturbance at home, cuss Lincoln and declare the war a failure." Now called "anarchists," he contended they were "the same breed of cats," whose chief aim was the destruction of the Union.

Bat recalled that as an adolescent in 1868 he heard a copperhead harangue a crowd in Illinois and declare the only good thing Lincoln ever did was attend Ford's Theater the night he was assassinated. "The same breed of character assassins who abused and vilified Lincoln and Grant are now busily engaged in the same line of mean and cowardly work against former President Roosevelt." He predicted that, having failed to destroy Roosevelt politically, his enemies would resort to murder. "The traitorous influences that finally succeeded in destroying Lincoln can be held directly responsible for the death of two other presidents—Garfield and McKinley." Within a thirty-six-year period the lives of three presidents had been "sacrificed by the same unholy and seditious influences." The nation had passed "from the era of copperheadism [to] that of anarchism. What the copperhead sought to do during the Civil War the anarchists are now seeking to accomplish." He added that the anarchists' goal was being aided and abetted by "certain newspapers, whose mission seems to be the tearing down of constituted authority," and by "the greedy rich who recognize neither law nor country."[7]

Bat was an early drumbeater for Roosevelt's presidential candidacy in the 1912 national campaign. As early as 1910 he predicted the large state and congressional Democratic victories in that year's elections signaled a repudiation of the Taft brand of Republicanism and that Taft, recognizing the direction of public opinion, would refuse the party's nomination for reelection in 1912. Roosevelt would then be a shoo-in as the Republican standard bearer and easily win the general election.

But after talking with the more politically astute Mike Sutton in Hot Springs several months later, Bat's rather naive belief that Taft would quietly step aside for Roosevelt was shaken. Although he was a firm Roosevelt adherent and still held out hope that the Republicans might nominate him again in 1912, Sutton could see a fissure in the party developing. According to his analysis, Taft would be the candidate of the conservative, standpat wing of the Republican Party, and that either Roosevelt or Senator Robert La Follette of Wisconsin would lead a revolt. He did not believe the differences between the two wings of the party could be reconciled and agreement reached on a platform. There was also an insurgent element in the Democratic Party, he said, but it lacked leadership. He believed the progressives in both parties preferred Roosevelt, but, in any event, if the Republicans nominated Taft, Sutton was convinced he would certainly go down to defeat.

By December 1911 Roosevelt still had not announced his entry into the presidential race, and Masterson was doing all he could to encourage him. In one of his columns he quoted a letter he had solicited from Mike Sutton, urging Roosevelt to run, and added, "It looks like a popular uprising to me."[8] He sent a copy of this column to Roosevelt, commenting only that Sutton was "one of the best posted men, politically, in the West."[9]

Roosevelt's response was noncommittal, but cordial: "That is an interesting letter from Judge Sutton. Do come and let me see you sometime."[10]

Roosevelt was faced with a difficult decision. It was not easy to challenge the incumbent president, a man of his own party, one who had faithfully served in his cabinet when he held the executive reins, and one who had been his personal choice to succeed him. But finally he yielded to the pressure from thousands of admirers like Masterson and Sutton, threw his hat in the ring, as he put it, and announced his candidacy for the Republican nomination.

In June 1912, shortly before the Republican National Convention, which he would attend as a Roosevelt delegate, Bat took advantage of Teddy's invitation. In a note requesting an appointment, he employed some prize-ring jargon: "It seems to me that the only place in which you have not slugged the bosses over the ropes is right here in New York, but you'll get to them in time and when I see them take the count maybe I won't laugh."[11] The two old friends met on June 4 in the offices of *Outlook* magazine, where Roosevelt was then working as associate editor. They discussed the forthcoming convention, and presumably Bat garnered some insight into Roosevelt's strategy.

The convention opened in Chicago two weeks later. The Old Guard, still in control of the party, rejected Roosevelt's bid and nominated Taft as the Republican presidential candidate. Bitterly disappointed, Bat returned to New York to pen a column on a convention he called "cold-blooded burglary" in which the better man had been defeated by foul tactics.[12]

The schism within the party that Mike Sutton had foreseen was now obvious. Roosevelt, refusing to accept his party's nominee and platform, bolted to the Progressives and prepared to run against Taft and Woodrow Wilson, the Democratic nominee, in the fall campaign. When someone inquired about his health and he replied he felt "fit as a Bull Moose," the Progressive Party quickly became known as the "Bull Moose" Party.

Bat Masterson, of course, followed his leader. In July he met with Roosevelt to discuss "a matter of importance in connection with the Progressive campaign," and presumably gave the colonel the benefit of his advice.[13]

The assassination attempt on Roosevelt's life Masterson had predicted in 1910 came to pass on October 14, 1912. A deranged man shot the former president as he began an address in Milwaukee. A spectacle case and a folded speech in a breast pocket over his heart absorbed much of the force of the bullet and saved Roosevelt's life. Teddy, displaying the courage and determination that endeared him to Masterson and millions of others, was undaunted, even with a bullet embedded four inches deep in his chest. He refused to leave his platform and delivered an impassioned fifty-minute address, remarking only that the gunshot wound might leave him a little "stiff in the morning." But his physicians ordered him to bed and kept him there for two weeks during the height of the campaign. The incident may have been critical to the outcome of the race.

In another strange turn of events, Vice President James S. Sherman, Taft's running mate, died suddenly on October 30, 1912, and on Election Day, less than a week later, three and a half million voters chose the Taft-Sherman ticket, half of which was deceased. Politically the ticket was completely dead. Wilson won easily over his divided opposition. Roosevelt came in second and Taft a distant third.

The following year Masterson kept in contact with Roosevelt, offering suggestions for the future success of the Bull Moose Party. Adherents were in turmoil after their candidate's defeat, and party leaders across the country were having trouble keeping them in line. Bat advised TR to "lay down the law."[14]

Roosevelt replied that he did not want "to lay down the law" anywhere at that time. He was just about to start for South America, and would have to take the matter up on his return. A few days before Roosevelt sailed on October 4, 1913, Masterson met with him again to pay his respects.

By the spring of 1914 Bat was urging Roosevelt to run for governor of New York on the Bull Moose ticket, an important step toward another presidential bid. "Colonel Roosevelt is as essential to the success of the Progressive Party in this country as Abraham Lincoln was to the Republican Party in 1860," he insisted. "The country appears to be badly in need of a Moses to lead it out of the wilderness at this particular time, and Colonel Roosevelt seems to be the only available Moses in sight."[15]

On May 19, 1914, Roosevelt arrived back in New York from his South American trip. The throngs who greeted him at the dock were shocked at his appearance. In the Brazilian wilderness the former president had contracted jungle fever and almost died. He had lost thirty-five pounds and was so weak when he got back that he had to be assisted down the gangplank. He would never regain his former vitality.

A few weeks later General Nelson A. Miles was quoted in an interview as questioning some of Roosevelt's highly acclaimed achievements, including his leadership in the famous charge up San Juan Hill in Cuba. Masterson rushed to TR's defense and, typically, attacked the attacker. He had served as a scout under General Miles in the Indian war of 1874, he said, and had joined the charge up a stoutly defended hill, but he didn't remember Miles leading the assault. In his interview Miles had predicted that Roosevelt would be the Republican nominee for president in 1916 and would be "snowed under" in the election. "General Miles perhaps thinks the Republican Party should nominate him for President instead of Colonel Roosevelt," Masterson scoffed. Roosevelt would not run as a Republican, said Bat, because he "has as much use for the Republican Party under its present leadership as General Miles appears to have for [him]."[16]

Later that month Bat made an appointment to meet with Roosevelt, but when he spoke with TR's secretary and learned for the first time the full extent of his friend's disabilities, he discreetly withdrew.

Those infirmities contributed to Roosevelt's decision not to run for governor of New York in 1914 as Bat had urged. Charles S. Whitman, on the strength of his celebrity as the district attorney who sent Charles Becker and four triggermen to the death house for the Herman Rosenthal murder, led a Republican sweep and was elected governor.

In 1916, with battles raging in Europe, President Woodrow Wilson ran for reelection with the slogan "He kept us out of war." The Republicans nominated U.S. Supreme Court justice Charles Evans Hughes as its standard-bearer, and the Progressive Party, still dominated by Bull Moosers, named Theodore Roosevelt. But Roosevelt, who had learned a bitter lesson in 1912 when his split with the Republicans had ensured a Democratic victory, declined the nomination and threw his support to Hughes.

In June Bat Masterson attended the Republican and Progressive conventions, both held in Chicago, and upon his return set forth his impression of the proceedings in a long Sunday feature story. It was a rambling, disjointed discourse in which he mixed complaints about escalated prices in the convention city (90 cents for a bacon-and-egg breakfast and $10 for a normally $4-a-day lake-front room) with wry comments on public drunkenness ("no longer confined to Democratic gatherings"), longing for Roosevelt's leadership (his withdrawal from political activity was "hardly thinkable"), and serious observations on the current political picture.

He then presented a rather cogent recapitulation of the historical tides that had brought the country to its current state of political turmoil. The country used to be divided into two groups of political thought, he said.

> In one group were men who called themselves Democrats, and in another men who called themselves Republicans. Individually these men were active only in local affairs. Their chosen leaders named national delegates, and as soon as a candidate was selected the rank and file rallied to his support. There was almost no such thing as party bolters. Voters were known as safely Democratic or safely Republican. Party lines were closely drawn and hard to pass. This is no longer true.
>
> The debacle began as far back as the early nineties, when the Populist movement took root in the West, and it would have progressed farther than it did had not the insane theories of Bryan been accepted by the Democratic Party, which in its mad career of repudiation stimulated a conservative reaction which well became a saturnalia. But in 1912, with an ex-President leading the forces of reform, the break-up was complete. The Republican Party went on the rocks and it would have beaten itself to pieces but for the apparent inertia of the Progressive leaders until almost time for the campaign of 1916 to open. The Old Guard had a chance to realign its forces under cover, and because of the general dissatisfaction in certain quarters with Mr. Wilson's foreign policies, the Republican Party came up stronger than the new organization that had bested it at the polls four years ago. . . . It remains to be seen how many Progressives of former Republican affiliations will vote for Mr. Hughes, how many will go to Wilson and how many will go fishing.[17]

With Roosevelt out of the race, the November election was very close. Hughes went to bed thinking he had won, but when the California returns came in, Wilson emerged victorious with 277 electoral votes to 254 for Hughes.

Despite winning on an implied promise to keep the nation out of the European conflict, then in its third year, Woodrow Wilson, within five months of his victory, asked Congress for a declaration of war against Germany. When Teddy Roosevelt announced that he wanted to lead an expeditionary force against the Germans, Bat requested a meeting with the colonel. He would bring Tex Rickard along, and the two of them would advise Roosevelt on how to organize his expeditionary force and win his battles, Bat said jocularly. "You know Tex and I are wonders in matters of this kind."[18] On May 19, 1917, Roosevelt welcomed Bat and Tex to his office and listened politely to their views. It was probably the last time Masterson and the former president ever met.

Wilson refused Roosevelt's request to raise a division of volunteers for the front. The colonel of the Rough Riders and hero of San Juan Hill had no opportunity to fight in what was called the Great War. His four sons all served, however, and one, Quentin, died in aerial combat.

Masterson was incensed when, a few months after the war, Christian Donhauser, the German pilot who shot down Quentin, expressed a desire to come to America and become a citizen. If the "cruel and barbarous Hun" came "strutting around in this country receiving the plaudits of the alien element," Bat said, he would likely "find a few thoroughbred Americans who would take great delight in hanging his hide on the fence."[19]

In another column Masterson extolled Theodore Roosevelt, observing that, like Washington, Jackson, Lincoln, and Grant, he would have to die before his greatness was recognized and appreciated. Although loved and admired by most Americans, Roosevelt had been constantly attacked by "pusillanimous character assassins." Great men "survive the slanderous and venomous attacks of those who thrive on malevolence and mendacity," however, and later generations would honor Roosevelt after his passing "from this sordid and selfish world of ours," and none would be left to vilify him.[20]

Roosevelt never fully regained his health after returning from his South American expedition. He died in his sleep only four months after Masterson wrote the above column. For Bat, the passing of the one national political leader he truly admired only increased his long-felt cynicism toward politics and politicians.

On his first visit to Washington in 1904 he had described members of Congress as "scrawny and unkempt" workmen "with nothing to do except to get together once in a while and frame up some pyrotechnics for the benefit of their constituents and then loll around until salary day."[21] Ten years later his low opinion of politicians as a class had not changed. In a 1914 column he cited a news report that a penitentiary inmate, when asked to name the highest and lowest professions to which a man could aspire, chose prizefighter as the highest and politician as the lowest. Psychologists declared the man mentally deficient, but Masterson thought he displayed "the mentality and wisdom of a Solomon."[22] Bat's contempt for political office-holders, whom he described as simply con men feeding at the public trough, only grew with the passing years. He had more respect for burglars, he said, because they had to have nerve and prowess, qualities utterly lacking in the politician's makeup.

Some of his closest friends shared his disenchantment with the state of politics in America. Laughing Ben Harris was not laughing in 1919 when he told Bat he had become a Socialist and would perhaps leave the country for good. Another friend also believed the country's survival lay in Socialism and predicted the left-wing political philosophy would continue to grow. "Don't be a bit surprised to see the Socialist party carry this country from one end to the other," he told Bat. "I look to see the Socialists elect the President in 1932."[23] (Many conservatives in the United States, after observing the huge growth of the federal government after Franklin D. Roosevelt assumed the presidency in 1932, might agree that Bat's friend was remarkably prophetic.)

Still disenchanted with the Republicans, and with the Progressive Party in complete disarray following the death of Teddy Roosevelt, Masterson, for the first time in many years, did not attend a national political convention in 1920. He sat out the campaign and offered the sour prediction that William Jennings Bryan would be nominated by the Democratic Party and would be elected in November. Humbuggery was in fashion, he said, and there were enough "boob Americans" and "alien criminals" to elect "old grape juice Bill."[24] Masterson was no better at predicting political outcomes than fight results: the Democrats nominated James M. Cox and Franklin D. Roosevelt as their candidates, and in November Republicans Warren G. Harding and Calvin Coolidge soundly defeated them. It was the last national election Bat would see.

— 13 —

WHEN HYPHENATES, HYPOCRISY, AND HYSTERIA RULED THE ROOST

What a crime it all is when a man becomes so thoroughly disgusted with his own country that he wants to leave it and never return. Conditions are certainly in a deplorable state.

W. B. "Bat" Masterson

As Heywood Broun recalled, the only consistent strong editorial position of the *Morning Telegraph* was its opposition to reformers.[1] The paper gained a powerful spokesman for its anti-reform views when it hired Bat Masterson, who shared Alfred Henry Lewis's cynical view that a reformer was "one who doesn't happen to be in with the other fellow's graft."[2] When the notion struck him, Bat dipped his pen in vitriol and skewered those who blocked or threatened to interfere with freedom of action. His primary targets were prizefighting opponents, prohibitionists, and advocates of woman suffrage, but forerunners of later restrictionists, anti-smoking fanatics and the like, also felt his barbs.

Often in the forefront of these reform movements were religious leaders whom Masterson attacked as "clerical humbugs." Evangelist Billy Sunday was a favorite target. Sunday toured the country inveighing against the evils of the saloon, and often cited Kansas, where liquor sales had been illegal since the 1880s, as a shining example of the beneficial effects of prohibition, an argument Bat found ludicrous. Having a far greater knowledge of Kansas saloons than the preacher, he could assure him from personal experience, he said, that saloons operated openly in Dodge City and other Kansas towns long after being outlawed, and no one in the state found it difficult to obtain a drink or a bottle. Sarcastically, he complimented Sunday for the fiscal success of his evangelical tour, saying he would like to take up a profession so financially rewarding, but lacked the audacity to be an evangelist.

Masterson attacked three muckraking clergymen of the time, the Reverends John Roach Straton, Canon Chase, and Wilbur F. Crafts, whom he compared to the "self-appointed prophets of God" of biblical times, who "worked a graft on the people."[3] As a outspoken opponent of boxing, Canon Chase came under particular Masterson fire. When Chase charged that those favoring legalized boxing were members of the criminal underworld, Bat suggested the clergyman check out the national crime statistics, which showed, he said, that laymen committed crimes at a rate of three per thousand, while the rate for clergymen was about thirteen per thousand.

Masterson delighted in reporting instances of disgraced churchmen. When the treasurer of a New Jersey church, a highly vocal opponent of prizefighting on "moral and religious grounds," deserted his wife for an eighteen-year-old waitress and ran away with the church funds, he gave Bat an opportunity to lambaste both the miscreant and his hypocritical ilk. As for the young girl, he had little sympathy. "It would have been bad enough had [she] run off with a horse player, crap shooter, or even a prizefighter, but to willingly hook up with a common church treasurer is not to be condoned."[4]

Interference by "clerical humbugs and sordid politicians" in prizefighting, a "most desirable sport" enjoyed "by all wholesome and virile men," always raised the Masterson hackles. He said the "mental misfits" who objected were part of an attack on the citizen's right to enjoy himself that could be traced back to Cotton Mather and the puritanical Sunday blue laws of New England, when the only pleasure permissible on the Sabbath was burning witches at the stake.[5]

Advocates of national prohibition were on the march during Masterson's New York years. Bat vehemently opposed prohibition, of course, arguing that not only was it another assault on individual freedom, but it was altogether impractical. In his columns he often returned to the example of Kansas, where after thirty years, he said, prohibition had proved to be an abysmal failure. As the country moved inexorably toward a national ban on alcoholic beverages, he wrote:

> Nationwide prohibition is the rage just now with the humbugs. Everywhere you go the hypocrites and picaroons of politics are preaching prohibition, although they are not practicing it to an alarming extent. . . . Prohibition is not democracy any more than the doctrine preached by Cotton Mather was democracy. Bigotry and intolerance cannot be made to conform with a democratic form of government. . . . The prohibitionist [is] an intolerant creature who seeks always to impose his dogmatic views on all. . . . He will resort to any means, no matter how unfair or despicable . . . , to force his narrow and selfish doctrine on his neighbors. . . . Temperance is a good thing . . . , but trying to legislate [it] into a freeborn and independent people can't result in anything but failure. . . . Prohibition everywhere it has been tried has proven a lamentable failure. . . . Worse than failure . . . , it has instigated crime and caused crime to be committed times without number.[6]

These were prescient words indeed, as the entire nation would learn in the years following ratification of the Eighteenth Amendment and passage of the Volstead Act in 1919, making the manufacture, sale, transportation, importation, or exportation of alcoholic liquors a federal crime. Saloons disappeared, but speakeasies quickly took their place. Thousands of people who previously avoided liquor now found it chic to drink. A crime wave swept the land. Political and law enforcement corruption increased many-fold. The deleterious effects of the "glorious experiment" remained long after repeal of national prohibition in 1933.

Bat Masterson only lived two years after passage of the Volstead Act, not long enough to see his predictions come true, but the success of the prohibitionists clearly soured him on America and its future. He believed Prohibition, forced on the nation by a fanatical minority, was a cancer eating into the body politic and heralded a fundamental change in the America he had known. Americans, he feared, no longer had the backbone to stand up for their liberties and constitutional rights. They had listened to "clerical humbugs and sordid politicians," had been corrupted by them, and had traded away personal freedom in their lust for the almighty dollar. Throughout human history great nations fell when the people became corrupt, and Americans, he sadly concluded, had become corrupt.

On the subject of woman suffrage the views of Bat Masterson and those of the *Telegraph* parted. The paper had long supported the feminist cause, but Bat, with his quintessential nineteenth-century American male perspective, was strongly opposed. When asked at the 1912 Republican Convention why he left Kansas, he replied: "I left when they got prohibition. I couldn't stand that. I went to Colorado and stayed until the women got to running things. Then I left there and went to New York. After Teddy came out for equal suffrage the other day I began to wonder where I would go next."[7]

Masterson opposed woman suffrage because he recognized that many of the same clerical and political "humbug" reformers who were forcing through national prohibition were in the vanguard of the feminist movement. As with prohibition in Kansas, he drew on his personal experience in Colorado, where women had voted since the early 1890s, to warn against national female enfranchisement. He devoted an entire column in 1910 to an explanation of his views.

He said that for about seven years after Colorado women gained the franchise, he lived in Denver, then the largest city in the United States in which women voted. He saw women "of lower intellectual and moral standards" and females of the underworld become dominant in the political arena, forcing out the better class of women. Soon ladies of refinement and intelligence stopped voting. Some of them, he said, even joined in the campaign to repeal woman suffrage in Colorado.[8]

Promises by advocates of woman suffrage that the female vote would improve and refine the electoral process had proved empty, he argued in subsequent columns. He claimed that after two decades of female participation in Colorado politics, corruption was worse than ever. No longer heard was the argument that women uplift and reform politics, he said, for women themselves, having shown "a particular aptitude for crooked politics," had made the position untenable. "Woman suffrage has accomplished no more for Colorado than prohibition has for Kansas. The only ones to be benefited by either institution are the political grafters, the hypocrites and the humbug reformers."[9]

Masterson took every opportunity to ridicule feminists and their cause. At Saratoga in 1914 he listened politely as suffragette speakers held a rally on the steps of the United States Hotel and made, he said, "the welkin ring with their fiery oratory." But he noticed no one claimed improvement of political and civic righteousness in Colorado and other states that had adopted women suffrage and suspected the speakers avoided the subject, knowing that the audience included knowledgeable anti-suffragists like himself. When the suffragettes departed, he said, the hotel was "thoroughly fumigated from cellar to garret."[10]

One night in 1915 a suffragette named Frances Brewer addressed the unruly crowd between bouts at the St. Nicholas Rink, or, as Bat put it, she was given an opportunity "to tell the men folk who are against woman suffrage what boobs they are." An attractive woman, described by Masterson as "built on symmetrical lines [with] a pleasant face and a winning personality," Brewer bravely finished her remarks despite an uproar from the "troglodytes" in the galleries. Bat, seated at ringside, was unable to hear a word she said because of the hoots and catcalls.[11]

A suffragette, far less comely than Brewer, was delivering a harangue on a city street corner one day during the war. The woman, described by Bat as "a militant suffragette with a mole on her chin, from which protruded a few straggling gray hairs," spotted a man sneering at her remarks. Enraged, she pointed a menacing finger at the man and demanded to know why he was not in the army.

"For the same reason, my good woman, that you're not in Ziegfeld's Follies," he responded. "I'm physically unfit."

Said Bat: "The shot must have hit the mark, for the suffragette fainted."[12]

Masterson could only watch with dismay as the Nineteenth Amendment, giving the vote to women throughout the United States, was finally ratified in August 1920, in time for the full participation of women in the national elections that fall. In the space of a year he had seen two monumental changes in American society, national prohibition and woman suffrage, become the law of the land. The "clerical humbugs, sordid politicians and hypocritical reformers" he so detested were winning the battle, and Bat Masterson was not at all pleased.

What he saw as another emerging threat to individual freedom, a growing campaign against smokers, troubled him also. A longtime cigar smoker, he took special notice when in 1915 Jimmy Johnston, then managing Madison Square Garden, announced that during an upcoming bout smoking would be banned at the fighters' request, as it impaired their abilities. While admitting that some cigars smoked at the Garden were pretty bad, with fumes strong enough to peel the paint from chairs, Bat contended that the cigars smelled no worse than some of the fights put on there. He himself smoked a better grade of cigar and usually enjoyed about three during a fight program. Although it would strain his nerves to forego the "solacing weed," he said he would comply with Johnston's edict.[13]

But a few years later when the Boxing Commission banned smoking on the main floor of the Garden, saying that the smoke obscured the view of the ring from the gallery, Masterson protested:

> Now here is where I come in with a kick. . . . I am a smoker and wouldn't give the solace I derive from a perfecto for all the fighters on earth. . . . If they want to give me the bum's rush for violating the smoking rule . . . , they'll actually have to take me by the neck and throw me out of the building to prevent me from smoking, and as soon as I land in the street I'll proceed to set fire to a perfecto and go on my way rejoicing.[14]

He never had to be forcibly ejected from the Garden; when he wrote this column he was less than a month away from his death.

Through the years Bat's diatribes against reformers, depending on his mood, ranged from simple indignation to despair to outraged calls for violent reaction. In the earlier years he looked with optimism to the future. "Clerical humbugs and sordid politicians are certainly giving the decent, liberty-loving people of this country a lively run for their existence," he wrote in 1910.

> How long this state of affairs will last is hard to tell. It is some consolation, however, to know that all civilized countries, where clerical humbugs and political rapscallions have dominated, succeeded in time in driving these human barnacles from power, and it's safe to predict that the time is not far distant when the free-born, American citizen will rise up in his might and go out for his rights. When that time comes, the humbugs and political grafters will be found scurrying to cover.[15]

He had seen no evidence of a national uprising by 1917, but thought perhaps America's entry into the European conflict might in some way trigger Americans, aroused by wartime patriotic fervor, to

GUNFIGHTER IN GOTHAM

sweep out the "parasitic reformers" who, he said, "tyrannized" state and national legislatures and forced through obnoxious laws. He predicted that the liberty-loving American would soon wake up, "and when he does the day of reckoning will be at hand."[16]

But the war was fought and won, and still the hated reformers moved relentlessly toward achievement of their goals. He ranted and raged in his columns, but saw little hope of changing the nation's direction through the electoral process. The American public, which he was now calling "the biggest aggregation of sapheads in the world," seemed to lack the will to drive out the "canting hypocrites" who, in his view, were destroying the country.[17]

He looked longingly at foreign shores. In the fall of 1919 as national prohibition loomed, he reported that 100,000 Americans were expected to winter in Cuba, where they could "enjoy a little personal liberty without being arrested and branded as criminals by the twisted mentalities in this country." He thought it tragic that Americans had to go to Cuba in order to escape tyranny in their native land.[18]

When a friend sailed for Europe in July 1921 and invited Bat to join him, he was tempted to go and remain abroad. "What a crime it all is," he said, "when a man becomes so thoroughly disgusted with his own country that he wants to leave it and never return. Conditions are certainly in a deplorable state."[19]

Too old to leave his country and increasingly frustrated by the direction society had taken, Masterson began calling for drastic, even violent, action. The "narrow-minded bigots" and "perverted creatures" riding roughshod over the nation had to be stopped by

an uprising of the people, a revolution as bitter and viciously contested as the world has ever known. . . . Americanism, although badly bent at the present time, is not altogether dead in this country. Some day the people are going to assert themselves, and when they do they'll make themselves felt with powder and lead if need be. When that time comes these intolerant human misfits who are masquerading under the cloak of religion had better have a care. The history of the world records many instances where bigotry and intolerance had to be put down by force of arms and history seems about ready to repeat itself in this country. Powder, lead and the bayonet are the only things these pernicious abnormalities are amenable to.

The nation was in a "helluva state," and a "revolution or something like that" was needed to save it. "The time is not far distant," he predicted, "when red-blooded men will get guns and use them, too." They had to rescue the country from the "modern witch-burners" and greedy politicians who were their minions. "Hypocrisy, rascality and cowardice have supplanted liberty, bravery and integrity" in America, he insisted. "Hyphenates, Hypocrisy and Hysteria rule the roost. . . . Dirty politics, treacherous politicians and profiteering reformers are in the saddle and ruthlessly riding down all that is left of Americanism in this country."[20]

— 14 —

THE BLACK SOX, THE GARDEN, AND TEX RICKARD

Tex Rickard is a stubborn sort of a cuss. He would rather put a dent in his bankroll than fall down on anything he started.

W. B. "Bat" Masterson

Bat Masterson's columns contained little sports news other than boxing. He was never a fan of baseball, a game he called "almost as weird a sport as football,"[1] despite the fact that John McGraw, manager of the New York Giants, was one of his Broadway cronies and these were banner years for New York City baseball; New York or Brooklyn teams were pennant winners in eight of the twenty years Bat lived in the big city. When he did mention baseball, it was usually to comment on the vast sums of money he saw being wagered on games throughout the season and especially on the World Series.

The pernicious effect of gambling on baseball exploded into headlines after the 1919 World Series, when it was learned that gamblers had conspired with Chicago White Sox players to "fix" the series and ensure a victory for the underdog Cincinnati Reds. The infamous Black Sox Scandal almost ruined major league baseball. Oddly, Bat never mentioned the affair in his column, though men he had known for many years were key figures in the affair. Arnold Rothstein, a prominent New York gambler, is still remembered as the brains behind the World Series fix, primarily through the fictional depictions of Damon Runyon and F. Scott Fitzgerald. Masterson certainly knew Rothstein, a well-known character in the Longacre Square district for twenty years and a nightly habitué of Bat's favorite hangouts. He probably was acquainted with others involved, former ball player Bill Burns, one-time boxer Billy Maharg, and Boston gambler Joe "Sport" Sullivan. But without question he knew former boxer Abe Attell, a key figure in the scandal.

Attell held the featherweight title for eleven years, from 1901 to 1912. While admiring his boxing skills, Masterson had a low opinion of the man's conduct and character. The little fighter, he said, engaged in phony bouts even as champion, because he was a compulsive gambler and constantly in financial difficulty. Bat was not surprised, therefore, when the former champion was named as a principal in the scandal, and he may have thought Attell got some well-deserved comeuppance when the clever Rothstein managed to make him the "fall guy" in the investigation. Indicted by a grand jury, Attell fled to Canada, where he successfully resisted extradition. (Never convicted for his part in the World Series fix, Attell in the 1950s was honored by the Boxing Writers of New York.)

Always distrustful of Attell, Masterson approved of the way his manager, Jack McKenna, controlled him during his prizefighting years. As Bat told it, after a bout McKenna would collect the purse and give his fighter only $2. If Attell objected, "McKenna whaled him over the head with a club. . . . Attell got a deal more of the club than he did money." That, Bat said, was the kind of manager Attell and other fighters like him needed.[2]

Hype Igoe, Wilson Mizner, and Jack Grace were other boxing managers he liked and admired.

Igoe managed Stanley Ketchel until the great middleweight left him to work under the guidance of Mizner. A flamboyant dresser, Mizner refused to tone down his attire even while working Ketchel's corner during a bout. He would appear, Bat said, "dressed as though for a party instead of a fight and did not soil his immaculate attire by swinging a towel or dashing water with a sponge."[3] (Four months after Masterson penned these lines, Mizner lost his prize pugilist. While in training at a farm near Springfield, Missouri, Ketchel moved into the bed of housekeeper Goldie Smith, replacing Walter Dipley, the farm foreman. Dipley took offense at this, got a gun, and shot Ketchel dead. Both Dipley and the lady were subsequently convicted of murder.)

Masterson and Jack Grace had been friends since bare-knuckle days. In later years Grace became a world traveler and a master of the tall tale. It was he who introduced Bat to the opprobrious expression "bohunk," which he said he had picked up in the Hawaiian Islands. Only a lightweight, Grace claimed to have won the Chinese heavy-weight title at Hong Kong in 1908 by knocking out the champion, Slung Wu, after eighty-seven furious rounds. Grace said he defeated the powerful and clever Asian by the use of his "scissors punch," which Slung Wu could not counter. He left China without defending his title, Grace said, and later Slung Wu regained the champion-ship at Singapore by knocking out Cannon Ball Smith in 192 rounds, the longest battle ever fought under Marquess of Queensberry rules. Masterson passed these stories on to his readers, but warned them that all he knew of Slung Wu and Cannon Ball Smith he had learned from Jack Grace, and he suspected all of it might be untrue.

Grace managed Jim Flynn at the time of the Carl Morris bout in 1911, the match that Bat exposed as a fake and led to his dispute with Frank Ufer and eventual lawsuit.

The scene of the Flynn-Morris bout, as well as many memorable prizefights in New York, was Madison Square Garden, a city land-mark. William Vanderbilt erected the original Garden in 1879 on the site of a P. T. Barnum museum. This building was razed ten years later and replaced by a $3 million structure designed by the famous architect Stanford White. The second-tallest building in New York, it contained the nation's largest auditorium (seating 8,000), a theater, concert hall, apartments, the most spacious restaurant in the city, and a roof cabaret where White, the building's creator, met his death at the hands of Harry Thaw.

Boxing matches, horse shows, bicycle races, footraces, wrestling matches, physical culture exhibitions, and political rallies were show-cased in the large auditorium. Upkeep of the huge building was expen-sive, however, and the place lost money year after year. In 1911 it was scheduled for demolition, but a real estate company purchased the fa-cility for $3.5 million and continued its operation until 1916, when the company went bankrupt. It then fell into the hands of the New York Life Insurance Company, which kept it going through the war years.

Veteran ring men Billy Gibson and Jimmy Johnston, the latter of whom was dubbed "the Boy Bandit" by Damon Runyon, managed the Garden and promoted fights there for a time in the late teens. It was during this period that Bat accused Boxing Commissioner Frank O'Neil of also having a secret financial interest in the place.

Madison Square Garden was always the premier boxing arena in the city. In the early years it attracted many middle- and upper-class boxing fans who were willing to pay higher admission charges to avoid the rowdy, roughneck crowds in the fight clubs. Later, gangs of "wild-eyed troglodytes," as Masterson called them, began to attend Garden fights, and their disruptive behavior was a major factor in the Garden's decline. Bat harshly criticized the Garden management and the city police for poor crowd control, until his pal Val O'Farrell was hired to provide security.

During boxing's lean years in New York the Garden managers turned to other sports to attract customers. For a while six-day bicycle races were popular, to the dismay of Masterson, who could find nothing exciting in watching bike peddlers endlessly circle the arena. Wrestling, ostensibly a physical combat between man and man, more closely approximated boxing, his first love, and he did attend wrestling programs at the Garden. Since boxing had fallen into such a low state, he saw little to differentiate the sports. "Fighters maul each other about with padded mitts on their hands," he said, "while the grapplers do their mauling without the mitts," and the "boob public" accepted both forms of flimflam.[4]

Although he didn't "take much stock in the grappling game," Bat found it hard to stay away from the Garden wrestling exhibitions. He was, he confessed, like those who attend bullfights in the hope of seeing the bull kill the matador. If two wrestlers simultaneously connected with their favorite grips and locked up until the ambulance arrived, he thought that might be a sight worth seeing.[5]

He enjoyed poking fun at the wrestlers who appeared in "grappling carnivals," as they were advertised. He thought the exhibitions were aptly named, for in Latin "carn" meant "flesh," and that was what a wrestling carnival offered: "Flesh, flesh, flesh! Pounds of it! Tons of it! A feast of it!" And tied to each ton was a name that sounded "like a hay fever victim's sneeze." There was Zkzrsty Nxrynz, Anton Przxmy, Wladek Zbyszko, and other names loaded with "jaw-breaking consonants." He suggested the referee wear a mask "to withstand the garlic and other gastronomic odors that permeate the atmosphere when these baby hippos" grappled in the Garden.[6] The difference between wrestling and a legitimate sport he likened to the contrast between three-card monte, a thieving con game, and faro or poker, high forms of gambling.

Madison Square Garden's fortunes turned in 1920 when Tex Rickard took a ten-year lease on the building at $200,000 a year.

George L. "Tex" Rickard and Bat Masterson had much in common, having started out as lawmen in frontier towns before turning to professional gambling, a vocation that eventually led them into the sport of prizefighting. Although a generation separated them—Rickard was born in Missouri in 1871, the year seventeen-year-old Bat left that state for Kansas with his father—the two were kindred spirits who held each other in great esteem.

Rickard had moved with his family to Texas in 1875. There he cowboyed and at the age of twenty-three became city marshal of Henrietta. Turning to gambling as a profession, he went to Alaska in 1895 and made and lost several fortunes operating saloons and gambling houses during the great Klondike gold rush. After returning to the States, he joined the next great mining excitement, the rush to Nevada, and opened his famous "Northern" gambling saloon in Goldfield.

A man of vision and imagination, Rickard always thought in large terms. He had first promoted prizefights as attractions to his establishments in the North, but in Goldfield he saw an opportunity to utilize the sport in order to spur nationwide interest in the Nevada mining boom, and at the same time make a little money. In 1906, by means of his considerable charm, persuasive powers, and a guaranteed combined purse of $33,500, an unprecedented amount for the time, he signed champion Joe Gans and Battling Nelson to meet in the remote mining camp for a lightweight title bout. Ignoring critics who said the project was doomed to failure, Rickard forged ahead with a campaign of shrewd promotion and ballyhoo. When the memorable battle was over—Gans won on a foul in the forty-second round—the enterprising gambler had achieved his objectives; the name of the mining camp of Goldfield was familiar throughout the nation, and he had turned a neat profit. In the process he had made a name for himself as an enterprising and risk-taking boxing promoter.

Rickard promoted his first heavyweight title fight in 1910 when he put on the epic Johnson-Jeffries battle at Reno, Nevada. Masterson was instrumental in the initial arrangements for Rickard's next title match. In early 1916 Bat brought together Rickard, Madison Square Garden manager Jimmy Johnston, and representatives of heavyweight champion Jess Willard and challenger Frank Moran to plan for what would be the biggest fistic event in New York in many years. After much wrangling over money, the various parties reached an agreement that Willard and Moran would meet in a title bout at the Garden for a total purse of $45,000. But within days the boxers reneged on the agreement, demanding a $70,000 guarantee.

In high dudgeon, Masterson withdrew from the negotiations and pleaded with Rickard to "chuck the whole dirty mess in the ash can." But Tex, described by Bat as "a stubborn sort of a cuss [who would] rather put a dent in his bankroll than fall down on anything he started," gave in to the fighters' demands. Calling it "a cold-blooded, underhanded, sneaking" holdup committed by the greedy fighters, Bat refused to affix his name as a witness to the final agreement, snapping that he was not in the burglary business.[7]

Rickard lost money on the match, as Bat feared, but that did not deter him from taking over management of the Garden four years later and turning it into a profitable enterprise. At the same time, he was developing outdoor fight promotions on a scale that dwarfed the Willard-Moran affair and left Masterson in absolute awe.

— 15 —

OUT OF THE PAST

The old-time Westerners are dropping out one by one with painful regularity these days. The time is not far distant when the Western pioneer will be but a memory.

W. B. "Bat" Masterson

Bat Masterson had full freedom to write anything that struck his fancy, and in the hundreds of newspaper columns he wrote for the *Morning Telegraph*, he had every opportunity to tell the story of his life in the West and give his own version of the exciting events that marked his career. But as Alfred Henry Lewis observed in his 1907 sketch of Masterson in *Human Life*, Bat would write biography, but not autobiography.

In the millions of words he composed for the paper, Masterson seldom touched on his former life, and only then when prompted by some outside influence—a visit from a western crony, perhaps, or increasingly, as years passed, the death of one of those friends.

He kept track of his western associates, and his personal correspondence was voluminous. In addition to old Dodge City cohorts like Ben Daniels, Bill Tilghman, Wyatt Earp, and Mike Sutton, he exchanged frequent letters with Bob Stockton, Billy Thompson, and other friends and supporters he still retained in Denver. He wrote Lou Houseman, W. A. Pinkerton, and Parson Davies in Chicago; Jefferson Davis Orear in Hot Springs; Charlie Mitchell in England; Snowey Baker in Australia; and dozens of other men associated with the boxing game around the country and the world. Sometimes a letter from one of his western friends would prompt a column on the stirring times he had experienced on the frontier.

After leaving Denver for the last time in 1902, Bat returned to the West—west of Hot Springs, Arkansas, that is—on only one occasion, to cover the Johnson-Jeffries fight in Nevada. On his way back home with Alfred Henry Lewis and Charlie White he stopped in Trinidad, Colorado, where he had served as city marshal in the wild old days. There he posed for a photograph with Lewis, White, and a group of Trinidad old-timers who greeted them at the depot. Two years later Trinidad honored Masterson and Lewis, both of whom had lived in the town in its early days and gone on to national acclaim, by encapsulating photographs of them in the cornerstone of a new courthouse.

Rolling eastward from Trinidad, Masterson was struck by the remarkable change in Kansas since first he saw it in the early 1870s. Where once he had hunted buffalo across miles of treeless grassland, he now saw orchards and fields of corn, wheat, and alfalfa. He had never dreamed, he said, that the Kansas plains could ever be made agriculturally productive.

The train stopped at Dodge City at eight in the morning, and passengers alighted to eat breakfast at the Harvey House. From the depot Bat could survey the scene of many of his adventures. When he arrived back in New York he allowed himself to reminisce a bit on Dodge, the little community where he had first achieved celebrity and which he remembered as "the liveliest town in the entire West." But his touch of nostalgia lasted for only a moment, and he quickly returned to boxing news.[1]

Thoughts of Dodge City still occupied his mind a few months later, however, and he devoted most of a column to Eddie Foy, the widely popular vaudeville headliner he had first met when Foy and his partner, Jimmy Thompson, appeared in the Kansas cow town in the summer of 1878. Foy sang comic songs, performed acrobatic dances, and in one of his best routines, Bat remembered, engaged Thompson in a four-round boxing match burlesque.

Foy was a hit as a performer in Dodge City, but, according to a story Bat related, he also gained the respect of the westerners when he refused to be intimidated by a gun-packing desperado who tried to bully him. "Eddie just let fly with his right and the bad man's head hit the floor first. Eddie was on him in an instant with both feet, and before the bad man realized what had happened Foy had disarmed him and booted him out of the place." When told that the fellow was a killer who would undoubtedly return with another gun, Foy snapped: "Very well, I'll wait, and if he can't shoot any better than he can fight I'll win myself another six-shooter."[2]

In New York, where Foy often performed as a topflight star, he and Masterson renewed their friendship. While always amused by Foy's antics on and off the stage, Bat scoffed at the comedian's assertion that he was an expert judge of prizefighters and their abilities. In late 1912 Foy was playing Boston and wired Masterson his predictions of the outcomes of several upcoming fights. Bat thought the choices "plumb daft" and telegraphed the Boston chief of police that he believed the comedian was suffering hallucinations and asked him to look into the matter. A return wire from the chief assured Bat that Foy was resting comfortably and evidently out of danger.

Always close to the theatrical business, especially after hooking up with Emma, Masterson in New York renewed acquaintanceship with many Broadway performers he had known in the old days. He remembered song-and-dance man Charley Ross as a jockey in the West before Ross turned to vaudeville. Bat recalled attending a theater leading actor Frank Keenan once managed in Wichita, Kansas. "The Great Lafayette," billed as "Europe's Greatest Mimic," performed his one-man act all over the world and earned $3,000 a week on Broadway; Bat remembered him as an archery expert who was lucky to net $50 a week with his exhibition in Denver. Tom Lewis and Sam Ryan, founding members and officers of the White Rats, an actors' social club, were successful vaudeville comedians Masterson had first seen perform in the Bucket of Blood saloon in Pueblo, Colorado. Maggie Cline, one of the first female vaudeville performers to work on stage alone, starred on Broadway as a comedy Irish singer; Bat remembered her as one of a troupe he had seen at Leadville, Colorado, in the early 1880s.

Although Bill Tilghman and Masterson were on opposite sides of the political fence, the two remained friendly over the years, corresponded regularly, and met occasionally after Bat went to New York. The first such meeting came about in 1904, when Tilghman, a lifelong Democrat and a delegate to the party's national convention in

St. Louis that year, was one of a group appointed to notify Alton B. Parker of Esopus, New York, of his official nomination as Democratic candidate for the presidency. Tilghman stopped in the big city and visited Masterson. The two old lawmen had not seen each other in many years, and their meeting was so memorable to Masterson that he mentioned it in a letter to Ben Daniels in 1905 and again in his article on Tilghman written for *Human Life* in 1907.

The two met again in Washington, D.C., in February 1909. This was the time Bat talked Tilghman and Chris Madsen into dressing in full formal attire for the gala affair at the White House and then hurriedly left town rather than joining them in what he considered a ridiculous get-up.

When Bat learned in 1910 that Tilghman had been elected to the state senate in Oklahoma, he publicly extended his congratulations in a column, and extolled him as a man of "indomitable courage and good generalmanship, cool-headed, fearless and virile."[3] In 1913 he again devoted much of a column to Tilghman, sketching his career as buffalo hunter, lawman, and political officeholder.

The two old lawmen met for the last time in 1921 when Tilghman and H. P. Myton, another veteran of early Dodge City, came to New York to attend the Dempsey-Carpentier title bout, and to promote a movie, *The Passing of the Oklahoma Outlaws*, which Tilghman had produced. Tilghman and Myton sought Masterson's help in promoting the movie production in New York, but Bat saw little chance of success for the film there. He did, however, offer his aid in acquiring a print of the motion picture of the upcoming fight and his help in their obtaining distribution rights in Oklahoma. With Bat's assistance Tilghman and Myton obtained a print of the fight and thwarted a federal statute that prohibited interstate transport of prizefight motion pictures by smuggling out the film in a specially made suitcase.

Back in 1911 Tilghman had written Bat, advising him that Quanah Parker, the mixed-blood Comanche chief who led the Indian assault against the buffalo hunter outpost at Adobe Walls, Texas, in 1874, had died in Oklahoma. Nearly 2,000 Indians and whites attended Quanah's funeral, the largest ever held in Oklahoma, Tilghman reported. He went on to say that he had often visited Quanah at his home near Cache, where the old chief provided details of the Battle of Adobe Walls from the Indians' perspective. For three days, Quanah said, the Indians suffered heavy losses from the accurate shooting of the hunters and their long-range, heavy-caliber buffalo guns. He himself was "cut almost in two" by one of the big bullets and barely survived. Tilghman passed along this information because he knew that Masterson, one of the participants in the fight, would be interested.[4]

Masterson shed no tears over Quanah Parker's passing. Although he respected the chief's record as a warrior and a leader of his people, he still saw him as a brutal enemy who had killed Bat's friends and destroyed their property. Only three months before receiving Tilghman's letter he had expressed outrage that Congress had appropriated $1,000 for a monument to Cynthia Ann Parker, Quanah's mother, and predicted that when the chief died additional government funds would be spent to honor him. Back in 1892 he had given a sworn deposition in support of friends who had suffered financial losses at Adobe Walls, and now, thirty-six years after that battle, the federal government still had not provided compensation for those losses. Instead, he said, Congress was voting funds for "a monument to the mother of the Indian chief who destroyed and plundered the white pioneers of the West." He found that deplorable.[5]

Thoughts of Adobe Walls and Quanah Parker led Masterson to an account of the subsequent military campaign against the marauding Indians in which he had served as a civilian scout. U.S. Army units under the command of Colonel Nelson A. Miles engaged the Indians for several months, he said, but managed to kill no more than a dozen warriors. "It will thus be seen that a score of buffalo hunters at the Adobe Walls killed about eight times as many Indians in that one battle than eight regiments of soldiers, supported by Gatling guns and cannons, killed in eight months." Perhaps, he suggested, the refusal of the government to reimburse the white men for their losses at Adobe Walls was due to jealousy and embarrassment.[6]

Billy Dixon, who had fought beside him at Adobe Walls and scouted with him in the Red River campaign, died at his Texas panhandle ranch on March 9, 1913. The story of his life, written by his widow, Olive, was published a few months later by Frederick S. Barde, of Guthrie, Oklahoma. Responding to a request from Barde, Masterson, on October 13, 1913, penned a tribute to his old compadre. Dixon, he said, "was a typical frontiersman of the highest order. The perils and hardships of border life were exactly suited to his stoical and imperturbable nature." Although at heart he was "kind-hearted, generous and hospitable," Dixon remained "cool, calculating and uncommunicative at all times." Bat's comments appeared in the preface to the Dixon biography, published in 1914.[7]

Two other celebrated scouts of the plains, William Mathewson and William F. Cody, were also held in high regard by Masterson, and he mentioned them from time to time in his columns. He first met Mathewson, the original "Buffalo Bill," at Wichita in 1871, when Mathewson was forty-one years old, a frontier veteran, and already a legend in Kansas. He made a strong impression on the teen-aged Masterson. Bat's admiration was still evident in 1911 when he learned that the old frontiersman had married at the age of eighty-one and publicly congratulated him. Mathewson died at Wichita in March 1916.

In 1871 Bat also met Cody, whose showmanship and flair for theatrics later made him internationally famous as "Buffalo Bill." When Cody brought his Wild West Show to New York he and Bat would always get together. In January 1916 Masterson wrote a feature story on the celebrated frontiersman for the Sunday magazine section of the *Telegraph*. Although he had announced his retirement six years earlier and had now reached the age of seventy, Cody told Bat he was negotiating to take over the 101 Ranch Wild West Show and had great plans for its expansion and improvement.

But just a year later, on January 10, 1917, Cody died. Masterson, who said he never had a better friend than the frontiersman and showman, eulogized him in an interview. "In his prime," he said, "Cody was the finest specimen of manhood I ever saw, standing fully six feet in height, and as straight as an arrow. He was strong as a lion and as nimble as a cat on his feet. . . . He was an expert horseman and could shoot a pistol with deadly accuracy while riding at full speed."[8]

The years passed and Masterson found it increasingly necessary to announce the death of another of his old friends. In May 1917 Bob Stockton, Denver sport and saloonkeeper, described by Masterson as a "true friend and a relentless foe," died suddenly. "The old-time Westerners are dropping out one by one with painful regularity these days," Bat wrote sadly. "The time is not far distant when the Western pioneer will be but a memory."[9]

When a year later he learned that Mike Sutton had passed away in Dodge City, Bat wrote: "One by one those valiant souls who comprised the vanguard of civilization in that vast and undeveloped territory lying beyond the Missouri River . . . are falling by the wayside. . . . In Judge Sutton's death the West lost an intrepid pioneer and Kansas one of its most highly-respected and substantial citizens." Sadly, he said, only a handful of those hardy pioneers who settled Dodge City in 1872 remained. "All have passed the three-score-and-ten limit [and] their cares and troubles, like those who have already preceded them across the great divide, will, no doubt, soon terminate in this old dump of a world of ours." They were, he said, "a grand set of characters."[10]

The veterans of the fight game—the pugilists, managers, promoters, and sporting men Bat had known since bare-knuckle days—were also dropping with frequency.

In October 1916 Billy Jordan, the peerless ring announcer whose stentorian voice had surmounted the crowd noise at Carson City when Corbett and Fitzsimmons met in 1897, and who, at the Jeffries-Johnson clash in 1910, Bat said, "spoke so plainly and with such tremendous lung power that a deaf person could have heard him," died in San Francisco.[11] When Bob Fitzsimmons cashed in his chips at Chicago on October 22, 1917, Masterson devoted four complete columns to the ring career of the great Australian fighter. Only a few months later, on February 2, 1918, John L. Sullivan died in Boston, and Bat reviewed the former champion's career in four more columns. Nineteen days after Sullivan's death, Billy Madden, who once guided John L.'s career and had been a close Masterson friend since 1881, passed on.

Few of the real veterans of the game remained. Charlie Mitchell and Parson Davies still hung on, but both were in poor health and might go at any time. "Soon the old-timers will all be gone and their like isn't likely to be seen again for a long time to come, if indeed, ever," Bat wrote in February 1918.[12]

Within weeks Masterson had to report that Charlie Mitchell, "the best of the lot," had joined the ranks of the departed. The old fighter died at his home in Brighton, England, on April 3, 1918, after a prolonged illness. A letter written to Masterson by Mitchell shortly before his death contained a note of the grim humor that endeared him to Bat and others:

> My dear Bat:
> Yours to hand and I was delighted to hear you and the Missus were well. I wish I could say the same for myself. You will perhaps read my obituary in the American newspapers before this reaches you. And let me assure you, that I would be greatly pleased to hop out anytime, for I have suffered the tortures of hell lately and I haven't a chance. You and I have been the best of pals ever since we first met thirty-five years ago, and I should have been delighted to have seen your old dial once more before flashing mine above or below. My blessing on you both.
> Your sincere pal, C. Mitchell.[13]

Although invalided for many years after a stroke, Charles E. "Parson" Davies was the last of Bat's close coterie of old-time sporting friends to go, "crossing the great divide" on June 27, 1920. Among other accomplishments, Davies had been Grand Exalted Ruler of the Order of Elks, and he died at the Elks' National Home at Bedford, Virginia. "For a quarter of a century," Bat eulogized,

> Parson Davies was the best-known sportsman in the Western Hemisphere. . . . His word was his bond. He never repudiated an obligation or failed to keep his word. Generous to a fault and as courageous as a lion, he battled his way up from a poor immigrant boy to the highest distinction in the realm of sports. . . . They are not growing any more Parson Davies these days. He was a grand man in every respect, the best ever. . . . No better pal ever lived than Parson Davies.[14]

When he wrote these lines, Masterson could not know that within sixteen months he, too, would "cross the great divide" to join the ranks of the great characters who had passed on.

Masterson was photographed on a New York City street about the same time as he appeared in the Savage automatic pistol ad. (Author's collection)

At the railroad depot in Trinidad, Colorado, on July 13, 1910, local residents welcome Masterson and others returning east from the Johnson-Jeffries fight in Reno, Nevada. *Left to right:* Tony Patrick, John English, Chicago sports editor Charlie White, Ben Springer, John Gysing, Masterson, John Conkie, Alfred Henry Lewis, E. B. Sopris, and Charley Hungerford. (Courtesy Old Baca House–Pioneer Museum, Colorado State Historical Society, Denver)

Sydney Burns, William A. Pinkerton, and Bat at the Hot Air Mine in Hot Springs, Arkansas, March 1911. (Courtesy Kansas State Historical Society, Topeka)

Photographs of Bat and Emma inscribed to "Their dear good friend Billy Thompson" and dated September 25, 1921, one month to the day before Bat's death. (Author's collection)

Bat Masterson stands behind western movie star William S. Hart, seated at Bat's desk in the *New York Morning Telegraph* building, October 7, 1921. (Courtesy Boot Hill Museum, Dodge City, Kansas)

Masterson and Hart pose together on the roof of the *Morning Telegraph* building, October 7, 1921. (Courtesy Jack DeMattos)

Bat Masterson's grave in Woodlawn Cemetery in the Bronx. The tombstone gives an incorrect birthdate of 1854 - rather than the correct date of 1853.

Bat was interred in this Woodlawn plot on what would have been Theodore Roosevelt's sixty-third birthday - October 27, 1921.

The gravestone of W. B. Masterson in the Woodlawn Cemetery in the Bronx, New York, contains two errors: the birth date of 1854 rather than the correct 1853, and the legend "Loved by Everyone." He was not. (Courtesy Jack DeMattos)

Emma Masterson, June 17, 1930. (Courtesy Roy Adams)

— 16 —

ALL WORK AND NO PLAY

Mr. Masterson is probably the best known newspaper writer in the country, [one who] never slops over and stands in the suds, [who] can pack a pause with feeling and put a pressure of power in the silence. His intellect is crystalline—his verb always fetches up. He says things.
                                                    Jefferson Davis Orear

While working at the *Morning Telegraph*, Bat Masterson regularly took two lengthy vacations a year. In the late winter or early spring he and Emma would spend a month or more at Hot Springs, Arkansas, and in August they would go to Saratoga during the racing season. For Bat these were always working vacations, for he continued to write his thrice-weekly columns from the resorts.

Masterson had first visited Hot Springs in the summer of 1878, when he was sheriff at Dodge City. He had been suffering from vertigo and sought relief at the popular spa. In following years he returned often, for he enjoyed the baths and believed in their salubrious effects. His columns from there often sounded as if they were composed by a chamber of commerce flack.

But the appeal of Hot Springs for Bat Masterson was more than the spa's health and climate benefits, for the citizenry there lived and conducted themselves by the western code to which he had always subscribed. In Hot Springs a man said what he meant and meant what he said, and if he happened to offend another in the process, he stood ready to defend his opinion with fists or guns if necessary. Bat felt at home in a town whose inhabitants still retained enough of the frontier ethic to respect and admire the man who had killed one or more adversaries in a stand-up gunfight, either in self-defense or in enforcement of the law. He, of course, was such a man, and this was his ethic. Those who did not take this view, he said, belonged "to that pusillanimous class which believes in assailing a man's character and then appealing to the law for protection." He contended that there was always a wholesome respect for character in a country where a man was held to personal account for public statements derogatory to another. "If there were more of this sort of spirit in this country there would be less vilification and blackguardism and fewer character assassins. . . . The man who will back up what he says with a fight if necessary is to be respected, while the one who assails character and then seeks refuge behind the law deserves nothing but contempt."[1]

Long recognized as a gambling center, Hot Springs became known as the "Monte Carlo of the Middle West" following the 1897 acquisition of the Southern Club by Dan Stuart. A number of other plush casinos were named for states: the Kentucky, the Arkansas, the Missouri, the Illinois, the Ohio, and the Indiana. Among the celebrated high rollers who visited the spa regularly were New York state senator Long Pat McCarren, who never tipped less than $5 and once dropped $100,000 at a Saratoga faro table; New York City gambling-house operator Davey Johnson, who helped Reginald Vanderbilt celebrate his twenty-first birthday in 1901 by winning $70,000 from him at faro and roulette; Pat Sheedy, best remembered for engineering the return of the stolen Gainsborough painting, *Duchess of Devonshire*, after its disappearance twenty-five years earlier; and legendary horse track gambler Riley Grannon, whose death in 1908 made national headlines when Tex Rickard and George Graham Rice turned his funeral into a well-publicized Nevada mining camp promotion scheme.

Bat Masterson quite naturally fit into this crowd. He never had the resources to make the enormous wagers of the biggest plungers, but he was a serious gambler and was for the most part successful. The *National Police Gazette* reported in 1903 that after a five-hour session in the Southern Club at a faro table he walked away with $10,000.[2]

For a few years at the turn of the century Hot Springs was also an important boxing center where Masterson refereed several bouts and top-notch boxers of the day, including Tommy Ryan, Kid McCoy, Joe Gans, Young Corbett, Battling Nelson, and Abe Attell, performed.

During the peak years of gambling activity at Hot Springs three horse-racing tracks were in operation and an enterprising liveryman named Simon Cooper piped thermal waters into a large pool and opened a bathhouse for the pampered equines.

Bat and Emma Masterson were in Hot Springs on the night of Saturday, February 25, 1905, when a terrible fire swept through the town. Starting in the Grand Central Hotel, it spread quickly, and before it was extinguished forty square blocks of the city lay in ruins. Destroyed were the homes of 2,000 residents, three hotels, two churches, the courthouse, and the jail. Hot Springs was like a second home to Masterson, and after witnessing the holocaust he devoted much of his time and personal funds to help rebuild the city and aid the devastated. A "high class vaudeville and sparring entertainment" he had planned on staging in the city's auditorium on Monday, February 27, was canceled, of course. Advance ticket sales had totaled $1,000. After deducting his expenses of $250, he donated the balance, $750, to a fund for relief of fire victims.

Most of the buildings were rebuilt, but the conflagration signaled the end of one of the last freewheeling communities in the nation. The reformers, so despised by Masterson, were on the march in Arkansas. Soon afterward they gained political control of the town and county and closed down the great gambling casinos.

The demise of Hot Springs as a gambling resort was part of a national trend. A few years after the turn of the century big-time high-rolling gamblers suddenly seemed as extinct as the dinosaurs. Masterson lamented their passing:

> There was a time in this country when men could be found who would bet their eyeballs out, and yours, too, on what they believed to be an even thing, but that was before barbering came into vogue. Now our big operators want a flash at your hole card before loosening up. The John W. Gateses, the Riley Grannons, the Pittsburg Phils, the Pat McCarrons and the Phil Dwyers were willing to take 1 to 2 for their money if they thought well of the proposition. But they are all dead . . . , supplanted by the barbering variety.[3]

In an earlier column he had given his philosophy on gambling in general and what constituted a "good sport" in particular: "Pretty much everything we do is more or less of a gamble.... The farmer when he sows and plants his crop in the spring . . . is gambling on what the harvest will be.... A good sport is a good loser and takes his medicine when, as the stage villain would say, the 'kirds' are stacked against him."[4]

Hot Springs experienced a short resurgence in 1910 when the clubs were allowed to reopen, but it was plain to Bat that the resort's days as a great sporting town were over. On his annual visit in 1911 he saw that a Catholic church had taken possession of the venerable Southern Club and was running a bingo game inside. He remarked sardonically that transition from "a high toned gambling establishment to a church bazaar" was not such big change after all; a man could be separated from his money in either place.[5]

By 1913 Hot Springs was, in Masterson's lexicon, "groggy and hanging on the ropes, waiting for the count." Hotel occupancy was down, but prices had risen. He refused to stay at the Eastman, his favorite hotel, when he found that weekly room rates had increased $21 over the year before. The Ohio Club had burned to the ground, the Arkansas Club was now an Elks Lodge, the Eagles were dickering for the Southern Club, and the Indiana Club had been turned into a nickelodeon. Unemployed dealers and casino workers wandered the streets.

Now the prohibitionists went on the attack. The state legislature in Arkansas enacted a measure banning the sale and consumption of alcoholic beverages, and the fifty-two saloons operating in Hot Springs were forced to close their doors. The gambling law had driven "the 'pikers' into the cheap hotels and boarding houses," Bat groaned, and now "the liquor law is sure to start a big boom in the blind tiger and bootlegging industry."[6]

Jefferson Davis Orear, eccentric editor of a singular local weekly magazine, the *Arkansaw Thomas Cat*, was Masterson's closest local friend in the "Valley of Vapors," as the Hot Springs area was called. The cover of Orear's magazine featured an artist's depiction of an angry feline. Below squatted a grinning gargoyle emblazoned with the words "Egotism, Bigotry, Hypocrisy, Superstition, Despotism, and Fraud," which was being attacked by a muscular man wielding a sledgehammer marked "Truth." The motto of the publication was

"God help the rich, the poor can beg," and its principles were "elevation of horse thieves and public morals; one country, one flag, and one wife at a time; and love your friends and brimstone your enemies."[7] A devotee of odd expression and alliteration, Orear called the *Tomcat* "a periodical for pensive people" and "a necromantic narrator of the nigescent, noxious, nozzling nuisance of a nation swollen with ignorance and pride."[8]

As a leader in the fight against those who were transforming Hot Springs, the iconoclastic Arkansas editor found a strong ally in Bat Masterson, who shared his dislike of reformers and held an incredulous, sometimes acerbic, view of the world. Orear mentioned Masterson frequently in his magazine, usually in his distinctively overblown prose. He described Bat, "probably the best known newspaper writer in the country,"[9] as one who "never slops over and stands in the suds, [who] can pack a pause with feeling and put a pressure of power in the silence. His intellect is crystalline—his verb always fetches up. He says things." The Masterson columns in the *Morning Telegraph*, he said, were "pregnant with fearsome facts, [loaded with] cocktail brilliancy and Tabasco sauce trimmings."[10]

Orear sometimes directed his humorous badinage at his journalistic friend from the big city. In 1917 he published a story purportedly lifted from the pages of "the Snagtown Torchlight," a fictitious Ozark Mountain newspaper. Like the paper, the story was entirely a figment of Orear's active imagination. It described a fire that raged through the offices of "the Swamp Valley Index," a temperance weekly edited in Snagtown by "a bald-headed, bow-legged cantankerous old critter" named Bat Masterson. When finally extinguished, the "disastrous conflagration" had wreaked damage assessed at $1.17, "a heavy loss for a plant worth only four dollars, all told." Bat enjoyed the joke and in his column quoted the story in full.[11]

Undoubtedly Masterson's greatest enjoyment in Hot Springs was seeing old pals, many of whom regularly vacationed at the spa in the spring also. Among those with whom he cut up old touches were Parson Davies, W. A. Pinkerton, Mike Sutton, and George Ade.

Davies, once "a strapping athlete, with a heavy shock of hair as black as the raven's wing, [who] could whip his weight in wildcats,"[12] as Bat remembered him, was now a white-haired old man shuffling about and suffering intense pain.

Bill Pinkerton, on the other hand, was in excellent health. The celebrated detective enjoyed horseback riding at Hot Springs and was often joined by New Yorker Sidney Burns, who claimed to have ridden to the hounds in his native England and never saw a fence he considered too high to jump. Not to be outbragged, Pinkerton said he had also hurdled some pretty high fences while chasing the James and Younger boys in Missouri forty years earlier. Masterson, who had once ridden a horse to death while a member of an Arizona posse with Wyatt Earp in pursuit of stagecoach bandits, declined to join in these saddle romps, explaining that he had his fill of horseback riding in his early days on the frontier.

George Ade was a young reporter for the *Chicago Record* in 1896 when he persuaded Masterson to write a column for him. Fourteen years later he had achieved national acclaim as a playwright and humorist, and Bat saw an opportunity to demand repayment in kind. Every spring in Hot Springs the Arlington and the Park Hotels tried to outdo each other in lavish St. Patrick's Day balls. Since reporting on social functions was not Masterson's forte, he decided to enlist the literary services of the talented and popular George Ade to describe the galas in a column for him.

Ade obliged, and in a humorous 1,500-word story admitted returning to the newspaper business only out of gratitude for the kindness and generosity shown by Masterson toward a "bewildered cub" years earlier.[13]

Now that boxing was just a memory at Hot Springs, horse racing had been outlawed, the clubhouses were closed, and to enjoy an alcoholic beverage a man had to commit a crime, there was little for Bat to do but take the baths, drink large quantities of Mountain Valley water, and listen to the hotel orchestra. "The only thing the town will have left before long will be the hot water and it's just possible that some one will try and stop that from running," Bat wrote sorrowfully in 1916.[14] The man who had once gambled with the highest rollers in the best sporting town in the land was now reduced to playing bridge whist at a penny a point. Nineteen nineteen would be the last year the Mastersons vacationed in Hot Springs.

For years Bat and Emma took a summer hiatus from New York City, spending the month of August at Saratoga Springs, 180 miles north, in the foothills of the Adirondacks. Like Hot Springs, Saratoga

Springs was a health resort, famous since the eighteenth century for its mineral waters. It also was a gambling center.

Shortly after the Civil War John Morrissey, New York prizefighter, gambler, and politician, built a gambling clubhouse and a racetrack at the spa, and for the next four decades Saratoga hosted America's richest and most powerful during the racing season each August. Professional gamblers owned and operated the racetrack until 1901 when a syndicate headed by William C. Whitney purchased the property and assumed control. The celebrated gambler Richard Canfield ran the clubhouse for a dozen years, but under pressure from reformers, it closed down in 1906. Operators of the Manhattan Club and the United States Club, the other major gambling casinos, soon followed suit.

As manager of the *Morning Telegraph's* Turf Advertising Department, Masterson necessarily maintained close ties with the track crowd. He liked to play the horses himself, although he complained often that he lost more than he ever won betting the nags. As he grew older and wiser, he tried to limit his bets to $5, but sometimes succumbed to the siren song of the "sure thing" tipster and risked $10 on a long-shot "sleeper." He did win occasionally, but his winnings, like his losses, were modest. He said he felt "like a microbe" among high rollers in the class of Abe Attell, who won $3,000 in one day at Saratoga. This amount, he added ruefully, exceeded his own best day at the track by $2,970.[15]

At Saratoga Bat reported on the comings and goings of the horse owners, breeders, jockeys, trainers, bookies, tipsters, and inveterate players who made up the racetrack crowd, all democratized by their shared love of the sport. He devoted columns to news of noted turfmen like Ed Bradley, whom he had known as a professional gambler in the frontier West. At his Idle Hour Horse Farm in Kentucky Ed Bradley bred many fine thoroughbreds, including four Kentucky Derby winners. A firm believer in the health benefits of the Saratoga mineral water, he transported it in barrels to his Idle Hour breeding farm, where he served it at his table and provided it for his horses to drink.

Stable owner Johnny Mayberry, on the other hand, was famous for giving his horses a glass of beer before they raced. When he did particularly well during the 1913 season, winning twice as many handicaps as any other owner, Bat concluded that there must be something to the beer treatment.

Masterson had a low opinion of jockeys generally and often blamed them for his losses at the track. Bookmakers also ranked low in his estimation, as evidenced by the story he told of a youngster who began making book at the track. One day the young man called on a friend and confessed that he was conscious-stricken and fearful that his mother would find out what he was doing.

"What are you doing?" inquired the friend.

"I'm booking races at the track."

"Well, what does your mother think you are doing?"

"She thinks I am a burglar," said the young bookie.[16]

Wilson Mizner, in the playwriting phase of his many-faceted career in 1914, told Bat he came to Saratoga to gather "atmosphere" for a new play to be called "How to Beat the Bookies." Masterson replied that if Mizner could solve that puzzle he should never divulge it on the stage, but use the knowledge to much better advantage at the track.

Of course the wealthy came to Saratoga and disported themselves in grand style. Diamond Jim Brady, "lit up like the Luna Park tower,"[17] and bedecked in a half-million-dollars worth of gems, was a perennial visitor during the racing season. Another attention-getting Broadway figure was Herbert Bayard Swope, the handsome *New York World* reporter renowned for his sartorial splendor. His appearance, noted Masterson, always caused a scurrying among the ladies.

The United States and Grand Union were the major hotels at Saratoga. The Mastersons always stayed at the venerable United States, built in 1824. Bat sometimes commented on activities there, as in 1914 when he remarked that dancing was going big in the hotel ballroom, and that a "Tango and Hesitation Carnival" was being well received. "Everybody seems to be taking a whirl at the sport," he said, but did not indicate if "everybody" included himself and Emma.[18]

Bat had predicted that without casino gambling Saratoga, like Hot Springs, would go into decline, but the resort prospered in the years just prior to America's entry into the world war. "Even when everything was wide open in Saratoga there never was as many visitors here as there are now," Masterson was forced to admit in 1915. The streets were packed in the evening, and hotel verandas were jammed. The vacationers were free with their money, which was good news to the natives, who spent "ten months of the year twirling their thumbs and discussing the best way to fry snowballs so as to make them nutritious and palatable."[19]

Masterson's last year at Saratoga was 1916. His visit that season began badly when he checked into the United States Hotel and was outraged to learn that a "plus," a daily $2 surcharge, would be added to his bill "because of the war in Europe." Then a few days later he became ill, poisoned, he said, by the hotel's drinking water. After a week confined to his room under a doctor's care, he decided that the Saratoga food and water were too much for his "poor old digestive apparatus" and returned to New York.

Human stomachs, he said, were not all alike. "Some are strong, durable and immune from diseased food, poisonous water, colic, cholera morbus or the yen yens. Others are weak, sensitive, and subject to spasms and convulsions when invaded by substances foreign to their delicately constructed tissues and membranes. The one we are toting round we suspect belongs to the latter system and that's why we're home." He blamed his hotel's ancient water pipes, idle eight months of the year and never cleaned, for his trouble. The experience, he decided, was another case of the old Mexican standoff—losing his money but saving his life. He asked sarcastically why any New Yorker would go to Saratoga when either Hoboken or Passaic was nearer and easier to get to, and vowed never to go to Saratoga again.[20]

A writer for the *Saratoga Sun* a few days later took him to task for what he called "a virulent diatribe" against the resort's hotels, and questioned just where he stayed at the spa. Bat replied in his column that he put up at the United States Hotel as usual, paid $17 per day for his room, a $2 increase over the $15 he had always been charged before, and was rewarded with poisoning by contaminated hotel plumbing.[21]

Two years later he was still angry and grumbling about Saratoga, where, he said, visitors could expect to be "plucked" and "plussed" of their money. He realized that the spa's permanent residents needed to make hay during the racing season and had to work fast, but he didn't care how fast Saratoga worked or who it worked, just so long as it didn't work him. He had "rubbed the Spa and its denizens off [his] visiting list."[22]

Having dropped Saratoga as a summer vacation spot, Bat and Emma the following year went farther north to Alexandria Bay on the St. Lawrence River. They stayed at the Thousand Island House, since 1872 the foremost resort hotel in the area, and it became their regular August retreat. Bat was delighted with the hotel and the area, calling it the best summer resort he knew "this side of the Pike's Peak country."[23]

Masterson extended an invitation to his "legion of anonymous correspondents" to write him while he vacationed. Letters from "this species of vermin" were always welcome, he said, as mail for the Thousand Island House was thoroughly disinfected before leaving the Alexandria Bay post office to protect hotel guests from contamination "by the insidious poison these vile communications carry."[24]

On the St. Lawrence Bat took up sport fishing, probably for the first time in his life. These were ideal fishing waters, and with a boat and guide he brought in fine catches of black bass, pickerel, muskellunge, and eel. He decided that no more enjoyable or relaxing day could be spent than on a fishing trip on those waters, followed by a shore dinner on one of the islands.

Another new experience awaited him at Alexandria Bay. There he flew in an airplane for the first and only time in his life. He had some business to attend to at Kingston, Canada, thirty miles away, and, seeing a plane at a hanger near the hotel, wondered if he might "take a fly." He looked up the pilot of the plane, who, surprisingly, turned out to be Charlie Rogers, whom Bat had known as a Texas cowboy forty years earlier.

"Get in and I'll drive you over and back," said Rogers.

"You'll not drive me anywhere," Bat retorted. "I might consent to go with you if you were on the hurricane deck of a Texas cayuse, the way you used to travel when I first knew you, but not up in the air in a flying machine, if you gave me every one of the Thousand Islands."

"Don't be afraid," Rogers laughed. "I have handled this sort of an animal a thousand times since I've been living here and never had the slightest accident."

After assurances by others that the former cowboy was a skilled pilot, Bat steeled himself, climbed into the two-seater, and they took off.

The thirty-mile trip to Kingston took only thirty minutes, but after they landed Rogers bragged that he could have made the flight in half the time if he had been in a hurry. After Masterson completed his business in Kingston, they again took to the air. At Cape Vincent, across the river from Kingston, they landed for refreshments and spent a convivial hour at a watering hole called the Devil's Oven. They were back at the Thousand Island House just three hours after their initial takeoff. "Not so bad," Bat marveled, considering half that time had been spent on the ground in Kingston and the Devil's Oven. Charlie Rogers might be "crawling along in years," Bat said admiringly, but he could still "steer an aeroplane" as skillfully as any man in New York State.

After Bat related his flying experience to William H. Warburton, proprietor of the Thousand Island House, the innkeeper informed him of his own aeronautical plans. He had ordered construction of a plane fitted out "with every modern convenience" and capable of carrying twenty-five passengers from his hotel to New York City in four hours. His pilot, Major Arthur E. Hume, planned "to sail his machine not more than 500 feet above the ground so as to avoid the different currents of air that usually prevail at a higher altitude." Takeoff and landing would be "from in front of Louie Cohen's ticket office on Forty-Second Street, near Seventh avenue," which Bat agreed was "a very convenient place, indeed."[25]

Warburton hoped to have his "aeroplane" ready for the next season, but Bat would never have an opportunity to fly in it. This was his last visit to the Thousand Island House; two months after his conversation with Warburton, Bat Masterson was dead.

During the five years Bat vacationed at Alexandria Bay he always spent part of his holiday journeying down the St. Lawrence to Montreal and Quebec, where, as was his custom, he stayed at the finest hotels available. In Montreal it was the Windsor, in Quebec the Chateau Frontenac. He was displeased with the latter, whose staff, he said, suffered from the "profiteering bug" and overcharged tourists, especially Americans. He preferred the Windsor at Montreal, although he complained that the dining room captains had to be tipped liberally in order to get a satisfactory table.

American visitors to Canada could stay at the finest hotels at reasonable rates before the war, he said, but those days were over. Canadians now openly fleeced American visitors with the excuse that Yankees cheated Canadians in America, and they were only getting even.[26]

On the whole, however, he rated Montreal the most democratic city on the North American continent, and predicted that if the United States continued on its foolish repressive road the Canadian metropolis would soon become to the Western Hemisphere what Paris had been to Europe. "When I get another $100,000 to add to the one I already possess, I'm going to live in Montreal," he vowed.[27]

Of course Masterson, with only eight weeks to live, never had an opportunity to add that additional $100,000 to his bank account and move to Montreal. Interestingly, the city he admired over all others was only thirty miles from the place of his birth. Ironically, he may have been totally unaware of that fact.

GUNFIGHTER IN GOTHAM

— 17 —

SLACKERS IN NONSHOOTABLE SUITS AND THE RISE OF JACK DEMPSEY

We would rather see boxing [banned] all over the country than to see one of these bullet dodgers get a dollar in his business.
W. B. "Bat" Masterson

In the years immediately preceding the United States' entry into what was first called the Great War and later World War I, a revolution in Mexico threatened to draw the nation into armed conflict on its southern border. Boxing was in the throes of the "White Hope" craze during this period, and, disgusted by the whole absurdity, Bat suggested that if war came, the big, strong White Hope heavyweights, hopelessly incompetent in the ring, might be productively utilized as packhorses for the military in a Mexican campaign.

In May 1914 a letter, purportedly written by four-year-old Eddie Salter, was published in the *Duluth News-Tribune*. Addressed to Secretary of War L. M. Garrison, the letter suggested that a regiment, patterned after Theodore Roosevelt's 1898 Rough Riders, be formed to fight in Mexico. Included would be E. R. Salter, Eddie's father; Teddy Roosevelt; boxers George Chip and Ad Wolgast; army general Frederick Funston; wrestler Frank Gotch; evangelist Billy Sunday; baseball player Ty Cobb; writer George Ade; songwriter George M. Cohan; actor David Warfield; and Bat Masterson. "Now these fellows are all good fighters and we'll soon whip Mexico," little Eddie assured Secretary Garrison. "My daddy is my secretary and is writing you this letter. . . . I understand Uncle Sam furnishes soldier suits free, so send on my general's suit at once."[1] Bat reprinted the letter in his column with no comment.

Masterson was skeptical about American military engagement on the Mexican border, but he strongly supported the nation's entry into the great conflict then raging in Europe. When the United States declared war on Germany in April 1917, Mike Sutton jocularly inquired in a letter if Bat intended to enlist. Masterson replied in all seriousness that he would sign up if he were twenty years younger. "It would be the height of folly for me to attempt military service at my stage of life," he said. "You know I'll be sixty-three in November and that puts me in the has-been class."[2]

One of the first war casualties on Broadway was the saloon free lunch. *A Morning Telegraph* headline announced in July 1917: GRATUITOUS GRUB NO LONGER A LURE TO THE THIRSTY WAYFARER OF NEW YORK. WAR ENDS FREE FOOD GRAFT.

Saloonkeepers and bartenders blamed rising costs and beer drinkers for the change. Whisky drinkers spent 15 cents per drink and ate nothing, they said, while beer guzzlers bought a 5-cent schooner to wash down 15 cents worth of free lunch. There were alarmist predictions that if the war continued for many months, prices would skyrocket, and 10-cent beer and 20-cent whisky would become the norm.[3] No one dreamed that within three years all the watering holes on Broadway would be closed.

Bat did not frequent free lunch counters, and the demise of the saloon tradition elicited no comment from him, but he did protest as the war dragged on and restaurant prices spiraled upward even as portions shrank. He blamed Federal Food Administrator Herbert Hoover for the problem. Hoover, a Republican and future president of the United States, was no Masterson hero.

During the war Bat urged greater effort by the fight crowd in war charity exhibitions and patriotic benefit programs. He himself participated in Liberty bond promotions, including a National Motion Picture Exposition held at Madison Square Garden in October 1918, with cinema celebrities William S. Hart, Mabel Normand, Harold Lockwood, Jack Pickford, and Viola Dana in attendance.

Masterson's only shots at the enemy came in his columns. When it was reported that some Germans had scoffed at the importance of America's entry into the war, he warned: "Germany is in the position of the chap who thought he had chilblains and found out it was only the smallpox."[4] In the last days of the war when the enemy was in full retreat he wondered who it was said Germans ran slow because they had big feet. "The guy who didn't think much of the sprinting abilities of the Boche will have to revise his dope. . . . The Allied armies have been right on the heels of the Teuton forces for the last two weeks and haven't caught up with them yet. And the faster the Allies go, the harder the Boche is to overtake. He is no longer hard to whip, when he is caught up with, but as a runner he manages in some way to keep in the lead."[5] (Perhaps Bat was reminded of another of German ancestry, Otto Floto, whose speed afoot down a Denver street once amazed him.)

Most of Masterson's war comments had to do with "slackers," men he believed avoided military service. He railed particularly against pugilists, supposedly fighting men, many of whom lacked the backbone, in his view, for a real life-and-death struggle.

He applauded Kid McCoy, who had put in a six-month hitch on the Mexican border and had again volunteered for service in the war against Germany. McCoy was one of only a few fighters, Bat said, who displayed true American patriotism. When Bat and Tex Rickard visited Teddy Roosevelt in May 1917, they learned that the colonel intended to make Kid McCoy his orderly and take him to France as part of his regiment. "We assured him," Bat said, "that he had made a wise selection, as McCoy was every inch a fighting man and would prove a soldier of unusual intelligence and unflinching courage." McCoy never got the orderly job, of course, as President Wilson rejected Roosevelt's request for a command, but McCoy told Bat he expected to earn a commission and was eager to get to the front. "What other New York prizefighter has joined the colors?" Bat asked, adding that McCoy stood in sharp contrast to the "mitt-wielding slackers" whose "ducking and sidestepping" tactics to avoid military service topped anything they ever showed in the ring.[6] A few days later McCoy appeared in uniform in a New York ring and exhorted the young men in the crowd to enlist in the army. Masterson was dismayed at the cool response he received and concluded that New York fight fans, like their boxing heroes, had no stomach for the trenches.

When boxer Jack Dillon enlisted in the navy he also received Bat's plaudits. Learning later that the navy had rejected Dillon,

Masterson speculated that it was probably because of his teeth: "Jack has a mouthful of gold grinders, and while they have an intrinsic value, they do not come up to military requirements. We never before suspected that soldiers fought with their teeth, but Uncle Sam seems to attach a great deal of importance to the maxillary section of a man's face."[7]

Many prizefighters soon discovered they could avoid actual combat by volunteering to "condition" recruits and instruct them in the manly art of self-defense. Jim Coffey and Benny Leonard were among the first to use this dodge, and both became targets for frequent vitriolic attacks in Masterson columns. Irish immigrant Coffey came in for special opprobrium. If America was good enough for the Irishman to live in, he chided Coffey, it was good enough to fight for.

The very notion that teaching soldiers to box would help them in a hand-to-hand fight with the Germans Bat found so ridiculous "it would make a horse laugh." When he learned that stateside boxing instructors in the military were receiving $150 a month and a doughboy at the front only $30, he insisted the army had it exactly backward—the soldier in the trenches was worth five times the amount the instructors received, not five times less.[8]

In column after column Bat predicted that the public would shun combat-avoiding prizefighters after the war. "These slackers with the yellow streak [will] not be able to get away with their pusillanimity," he predicted. When those young men who had done their duty for their country returned home after the war, he said, the slacker would get what was coming to him "and get it with a vengeance."[9]

Throughout the war years Masterson's assault on slacker pugilists continued unabated, colored by increasingly immoderate language. They were, he said, "a craven-hearted, low-down set of measly microbes, hare-hearted fakers," who, by their "poltroonery," had disgusted all decent Americans.[10] He believed "slacker virus" had infected boxers like the influenza epidemic then sweeping the country and had an even more enervating effect. A fighter, stricken with the slacker virus, he said, lost all his virility and became "womanish and unmanly."[11]

When news of the armistice was received on November 11, 1918, Bat Masterson exulted with all America:

Humanity all over the world is rejoicing over the termination of the bloody and barbarous conflict which has drenched the earth with blood for more than four years. Autocracy and the ruler by divine right will have passed into oblivion by the time our victorious troops come sailing home. Democracy, justice and civilization are destined to rule the world hereafter. All who aided in bringing about this glorious state of affairs will receive their full meed of praise and appreciation from a grateful world. They did nobly and humanity will not forget them.[12]

He turned a jaundiced eye, however, on the crowds who celebrated on Broadway. The armistice, he said, brought out every "long-range, safety-first warrior" in New York City. Of the thousands of men parading Broadway, many were of draft age and apparently physically fit:

They were not an inspiring spectacle. . . . We thought of the boys "over there" who were driving the despicable Hun out of France and Belgium at the point of the bayonet and felt proud of them. . . . Then we took another look at that unwashed mob on the street, nearly all of whom were pro-German in sentiment, and slackers of the first water, and we hastily beat it for the back room in disgust and remained there until the hoi polloi patriots crawled back into the dingy recesses from which they had so suddenly emerged.[13]

But the boxers who had dodged combat service and enriched themselves with plush recruit conditioning jobs and fake fights during the war remained the major focus of his disgust:

These get-rich-quick ginks of the glove game . . . who refused to take a chance on the Western front . . . will soon be called upon to explain [their] derelictions during the great crisis. . . . The public is going to have something to say [and] the boys who have been over there will be the first to [protest] the slacker prizefighters when they [return]. The Jack Dempseys, Benny Leonards, Ted Lewises and their kind will be glad to get anything they can get for their services. [Promoters] should pass them up, for they don't deserve to be patronized. They are a mean, cowardly bunch of slackers, who should not be countenanced by patriotic citizens anywhere. . . . They refused to fight for their country when their services were badly needed [and should] not be allowed to fight in the ring in the country in which they disgraced themselves by their poltroonery. . . . We would rather see boxing [banned] all over the country than to see one of these bullet dodgers get a dollar in his business.[14]

Within months, however, Masterson's worst fears materialized. The public did forget, promoters signed up notorious "slacker" boxers for important bouts, and boxing continued as if the war had never happened and Bat's opprobrium had never been aired. "Slackers go big in this country, especially the alien ones," he growled sourly nine months after the armistice. "They get the raspberries in England, France, Canada and Australia [where] these yellow-hued birds are not allowed to take the public's money for their phony ring work. [But here] the slacker, the profiteer and the alien criminal generally receive unstinted adulation wherever they appear. . . . So there you are."[15]

The boxer who would become the focus of Masterson's scorn of slackers was a tough young heavyweight from Colorado who was just breaking into the ring game under the name Jack Dempsey.

Bat had known the original Jack Dempsey prizefighter, billed as "the Nonpareil," back in the 1880s when he held the middleweight title. Most ring historians still agree with Masterson's assessment that this Jack Dempsey was one of the greatest fighters in his class.

Late in the year 1914 another boxer calling himself "Jack Dempsey" showed up in New York and caught Masterson's attention. "There is a new welterweight in town, Jack Dempsey by name . . . , who is the real Tabasco, so the experts say," he noted in his column. Ben Rosenthal, Dempsey's manager, claimed his man would "eat up every welterweight [around] inside of ten rounds [and] what Rosie says goes without salt."[16] Newcomer Dempsey scored a couple of impressive wins and seemed to have bright prospects, but, matched with a hard-hitting welterweight named Tommy Robertson, suffered a severe beating. Bat decided this new Jack Dempsey was just a mediocre fighter who would never be a top contender.

He was right, of course, because the second "Jack Dempsey" was actually Bernie Dempsey, a boxer from Colorado with impressive ring skills, but a glass jaw. Out of respect for the legendary "Nonpareil,"

GUNFIGHTER IN GOTHAM

he had adopted the name "Jack Dempsey" for the ring. William Harrison Dempsey, his younger brother, substituted for him in one of his bouts and thus also became "Jack Dempsey." It was this brother who would lead the boxing game to unimagined heights and make the name "Jack Dempsey" famous throughout America and the world.

The future heavyweight champion of the world fought three preliminary bouts in New York City in the summer of 1916 but failed to impress Bat Masterson, who ignored the Dempsey New York debut in his column. The first Masterson mention of the future ring great came in March 1917, when Bat noted that the old Pueblo Fireman, Jim Flynn, had "stiffened in about a minute" a heavyweight named Jack Dempsey in a Utah bout.[17]

That year a series of four-round bouts to a decision was held in the San Francisco Bay Area. Dempsey appeared in many of these, performed well, and began to attract the attention of Masterson and other ring followers. "They have a big fellow out in San Francisco named Jack Dempsey, who is going great guns in the four-round game just now," Bat noted in September. Bat's old pal Jack Grace had seen Dempsey perform and said the boy was a world-beater over a short distance. What he could do if extended was hard to tell, said Grace, but in four-round bouts he was a whirlwind. Bat, unconvinced, reminded his readers that Dempsey was the same fellow the old Fireman Jim Flynn put away in one round.

In the next two months Dempsey won four-round decisions over two veteran heavyweights, Gunboat Smith and Carl Morris. After the Morris victory, Jack "Doc" Kearns, Dempsey's manager, fired off a telegram to Bat: "Carl Morris was no match for Jack Dempsey, the submarine destroyer. Jack gave Morris a terrific beating and easily out-pointed him and all but knocked him out in the fourth round. The bell was all that saved Morris, as he laid helpless on the ropes when the bout was over."[18] In a follow-up letter Kearns said he had challenged Jess Willard to a title match on behalf of Dempsey. Masterson thought Kearns had little chance of success, as Willard wanted $50,000 to defend his title, a figure no promoter would consider. In addition, there were other, better-qualified heavyweight title aspirants out there.

Foremost challenger for Willard's title in Masterson's opinion at this time was gold-toothed Jack Dillon, claimant to the light-heavyweight title since 1908. Throughout the year 1916, Bat touted Dillon as "strong as a bull, courageous as a lion, a fast and skillful boxer and a smashing good hitter" who had never been knocked down. Bat thought Dillon was, pound for pound, the most formidable fighting man he had seen in thirty years.[19] But Dillon blew any hope for a shot at Willard's title late in 1916 when Battling Levinsky out-pointed him in a twelve-round bout in Boston and took his light-heavyweight championship.

Masterson's next choice as the man to dethrone Willard was Fred Fulton, a big, strong ex-plasterer from Minnesota, standing six feet four and weighing 215 pounds. After the demise of Dillon, Bat began beating the drums for "Elongated Frederick," who, he predicted, could roll over Willard "like the Empire Express passing a tramp."[20]

While Bat was boosting Fulton, Jack Dempsey was touring the country, running up an impressive record of knockout victories. His growing army of fans waxed ecstatic when within a month he knocked out Homer Smith in one round, won from Carl Morris on a foul in six, avenged his loss to Jim Flynn by stiffening the Pueblo Fireman in one round, and put "K. O." Brennan away in six.

After the Brennan bout Bat received another wire from Doc Kearns, who was obviously trying to get the New York ring pundit on the Dempsey cheering section: "Jack Dempsey, the sensational Coast heavyweight, proved to the boxing world . . . he is the man to dethrone Jess Willard."[21]

Bat was unimpressed by the Dempsey wins over Smith, Morris, and Flynn. The first two he considered human punching bags, and Flynn was long over the hill. But, according to press reports, Brennan's ankle had snapped when Dempsey put him away, and grudgingly Bat had to concede that "hitting an opponent on the head with sufficient force to knock him down and break his ankle is going some."[22]

Sportswriters across the nation were joining Kearns in demanding a Willard-Dempsey title match, but Masterson argued that Dempsey should first face Fred Fulton. Despite the Colorado fighter's well-publicized knockout record, Bat said he doubted if he could beat the big ex-plasterer. Long suspicious of Dempsey's knockout string, Bat charged Kearns with "pulling some queer-looking stuff," arranging a series of mismatches and set-ups to build that impressive record.[23]

Kearns ignored the Masterson barbs as Dempsey continued to pad that record, putting away in his distinctive whirlwind style a string of unknown and over-the-hill heavyweights: Tom Riley in one round, Dan Ketchell in two, Arthur Pelkey in one, Kid McCarthy in one, Bob Devere in one, and Porky Flynn in one.

Only a no-decision bout Dempsey fought with Billy Miske at St. Paul, Minnesota, in May impressed Masterson, for Dempsey held his own for ten furious rounds with Miske, an authentic heavyweight contender. Strangely, Dempsey considered the Miske fight one of his worst exhibitions. "We stank up the joint," he told a biographer. "It was just one of those things."[24] Dempsey never admitted to engaging in a faked fight, but it is interesting to note that he used the phrase "just one of those things" in reference to the Miske bout, as this was Bat's favorite euphemism for a fistic set-up, and he used it often in commenting on Dempsey's ring victories.

Masterson still had not seen Dempsey fight, and to assess the young heavyweight's real ability he had to rely on the opinion of those who had seen him perform and whose judgment Bat respected. Many were certain Dempsey was "the real thing," but to Masterson the ballyhoo surrounding his spectacular rise still invited suspicion. He found it reminiscent of the ascendancy to ring stardom of John L. Sullivan, who planted "marks" around the country to score easy knockouts. Dempsey, he said, was a "ripsnorting gasconader" who did not deserve a title match until he had faced Fred Fulton.[25]

Bat kept up his own gasconade on behalf of Fulton, constantly touting "elongated Frederick" for a title shot. In March 1918 he thought he had been successful and happily announced that articles had been signed calling for a Willard-Fulton title battle on the Fourth of July, but a few days later Willard backed out of the agreement. By July Masterson was saying that Fulton stood alone as a heavyweight contender and that if a bout could be arranged Willard would be "a little tapioca" for him. He added that Dempsey would also be "tapioca" for Fulton if the two ever met.[26]

Just three weeks after Bat penned these lines Fulton and Dempsey did meet. Promoter Jack Curley signed them to a match to be held at Harrison, New Jersey, on July 27. During those weeks Bat smelled a rat. He thought it strange that Mike Collins, Fulton's manager, with whom he was very friendly, never stopped in to see him, although meeting frequently with Jack Kearns and many of the "we boys" in Curley's office in the Fitzgerald Building, only 200 feet from Masterson's place of business. Bat thought this peculiar. To anyone with an understanding of the "ins and outs" of the fighting game, he said, this had a suspicious look.

Despite his doubts, he still thought Fulton would win if he survived the first round. A slow starter, Fulton often took some hard shots in the early going. The first round, Masterson concluded, might well decide the outcome. He was certainly right on that score; eighteen seconds into the fight Dempsey landed two quick punches, and Fulton went down for the count.

Masterson was infuriated. He charged in his next column that the affair was a travesty, "another one of those things" in which the principals played their parts well. He said he was really not surprised, for shortly before the fight he had been "tipped off that it was to be Dempsey in a walk. Fulton was to get the money and Dempsey the fight." He did not know if Fulton got all the money, but it was certain Dempsey got the fight. He reminded his readers that he had warned them "the match had a drab color," and his suspicions had grown when he saw sure-thing gamblers betting heavily on Dempsey. The phony knockout was pulled off so quickly, he said, that few observers knew exactly what happened. "Fulton and Dempsey turned the trick in the only safe way it could be turned without arousing suspicion. Had they [dragged] the affair along for a few rounds, it is almost [certain they] would have [exposed] the whole dirty mess." The blows Dempsey struck "would not have knocked a lightweight off his feet," but they served their purpose. Fulton knew what to do, and he did it in fine thespian fashion, stretching out on the canvas, "playing 'possum." It was enough to make a decent man sick, and he doubted if Fulton would "ever have the effrontery to look an honest man in the face again." In his many years of viewing fights he had seen many an odorous exhibition, Bat said, but nothing as brazen and bold as the Dempsey-Fulton fiasco.[27]

A day or two later the fighters' managers, Jack Kearns and Mike Collins, visited Masterson in his office and vehemently denied any prearrangement or collusion. After hearing them out, Bat accepted their statements, but still did not believe there had been a true knock-

GUNFIGHTER IN GOTHAM

out. If there was no fix, he told his readers, then "Fulton quit like a yellow cur." Evidently the Dempsey newspaper ballyhoo took all the fight out of him, and "the big fish-eyed sea cow flopped before he was hurt." As far as Bat was concerned, Fulton had consigned himself to "the pugilistic discard," and that is where he would remain. Thereafter "Elongated Frederick" became "the big fish-eyed sea cow" in the Masterson lexicon.[28]

The first time Masterson met Jack Dempsey was about a week before the Fulton bout when he and Doc Kearns called at Bat's office. Dempsey looked like a fighter "from his heels up," Bat admitted. Dark complected, he seemed to Bat to have a trace of Italian blood, but he spoke "English like an American." He comported himself well, with no hint of braggadocio. Bat was left with the impression he was "a real, sure-enough scrapper."[29]

Bat's surprise that Dempsey had no accent and spoke English "like an American" was due to a rumor he had picked up on Broadway and repeated in a column some months earlier. Dempsey was said to be Polish and his true name "Julius Shinsky." A man named Harry Lefkowitz, claiming familiarity with the entire Dempsey family, later informed Bat that the fighter was indeed of Polish descent, but that his name was neither Dempsey nor Shinsky, and "it would take a Russian scholar of high attainment to pronounce [his] right name." These stories were false, as reporters later determined. The fighter's true name was William Harrison Dempsey, and he was born near Manassa, Colorado.

In discussing this name business, Masterson informed his readers that the original Jack Dempsey, "the Nonpareil," was known as John Kelly before he left Ireland for America. So, Bat said, "the present Jack Dempsey, or Julius Shinsky, whichever it may be," had a good model "when he made the shift in his moniker. . . . But a rose by any other name would probably smell just as aromatically, so what care we."[30]

The initial meeting with Jack Dempsey in July 1918 may have dispelled Bat's belief that Dempsey was "foreign," but it did nothing to allay his conviction that the fighter's remarkable ring record was based on a series of "jug-handled" setups. Much of Masterson's suspicion and personal dislike of Dempsey stemmed from his distaste for the people with whom the fighter had been associated in his rise to prominence. He detested John "the Razor" Reisler, an early Dempsey manager. Jack Kearns, who wrested Dempsey away from Reisler, rated scarcely higher in his estimation; Bat openly accused him of drug addiction. When he learned that Dempsey's early career in Colorado had been guided by none other than Otto Floto, and that his old Denver enemy reportedly still retained a financial interest in the fighter, Masterson's animosity toward Dempsey was compounded.

Unsavory managers and a dubious fight record aside, the issue on which Bat belabored Dempsey relentlessly was that of slackerism. "Nobody ever called me a slacker to my face," Dempsey later told a biographer. "Nobody ever made the charge in print. But they hinted at it in a way that said as much but was libel-proof."[31]

It is not known if Masterson ever called Dempsey a slacker to his face, but he made the charge repeatedly in print. Before the Fulton fight "the Manassa Mauler," as Damon Runyon had dubbed the Colorado heavyweight, was only one of many prizefighters who came under Bat's assault, but thereafter Bat focused his attack on both the fighter and his manager. Shortly after that fight newspapers carried photographs of Dempsey and Kearns in overalls at a Philadelphia shipbuilding plant where they had reportedly taken essential defense jobs. More than just a promotional stunt, Bat fumed, this was a "mean and cowardly subterfuge" by the pair to avoid military duty.[32]

When the war ended about ten weeks later, Masterson's campaign against despised slackers did not abate. If he had his way, he said, "the two Jacks, along with the other slacker prizefighters in the country, would be in jail and the key thereof thrown into the ocean." The "bunkerenos" and "rank slackers" who had "adorned themselves with nonshootable suits during the war" deserved nothing better.[33]

Despite Bat's harangues Dempsey's march to a title match under the guidance of Kearns continued. He disposed of eleven contenders and pretenders by the knockout route in the eight months after the Fulton fight. Masterson, still unimpressed, observed sourly that these Dempsey victims were all setups arranged by Kearns. When Dempsey lost a four-round decision to flabby club fighter Willie Meehan, Bat jumped on the loss to a "fat and paunchy slob" as proof that the Manassa Mauler was an overrated phony.[34]

Wily promoter Tex Rickard, however, recognized that Dempsey's string of quick knockouts and all that "press agent ballyhoo" could lead to his greatest fight promotion yet. He had been trying to promote a title match since Willard became champion. As early as 1916 he had secretly tried to arrange a title bout between Willard and Georges Carpentier, the popular French champion. Negotiations collapsed, however, when Tex would not meet Willard's demand for a $50,000 guarantee. Rickard had also planned to match the champion with the highly touted Australian heavyweight Les Darcy, then touring America, but Darcy took sick and died suddenly in May 1917. And, of course, the Willard-Fulton title match Bat had so delightedly announced in March 1918 never came off. To defend his crown Willard still set his price high; he wanted a $50,000 guarantee, plus 50 percent of the revenues from any fight pictures. Masterson called this an outrageous demand, "the sublimest display of unadulterated gall, [making] such enterprising gentlemen as Jesse James, Black Bart, Bill Doolin and the Dalton boys look like the cheapest sort of pikers in comparison."[35]

But to Bat's utter amazement, the ever audacious Rickard, determined to get the champion in the ring with Dempsey, doubled Willard's figure, offering him a $100,000 guarantee, and quickly signed him to a contract. Tex then offered the challenger $15,000, but Kearns held out for $50,000. Rickard and Kearns, both brilliant publicists, came up with a scheme to settle the dispute and at the same time kick off a hype campaign for the big fight. They had Bob Edgren assemble a panel of newspapermen to hear the arguments of the promoter and the manager and decide the issue. Edgren called in a bunch of his colleagues, including Bill Farnsworth, Jim Dawson, Eddie Frayne, Gene Fowler, Grantland Rice, Rube Goldberg, Hype Igoe, and Damon Runyon.

Conspicuous by his absence was Bat Masterson, who, of course, Edgren had not invited. The writers settled on $27,500 as a fair figure for Dempsey's end, and Kearns inked the contract. The fighters were to meet on July 4, 1919, in a twelve-round contest to a decision at a site to be announced.

Masterson had made it abundantly clear that he believed Dempsey to be greatly overrated, a product of press agentry who had never really proven himself in the ring with a worthy opponent. His evaluation of Jess Willard's fistic prowess had been much less consistent, fluctuating considerably in the four years since the big fellow's decisive defeat of Jack Johnson at Havana. Following that victory, Bat had called Willard "the greatest heavyweight pugilist that the Queensberry game ever knew, not even barring the great Jim Jeffries." But, disappointed by Willard's lackluster performance in his ten-round no-decision match with Frank Moran at the Garden in 1916, he advised the champion to retire from the ring and go back to cowpunching.

Months and years passed, and it became evident Willard had no great desire to defend his title. But he was not ready to retire to Kansas either, as he was still cashing in on his fame as the champion who had whipped Jack Johnson. At one point he was making $500 a day as a circus attraction. (This was, Bat noted with tongue in cheek, even more than he made.) Exempted from military service during the war because of his size, Willard still came under his share of Masterson opprobrium as just another prizefighting slacker.

By 1918 Bat concluded that Willard was too old and out of shape to ever again reach the form he had shown against Johnson. "A corking fighter" at Havana, he had now descended to "the dub class" and would be a "push-over" for the first opponent he met with minimum fighting skills. He doubted that even the blandishments of some "boob promoter" would lure the big man into a title defense. Without question, he decided, Willard was through.[36]

Those who still held out hope that somehow a heavyweight title fight could be pulled off by old master promoter Tex Rickard were disheartened when Rickard and his wife sailed for Buenos Aires in February 1918. Rickard announced that he no longer was interested in boxing and expected to spend the next five years attending to his ranch in Argentina. Within months he was back in the States, however, and angling for the Willard-Dempsey bout.

Once Bat learned in early 1919 that Rickard had indeed signed Willard and Dempsey to a contract and a championship bout was to become a reality, he crawled up on the bandwagon and backed Rickard's promotion to the hilt. When some sportswriters questioned Rickard's ability to pull it off, Bat rushed to his defense, declaring that Rickard "possessed a sufficient amount of strategy and gray matter to enable him to fight rings around the knockers and schemers without even soiling his shirt collar with perspiration," and issued a thinly veiled warning: "There is a sporting writer or two out West who had better have a care about the way they attack Rickard and the big match or they will hear something about themselves some day that wouldn't look good in print. A word to the wise is sufficient, or at least it ought to be."[37]

Again Masterson did an abrupt about-face with regard to Jess Willard's ability. Once more the big man was the greatest heavyweight who ever lived the day he defeated Johnson. Bat predicted that the champ, if only half as formidable as he was when he won the title, would defeat Dempsey easily.

— 18 —

THE BATTLES OF MAUMEE BAY AND BOYLE'S THIRTY ACRES

There are so many "experts" here now cluttering up our streets and hotel lobbies that ordinary newspaper slaves are elbowed off the sidewalks and shoved back into hotel nooks and crannies.

Toledo News-Bee

Boxing had not yet attained national recognition as a legitimate sport in 1919, and Tex Rickard's first problem after signing Willard and Dempsey was to find a favorable battle site. Powerful political forces opposed to prizefighting still dominated in the populous eastern states. The more free-and-easy but sparsely populated West beckoned, but Rickard needed a big attendance to cover his up-front expenses, most notably the guaranteed $127,500 for the fighters. He finally settled on Toledo, Ohio, a growing city close to the large metropolitan areas of Detroit, Chicago, and Cleveland, and within a day's train travel for East Coast ring fans. After receiving assurances from local and state authorities of full cooperation and no interference, he ordered construction of an 80,000-seat arena on the outskirts of Toledo near Maumee Bay, an inlet of Lake Erie. The $100,000 structure required 1.75 million feet of lumber to construct and had several innovations, including a small emergency hospital at one end and a special barbed-wire enclosed section for female spectators. The *New York Sun* called it "the most remarkable structure of wood ever erected for a sporting event." Rickard envisioned the first million-dollar gate in sports history and spared no expense.[1]

Excitement grew among ring fans in the months preceding the big bout, when all were free to opinionate and speculate about the fighters, their managers, the promoters, the stakes involved, the contest site, and any possible repercussions from church or government authority. A poll of prizefighters, promoters and managers, major league baseball players, sports editors, actors, racetrack men, and wrestlers, conducted by the *National Police Gazette* in June, found these "ring experts" about evenly divided as to the outcome, with 172 favoring Dempsey, 144 choosing Willard, and 20 undecided.

Masterson, of course, had long since made his choice. Dempsey, he repeatedly declared, was a "false alarm" who did not stand a chance against the much bigger, more powerful champion. He expected Willard to put Dempsey away with the first solid punch he landed. If by some miracle the challenger managed to beat Willard, Bat said he would tip his hat and acknowledge Dempsey as "not only the best heavyweight now in the business, but the best the American prize ring ever produced."[2]

On the evening of June 24 Bat took the overnight Pullman to Toledo, a city he had never visited but had been assured was "far from being a boob town." Accompanying him was *Morning Telegraph* sportswriter Weed Dickinson, who would also provide daily on-the-scene reports for the paper. Masterson assured his readers they would receive "intelligent and trustworthy" news coverage from the scene, with no "dressing up" to look well in print. He would leave that, he said, to "the geniuses of the sport writers' fraternity" who were already on the ground in "a swarm."[3]

That "swarm" of "geniuses" was composed of perhaps the most talented array of American sportswriters and artists ever assembled. On hand were Bugs Baer, Ed Bang, Heywood Broun, Ned Brown, Casey the Bear, Irvin S. Cobb, Tad Dorgan, C. W. Dunkley, Nat Fleischer, Rube Goldberg, Sandy Griswold, Sam Hall, Harry Hocksteder, Hype Igoe, Walter C. Kelly, Ring Lardner, Charles MacArthur, Bill Mc-Geehan, Ray Peason, Bill Peet, Edgar "Scoop" Gleeson, Grantland Rice, Robert Ripley, Damon Runyon, and Lamber Sullivan. Also in attendance were three Masterson foes of long standing: Otto Floto, Walter St. Denis, and Bob Edgren.

"There are so many 'experts' here now cluttering up our streets and hotel lobbies," grumbled one Toledo sportswriter, "that ordinary newspaper slaves are elbowed off the sidewalks and shoved back into hotel nooks and crannies."[4]

Bat genuinely admired and liked a few of the newspaper corps— Sandy Griswold and Damon Runyon, for example—but he disdained the group as a whole. Newsmen, especially sportswriters, had long been notorious as a hard-drinking crowd, and at Toledo they did nothing to dispel that reputation. Tex Rickard opened a free bar for the newsmen in the Secor Hotel, where they headquartered, and they took full advantage of it. "The way they carried on was enough to make a decent man sick at the stomach," Bat later wrote. "Some of them got drunk as soon as they hit Toledo and remained in that condition until they left it. And all the time they were sending out their maudlin inventions to the papers they represented."[5]

After watching the fighters work out at their training camps, Masterson reiterated his conviction that Willard would win "in a walk."[6]

Bat reported daily on the doings in Toledo, the arrival of celebrities, the selection of officials, the anticipated attendance, and the oppressive heat blanketing the city. He complained about restaurant price gouging ("food emporiums are charging $7 for a plate of wheat cakes and a pot of coffee") and interlopers ("guests of other hotels and an unwashed mob of street loafers") occupying seats in the Secor lobby. But especially he kept track of the betting—or lack thereof—on the fight.[7]

He reported that bettors, especially Dempsey backers, were "conspicuous by their absence," while noting that he himself managed to get down "a stack of whites" on Willard.[8] A story went with that "stack of whites." Masterson related it many months later:

> One day I made up my mind to have a little wager on Willard, just to show that the Dempsey chatter had not frightened me in the least. . . . I hunted up Tex Rickard one morning and handed him five one hundred dollar bills and told him to bet it for me on Willard. . . . That evening Tex told me he couldn't find any takers for my money, although he had tried very hard to do so. The next evening Tex told me the same story. "No Dempsey money in sight anywhere," was what he said.[9]

A little later Bat ran across Damon Runyon, whom he knew to be a strong Dempsey partisan, and needled him about the Dempsey supporters not backing their fighter with hard cash. Runyon said he knew of the $500 Bat had with Rickard, for the news was all over town. He was trying, so far without success, to get it covered. Finally an envelope addressed to Otto Floto arrived from Denver. It contained a $500 certified check and a note instructing Floto to take the Masterson bet at even money. Floto deposited the check with Rickard to cover the Masterson wager placed sixty hours earlier.[10] (When Bat later told this story, he did not reveal, or perhaps did not know, who sent the check, but it probably came from his other longtime Denver adversary, Pat "Reddy" Gallagher, who had grown wealthy in the Mile-High City.)

Masterson reported that Willard remained a heavy favorite in the betting, and Dempsey money was hard to find almost up to fight time. But then, on July 3, the day before the big event, all this changed. Betting became brisk, and Dempsey partisans suddenly were willing to back their man at even money. Masterson found the situation very peculiar, and without precedent in his experience. The idea of a challenger, he considered "virtually an unknown quantity," being made an even money choice against a much bigger and more powerful champion, Bat thought, was "the most surprising thing in the annals of the prize ring."[11]

An informal poll conducted by a *Toledo Times* reporter found that the visiting ring experts were about evenly divided in their predictions of the outcome. Bat, quoted as saying, "If Willard doesn't win, I sure am a poor piker," found himself in rare agreement with Bob Edgren, who thought Willard had it "over Dempsey in every way."[12]

Damon Runyon, unlike Bat, was close to Doc Kearns, who tipped him that he had placed a $10,000 bet at ten-to-one odds that Dempsey would knock out Willard in the first round. Gambler John "Get-Rich-Quick" Ryan had taken the wager, and Kearns stood to win $100,000 if Dempsey could pull it off. It sounded like a good thing to Runyon, who scraped up all the cash he could and made the same bet with Broadway theatrical man Sam K. Harris.[13]

Despite the strange and sudden influx of Dempsey money, Masterson remained steadfast in his opinion on the eve of the fight. He expected Dempsey to lose heart after Willard warded off his whirlwind early attack, and after that to become an easy mark for the bigger, stronger man. His "stack of whites" still rode on the champion, and he made no effort to "lay off" his bet.[14]

About eight o'clock on the evening before the bout Willard's automobile pulled up at the Secor Hotel, and his driver, Joe Chip, sought out Masterson. Willard, who was accompanied by his sparring partner, Walter Monaghan, asked Bat if he would join him in a ride around Toledo. Masterson accepted the invitation, and they all drove off. During their discussion the champion expressed amazement that Dempsey's supporters were making him an even choice in the betting. Supremely confident, Willard said, "I ought to beat this fellow in four or five rounds."

"Let's hope you beat him in one round," Bat replied.[15]

There had been much speculation in the press regarding referee selection for the big fight. Many names had been put forward, including Bob Edgren, a suggestion that sent Masterson into a tirade against "the late editor of the best sporting page in New York." In the end, Ollie Pecord of Toledo got the assignment, with Jack Skelly as alternate. Tex Rickard and Major A. J. Drexel Biddle would act as judges. The official time was to be kept by future U.S. senator W. Warren Barbour with the aid of four precisely regulated, split-second watches. Time would prove to be a crucial factor in the forthcoming battle.

In one of his autobiographies Jack Dempsey said that standing outside the arena on the day of the battle was Bat Masterson, "a somewhat stocky, spruced-up guy with a curled mustache and carrying a fancy cane [who] had appointed himself Official Collector of all spectators' guns and knives. His assistant was a balding Wyatt Earp. . . . Between the two of them, they got things done. At first all equipment was placed neatly in piles, but by fight time the guns and knives were in a disorderly heap. Some of the rowdier boys refused to relinquish their six-shooters without a scuffle."[16]

Dempsey could not personally have observed this quaint scene, as he was in his dressing room preparing for the fight, but, of course, it never happened anyway. In 1919 Bat was long past his days as a prizefight security chief, his moustache (never curled) and his "fancy cane" were only memories, and Wyatt Earp was not present at Toledo. One suspects that Dempsey and his coauthor drew on hazy memories of the fictional *Bat Masterson* television series rather than the fighter's recollections for this vignette.

The heat wave continued, and Independence Day, 1919, dawned extremely hot and humid in Toledo.

(The oppressive heat led to one of the many legendary stories surrounding this event. Battling Nelson, according to the tale, got drunk the night before the bout and, suffering intensely from the heat, immersed himself in a tub of cool liquid and fell asleep. It seems the tub contained a concoction of lemon syrup and ice, which was to be peddled as lemonade the next day. Discovered in the morning, Nelson was ejected from his comfortable slumbering quarters, and the lemonade sold to an unsuspecting public.)

When the first preliminary bout began at eleven o'clock the temperature at ringside stood at 101 degrees. By three-thirty, scheduled start of the featured bout, it measured 114 degrees. Sap dripped from the green pine arena seats. Before the main event a squad of U.S. Marines performed a drill exhibition in the ring, disturbing the ring canvas to such an extent that a second canvas had to be stretched over it. A loose stay rope from this additional covering fouled the timekeeper's bell, contributing significantly to the wild scene soon to ensue.

As was customary, the fighters donned gloves after entering the ring. This convention provided the basis for a controversy that would rage for years. When the combatants were introduced in the ring, Dempsey, deeply tanned and well muscled, still looked like a small boy standing beside the towering, powerfully built champion. Willard outweighed Dempsey by sixty pounds and stood half a foot taller.

Because of the rope entangled in timekeeper Barbour's bell, neither fighter heard the signal for the start of the first round. They remained in their corners, looking in confusion at Barbour until he motioned for them to begin. Finally the two men moved forward, the fight was on, and the wildest scene in the history of boxing began. For about a minute no real blows were struck as Willard pawed with his left hand at the challenger, who circled, looking for an opening. Suddenly Dempsey lashed out with a flurry of blows. Willard went down, his jaw broken and his face a mass of crimson. He struggled to his feet, only to be dropped again by savage punches. The match turned into a brutal spectacle as Dempsey stalked the big man, hammering him to his knees with devastating punches.

Willard went to the canvas seven times in that first round. After the last knockdown he sat slumped in a neutral corner, his arms dangling over the lower ropes. Referee Pecord tolled the count over him. Midway in that count Barbour rang the bell ending the round, but no one heard it.

Pandemonium reigned when Pecord reached ten. At ringside, Damon Runyon's normally dour face split into a wide grin. He flung his hat in the air to celebrate the apparent first-round Dempsey knockout that made him suddenly wealthy. Doc Kearns, sure that he had just won $100,000, bounded over the ropes and began dancing with glee. Pecord raised Dempsey's hand as Willard's handlers dragged their battered fighter to his stool. Thinking the fight was over, Dempsey left the ring and pushed his way through the madly cheering crowd toward his dressing room. But above the din Pecord heard Barbour screaming that the round had ended before Willard was counted out. He grabbed Kearns and shouted that the fight was not over, and if Dempsey did not get back in the ring he would be counted out. Kearns, gesticulating frantically, got Dempsey's attention and waved him back. After a delay of more than a minute, a second round began.

With amazing bravery, Willard, his jaw broken, two teeth knocked out, and his ribs cracked, survived this round and yet another. Dempsey, arm-weary and amazed at the raw courage that kept his opponent still on his feet, did not score another knockdown. Willard, finally conceding defeat, did not come out for the fourth round, and the world had a new heavyweight champion.

Bat Masterson was so shocked that he did not write the initial story of the fight, but left that dismal chore to Weed Dickinson. In a dispatch to the *Telegraph* the next day, he attributed the Dempsey victory to the "tremendous power" the man carried in his fists. He said he had never seen a fighter with the hitting power in either hand that Dempsey displayed. The outcome of the battle had been determined by the first solid blow the challenger landed, a left hook that split open Willard's cheek, knocked out several teeth, and broke his jaw. The champion, who had never even been staggered in his previous fights, went down "as if he had been hit on the head with a maul." Bat said he was amazed that any man could continue fighting after receiving such a blow, but Willard, stout hearted and courageous, got up time after time to absorb more punishment. Dempsey, Masterson had to admit, was "a champion in everything that the term implies."[17]

Resuming his regular column back in New York, Bat said he had been plagued by "I-told-you so" pests who were more plentiful "than the mosquitoes over in the Jersey swamps." This led him into a tirade about a wild exhibition of hero-worship he had witnessed in the Secor Hotel dining room the evening of the fight. When Dempsey entered the room "old men and middle-aged women, young men and girls in their teens all left their tables and made a mad rush for the victor." Women "grabbed him around the neck and hugged and kissed him," while male "sapheads" behaved in an equally "disgusting" manner. Observing the scene from a nearby table, Bat said he felt like crawling under it.[18]

The Willard-Dempsey fight turned out to be a big disappointment for Tex Rickard. He had hoped for a million-dollar gate, but his 80,000-seat arena had only been half filled, and his gross receipts barely covered expenses. Some critics blamed high admission prices for the low turnout. Seats in the farthest stands were priced at $10, a week's wages for the common working man, and it cost six times that amount to sit anywhere near the ring. But Masterson blamed the poor turnout on the prefight ballyhoo of other sportswriters, whose talk of a million-dollar gate and huge attendance had discouraged many from coming to Toledo. Nevertheless, he said, Rickard's promotion was "the biggest thing of its kind ever staged anywhere," and would "stand as a record-breaker in pugilism for all time." If he netted nothing from the Toledo affair, Tex could savor the knowledge that he had promoted the greatest event in boxing history. "Nothing like it will ever again be seen in this country," Bat concluded.[19]

Masterson was one of the first to raise a question about the fight that has been an issue of controversy among ring historians since that torrid day in 1919. After pondering what he had witnessed in Toledo for several days, Bat came to the conclusion that there was something wrong somewhere. In that brutal first round Dempsey not only knocked Willard down repeatedly, but "slashed and bruised his face as if he were using an ax." Perhaps, he suggested, Dempsey's hands had been wrapped with electric tape laced with cement. The "loaded glove," "mailed fist," or "big mitt," as it had variously been called, was not new to the fight game, he reminded his readers. It could be traced all the way back to the Romans, who called a leather strip loaded with metal on a boxer's hand a "cestus." Bat had seen it used before, and now suspected he had seen it again in Toledo.

In later years Masterson's suspicion became conviction. Dempsey's left fist, he declared, had been "loaded for bear." That first left hook to the jaw landed by Dempsey dropped Willard "like a ton of brick," and all the later damage came from that hand. "The battered condition of the right side of Willard's face proved this conclusively. [Dempsey] failed to bruise or even blacken Willard's face with all the punches he landed with his right and you could hang your hat on the lumps raised on Willard's face with Dempsey's left." A two-handed puncher who hit equally hard with either hand, Dempsey "didn't even bark Willard's face with his right, while he cut him to the bone in several places with his left."[20]

A year and a half after the fight Masterson explained that he "would have sprung the leaded fist story immediately" had it not been for the $500 bet he had lost. "The money I had bet on Willard put the muzzle on me and I still would be muzzled were it not that so many are now broadly insinuating that maybe Dempsey did employ foul means to beat Willard at Toledo. Had I [written] what I really believed to be true, every Dempsey shouter in the country would have characterized me as a bad loser who was bellyaching because I had lost a bet."[21]

When Tex Rickard signed Dempsey and Georges Carpentier to a title match in 1921, Bat predicted that the French champion and his manager, Marcel Deschamps, would watch carefully as Dempsey's hands were bandaged, for they knew all the tricks of the game. "In this respect they'll be different from Willard and his coterie of handlers at Toledo. Willard was so cocksure of winning that he didn't seem to care what means Dempsey resorted to. Mailed fist or no mailed fist was all the same to big Jess. With him Dempsey was just a common mug whom he would bowl over whenever he got ready." Bat said Willard did not change his mind until after the first knockdown, "and then he didn't have much mind to change."[22]

Certain now that Willard's title had been taken by means of the illegal "mailed fist," Bat predicted a quite different outcome if the two men met in the ring again. "I lost $500 at Toledo on big Jess and stand ready to risk the same amount on him [again] if Dempsey will take one more chance." But he doubted that day would come: "Willard is one baby Dempsey is going to sidestep for all time."[23]

In the following months Doc Kearns matched his fighter against a pair of heavyweights Dempsey had already defeated in his march to the championship. Dempsey knocked out Billy Miske in three rounds at Benton Harbor, Michigan, and put Bill Brennan away in twelve at Madison Square Garden. After watching Brennan absorb all the punishment Dempsey could deliver before going down for good in the twelfth, Masterson remarked that without the "horseshoe in his glove" he used in Toledo, Dempsey could not even bloody Brennan's nose. Lacking a cestus, he decided, Dempsey was just an ordinary fighter.

Masterson disliked both Dempsey and Kearns, "the two Jacks" as he called them. This antipathy may have originated in his disdain for the managers Dempsey had chosen, but the "slacker" issue certainly exacerbated it. He was angered and dismayed that "slackers" Dempsey and Kearns were acclaimed throughout the country and "disgusting" scenes of hero-worship like the one he had witnessed in the Secor Hotel dining room became commonplace.

Long after the war ended Bat continued to inveigh against slacker prizefighters as a class, and Dempsey and Kearns in particular. "That Jack Dempsey and his manager are both slackers goes without saying," he charged unequivocally, and the public should be ashamed of itself for making heroes of this "impudent set of swindlers." Only "troglodytes" and German sympathizers defended Dempsey's behavior during the war, he said. "If Dempsey is guilty of scheming and resorting to questionable means to avoid performing his solemn duty to his country . . . , he is no better than a traitor and should be dealt with as a traitor."[24]

Early in 1920 the American Legion, reacting to the outcry from Masterson and others about Dempsey's slackerism, came out strongly against the champion and advocated barring him from further matches. Bat applauded the stand, but warned that "pro-Germans" and "other alien criminals" would "set up an awful howl."[25]

About this time Maxine Cates Dempsey, the champion's former wife, charged publicly that the fighter had not contributed to her support during the war and had falsified his draft papers. Reacting to a growing public protest, the Army, Navy, and Civilian Board of

Boxing Control met in February to review the charges. When Bat learned that his old foe, Bob Edgren, sat on the board, he expressed doubt that sanctions would be brought against Dempsey. By encouraging prizefighters to become boxing instructors, Edgren had been a major contributor to prizefighter slackerism, Bat charged.[26]

Concurrent with the board hearings, a federal grand jury held hearings on the criminal charges against Dempsey. On February 27, 1920, he was indicted for draft evasion. As much as Bat had railed against Dempsey as a slacker, he thought in all fairness he should not be convicted on the charge while other violators of the statute were being ignored. Perhaps the jury agreed with Masterson's reasoning, for after only fifteen minutes of deliberation it rendered a verdict of acquittal.

Aware that Dempsey and Kearns were financially strapped after the court battle, Masterson surprised his readers by announcing publicly that he would lend them money in their time of need and wouldn't even ask for an IOU. "They can swing on me for a touch if it isn't too big a one," he said. "A few hundred dollars won't distress me and they can have it by merely asking for it. . . . Now, boys, this is no bluff—it goes, and if you have any doubts about it come around and try me."[27] Evidently neither of "the two Jacks" ever took Bat up on his offer.

Dempsey and Kearns came under criticism in some quarters for not giving the fine black heavyweight Harry Wills a shot at the title. Dempsey reportedly had "drawn the color line." Some ring followers found that curious, for Dempsey had fought black heavyweight John Lester Johnson when he first came to New York and often used black sparring partners. Many believed the champion's refusal to face Harry Wills was based not on racial prejudice, but on fear and respect for the fighting ability of the redoubtable black heavyweight. Dempsey would later deny color bias or that he avoided Wills out of fear. Rickard, he said, refused to promote a black-white title fight because of criticism he had received after the Johnson-Jeffries fight. In addition, New York State Boxing Commissioner William Muldoon, certain that a Dempsey-Wills match would lead to race riots, would not sanction the fight within the state.

Masterson took a different slant. Wills was undoubtedly the best in the field of heavyweight contenders, and it was wrong to exclude him from a championship bout because of his color, he said. He condemned race discrimination but doubted if Wills or any black fighter would ever get a shot at Dempsey's title, for the simple reason fight fans had been disgusted by the behavior of Jack Johnson and would not patronize such a match. "One colored man held the heavyweight championship, and that will do for a long while to come," he said.[28]

Talk of a Dempsey title defense against the popular French boxer Georges Carpentier had been rife since the Willard fight. But Kearns was demanding $175,000 to match Dempsey with Carpentier, a figure Bat considered ridiculous. He was sure that no promoter, not even the daring Tex Rickard, would guarantee the champion that kind of money to take on Carpentier. It would require a million-dollar gate, he pointed out, and the Toledo fight had grossed only about $400,000, a figure that would "stand as a record for a long time." A Dempsey-Carpentier match "might draw a million dollars in Paris, but never in a thousand years in this country or England." Bat took the opportunity once again to assail Dempsey's character by comparing his war record with that of the popular Frenchman. Carpentier, he said, was idolized in France, not only because of a fine ring record but also because of his heroic war service. Dempsey, on the other hand, was "a stench in the nostrils of all patriotic citizens." He was "a poltroon of the meanest type," commanding no one's respect except pro-Germans and other enemies of his country, and had "no business in a ring with a man like Carpentier."[29]

In March 1920 Carpentier, the handsome, dapper European heavyweight champion and war hero, arrived in the United States, accompanied by his bride of a few weeks; his manager, Marcel Deschamps; and a personal retinue. Everywhere he appeared he received great public acclaim. Bat called it the most cordial welcome any foreigner had received in a hundred years.

The following October at Jersey City, New Jersey, Carpentier knocked out Battling Levinsky to win the world's light-heavyweight championship. After that victory the clamor for a heavyweight title match between the French champion and Dempsey increased. Sensing another opportunity to achieve his long-held ambition to promote a million-dollar match, Tex Rickard went to work. To Bat Masterson's great consternation, he signed Dempsey with a $300,000 guarantee, Carpentier with $200,000, and began construction of a huge 90,000-seat stadium in Boyle's Thirty Acres at Jersey City, New Jersey. The bout was scheduled for July 2, 1921.

Sportswriters ballyhooed the fight as a clash of titans, but Masterson was unexcited. Dempsey and Carpentier did not impress him; he believed Jeffries, Fitzsimmons, Corbett, or Johnson would have handily disposed of either one.

As early as May Dempsey backers were offering two-to-one odds on their fighter to win. When he read press reports that twenty-to-one odds against Carpentier scoring a knockout were being offered with no takers, Bat's sporting blood surged. In his column he said he would gladly take ten-to-one on Carpentier to score a knockout, and would "go quite a distance at these figures." He invited anyone wanting to make that bet to come to his office and bring his money. When no one took his offer, Bat spread the word in betting circles that he would accept five-to-one on the proposition, but never found a taker.[30]

Only once had Masterson seen Carpentier in action—in his victory over Levinsky—but he rated him a clever boxer with a powerful right-hand punch, and believed he could whip Jack Dempsey, who, he was now convinced, had been greatly overrated. He claimed his conclusion was based on his long ring experience, but admitted a certain amount of personal bias. "To be candid about it," he said, "my feelings are all with Carpentier, and I hope he wins." He was sure every "genuine American" shared his view: "One hundred per cent Americans are with the French war hero to a man. Trying to work up a sentiment for Dempsey on patriotic grounds is the bunk." Among Carpentier's strong supporters, he noted, were his own countrymen and the American Legion, a combination of which Dempsey could not boast.[31]

As usual, referee selection became an issue. Among those considered by the two camps were the old champions Jim Corbett and Jim Jeffries. When he heard that Jack Kearns was pushing for Otto Floto or Bob Edgren, Masterson said the idea of either of that pair refereeing a match of this importance was too ridiculous to even elicit a comment. The parties finally compromised on Harry Ertle as referee and Edgren as stakeholder.

To Masterson's amazement, Tex Rickard achieved, and even exceeded, his million-dollar gate with the Dempsey-Carpentier bout. More than 90,000 fight fans came to Boyle's Thirty Acres and paid $1,800,000 to see the battle between "the Manassa Mauler" and "the Orchid Man," as the press had dubbed Carpentier. It was said to be "the greatest multitude ever gathered in a single structure in American history," with fight fans on hand from China, Japan, South Africa, Australia, and "the farthermost points of South America and Europe."[32]

Celebrities abounded. No longer were women banned or confined in sections enclosed by barbed wire. The Roosevelt family had a private box in which were seated a daughter and two sons of the late president and their spouses. Others of prominence from many fields included George Ade, Vincent Aster, Bernard Baruch, Rex Beach, David Belasco, William A. Brady, George M. Cohan, James J. Corbett, Attorney General Harry Daugherty, Douglas Fairbanks, William Farnum, Henry Ford, Jay Gould, Mose Gunst, Sam K. Harris, Al Jolson, John McCormack, Tom Mix, Wilson Mizner, J. P. Morgan, Tom Pendergast, William Pinkerton, John Ringling, John D. Rockefeller, Arnold Rothstein, Charles Thorley, and Senator James J. Walker.

"No social lines [were] drawn in that great human maelstrom," wrote Bat. "The 'dis and dat' guy from slumland" rubbed elbows with the highbrow. Only ticket price separated classes; $50 ticket holders sat hundreds of feet nearer the ring than those in the $5 seats. It was, Bat thought, "a great gathering of democrats."[33]

The *Morning Telegraph* was represented by three writers: Thomas B. Hanly wrote the lead story, Weed Dickinson provided color, and Bat Masterson did the expert analysis.

There would be no "mailed fists" in this fight. The combatants' hands were taped and the gloves donned in the ring under the watchful eye of opposing cornermen. The battle lasted less than a dozen minutes of furious fighting. In the second round Carpentier staggered the champion with a right-hand smash, but he also broke his thumb. In the fourth Dempsey dropped Carpentier twice, the second time for the full count.

Masterson was impressed and finally acknowledged that he had underestimated both the fighting ability of Jack Dempsey and the amazing promotional skills of Tex Rickard. Dempsey had proved to his satisfaction that he was a champion who ranked with the great heavyweights of the past, but nothing in the past could remotely compare with what Rickard had achieved. The promoter had managed to more than double the attendance and quadruple the gate receipts of the Toledo promotion, a fight that Bat believed had set records for all time. "There never has been anything like it in the history of the prize ring," he wrote in awe. "Tex Rickard is the greatest fistic promoter on earth. . . . The Dempsey-Carpentier battle, in point of attendance and the money taken in, has never been equaled and probably never will be."[34]

Bat would not live to see Rickard top himself again and again. In 1923 Dempsey's title defense against Luis Firpo drew 82,000 spectators and another million-dollar gate; 120,000 people paid nearly $2,000,000 in 1926 to see Gene Tunney take the title from Dempsey; and gate receipts for a rematch in 1927 totaled an amazing $2,658,000. Masterson, of course, never dreamed of closed circuit television and the multimillion-dollar boxing promotions of the late twentieth century.

— 19 —

"A STRANGELY QUIET CLOSING"

I play the hero that Bat Masterson inspired. More than any other man I have ever met I admire and respect him.

William S. Hart

Bat Masterson and his wife, Emma, had seen years of deprivation, if not abject poverty, but their lives together after moving to New York City were economically untroubled. In Denver the couple had lived in a succession of rented homes on Larimer, Lawrence, Arapahoe, and Curtis Streets, never far from notorious Holladay Street, heart of the city's tenderloin. In New York they resided in a succession of fine locations, all in the Longacre Square district. They stayed at the Delevan Hotel for four years before taking an apartment at 253 West Forty-Third Street, where they remained for another four. In 1910 they moved two doors away, to a larger apartment at 257 West Forty-Third. Then, on April 1, 1918, they moved into commodious five-room quarters at the Elmsford, a 108-unit apartment building at 300 West Forty-Ninth Street, at the corner of Eighth Avenue, only a block from the *Morning Telegraph* offices.

Today's New York apartment dwellers might be astonished to learn that for this spacious apartment Bat initially paid only $63 a month. Inflation soon began its insidious growth, however, and six months after they moved in, the rent was increased by $4 a month, and a year later by another $9. Masterson complained bitterly at what he called extortion by "a grasping and soulless landlord." In a 1919 column he bewailed the fact that his rent was costing him $156 more a year than it had eighteen months previously. His tailor, he said, could make him three fine suits for that amount. The recipient of only a "modest" salary, he said he was not one of "the idle rich" who could afford such graft.[1]

Masterson was known for his generosity, and members of the sporting fraternity considered him a "soft touch" when they were down on their luck, but he could get tightfisted when he believed he was being "gouged" by restaurateurs, innkeepers, or landlords. He may have considered his salary "modest," but he was very well fixed financially. What actually was modest was his comment in a 1917 column that he was "not suffering for the necessities of life."[2] His remark a few weeks before he died that he hoped to double the $100,000 he had in the bank was not entirely facetious.

The Mastersons were sufficiently well-off to afford servants. When Zoe Anderson Norris of the *New York Times* called at the Masterson home in April 1905, she was met at the door by a butler, "a black and urbane servitor," who ushered her into the living room for her interview with Bat.[3] A live-in maid was later hired.[4]

Emma accompanied Bat on his annual sojourns to Hot Springs, Saratoga, and Alexandria Bay; stayed with him at the finest hotels; and dined at the best restaurants. She attended motion pictures, stage plays, and vaudeville shows with him in New York, but she could never be a part of much of his life, necessarily spent in sweaty gymnasiums, smoke-filled boxing clubs, and bars and cafés. She did not go with him on his out-of-town journeys to witness important fights. Nor was she invited to all-male recreational functions like the clambake Bat attended annually at Frazier Price's hotel at Pleasure Bay, near Long Branch, on the Jersey coast.

Masterson was one of some three-dozen male club members who assembled every year at the resort and there devoured clams, lobsters, and corn on the cob, "and killed the amber brew." Other members included prizefighter Charlie Mitchell, comedian Leo Donnelly, renowned gourmand Jim Collins, author Alex Moore, actors Otis Harlan and Charlie Ross, Wall Street broker Jim Jordan, vaudevillian Eddie Dowling, and turfmen Ollie Power and Bob Arthur. Members and invited guests would gorge themselves on the delicious comestibles until all were "stuffed to the esophagus, like a Christmas turkey."[5]

GUNFIGHTER IN GOTHAM

Bat, a member of the club since 1905, never missed this event. He attended his last one in September 1921, a month before his death.

Masterson was a longtime member of several fraternal lodges, but he never joined any organization of newspaper writers and did not attend their functions. A number of prominent New York sportswriters, including Damon Runyon, W. O. McGeehan, Irvin S. Cobb, and Bozeman Bulger, joined ball players Babe Ruth, Joe Kelley, and Wilbert Robinson in annual winter hunting sessions at Dover Hill, Yankee owner Cap Huston's Georgia shooting lodge, but Bat never attended. He may not have been invited because of his dislike for baseball, but he would have declined an invitation anyway as some of the "we boys" crowd might be there, and he would not socialize with them.

On at least one occasion he attended a roast at the Friars' Club. In December 1913 he was an invited guest when the organization roasted David Warfield at the Hotel Astor. Other guests included W. E. Lewis, DeWolfe Hopper, Rhinelander Waldo, and Lew Fields. Some of the foremost vaudeville stars of the day—Eddie Foy, Irving Berlin, and Gus Edwards' Kids (including Eddie Cantor and George Jessel)—provided the entertainment.

One of the joys of life for Bat Masterson was the smoking of fine cigars, and he sometimes commented on the pleasure he derived from the habit, while chiding others who smoked cheaper stogies. In a 1917 column he quoted one of Jeff Orear's fanciful pieces in his *Arkansaw Thomas Cat* in which Orear claimed to have suffered a near-fatal accident. He had slipped on a banana peel and fell, driving "the bouquet de glue-factoro cigar" in his vest pocket through the breastbone, almost piercing his heart. He had almost died, he said, but was happy to report the cigar was undamaged.

His friend Orear must have gotten one of Jack Grace's brand, Bat suggested. Grace, he said, smoked the most evil kinds with apparent relish. In an attempt to cure him, friends in Denver once presented him with a box of specially prepared cheroots, rolled with "horse hair, strips of bacon rind and other things equally nauseating." Lighting up and puffing away with gusto, Grace was soon "enveloped in a cloud of black smoke that smelled worse than a tan yard." The effort to educate him, Bat said, had proven an abysmal failure.[6]

Another Masterson pal who smoked noxious stogies was Eddie Foy. Bat said he tried one of Foy's brand and when he "got out of the hospital" swore he would never smoke another. He passed on Foy's offerings to Jack Grace, who would smoke anything.[7]

Once a cigar ignited a ruckus between Masterson and an Eighth Avenue streetcar conductor. Boarding the car with an unlit cigar in his mouth, Bat was informed by the conductor "in a rough and uncouth manner" that no smoking was allowed. Bat replied that the cigar was not burning.

"Well, then, take it out of your mouth," snapped the conductor.

"I'll do nothing of the kind," Bat retorted. "This cigar is mine and I'll do what I like with it so long as I don't violate your rules against smoking."

The "militant commander of the car" then made some "uncalled for remarks," and Bat called him "an impudent bum."

In an earlier day a confrontation like this would surely have precipitated some sort of physical scrimmage, but age had brought discretion to Masterson. "Being aware," he said, "that my fighting days are long since passed, owing to the fact that I'm well on the way to the three-score-and-ten mile post, I said no more for fear of receiving a mopping up." He merely took down the conductor's number in order to report him to his superiors, and exited the car at his stop, happy that he had made a "lucky escape."[8]

Masterson had always been a moderate drinker. His tirades against national prohibition were prompted more by a deeply felt abhorrence of constraints on individual freedom than any personal interest in alcohol consumption. When it became obvious that prohibition was coming in 1918 he wrote that as far as he was concerned, it didn't make a particle of difference, for he was not a boozer, never was one, and never expected to be one. He enjoyed an occasional glass of beer until the price went to $1.50 a quart and he gave that up. He now drank buttermilk, but since the price had shot up to 55 cents a quart and sweet milk to 40 cents a pint he suspected that prohibitionists now controlled the retail milk business.

Like all ordinary men, Bat suffered the infirmities that age brings. As early as 1911 his vision was weakening, and he needed glasses for close work. He lost his spectacles one night at a boxing club and sent out a distress signal in his next column:

If the gentleman who picked up a pair of gold-rimmed eye-glasses, enclosed in a Morocco leather case, at the Twentieth Century Athletic Club Tuesday night will either return them to this office or notify me where they can be had, he will receive the grateful thanks and maybe a perfecto from their owner, who is badly in need of them all the time. The glasses were lost in or about one of the ringside boxes. Come on boys! I need them ever so much.[9]

His hair, already thinning noticeably during the Denver years, re-treated from his forehead and turned white in New York. Always a meticulous dresser and fastidious about his appearance, he did not seem bothered by hair loss, and apparently found it amusing. In 1917 he repeated a story credited to an American entertainer named Mabel Lambert, who was a hit in the London music halls. Mabel convulsed her English audiences when she told them she had left America because of a new law requiring men to dress according to their hair color; black-haired men should wear black clothes, brown-haired men should wear brown, gray-haired men gray, and so on. "But," said Mabel, "America is full of baldheads—well, I just had to leave the country, that's all."[10]

The idea of wearing a toupee he thought ridiculous and kidded Danny Morgan when he began sporting one. "Before Danny staked himself to that toupee," Bat said, "he didn't have to remove his hat when he had his hair trimmed."[11]

Bat claimed to have had "every kind of physical infirmity a man could suffer and survive,"[12] but his health, up to the last few years of his life, had actually been excellent. The vertigo that afflicted him in 1878 and sent him to Hot Springs apparently never returned. His susceptibility to seasickness was probably a symptom of the "weak, sensitive" stomach that incapacitated him at Saratoga. On rare occasions he complained in his column of personal illness. In 1919 he remarked that "the penalties of old age, neuritis, lumbago and float-ing kidneys," had afflicted him for two weeks, and a year later that a thirty-five-mile trip in a friend's Packard over bumpy roads had "pretty well jolted out" his lumbago, which had been bothering him for a week.[13] Unmentioned were any aches and pains he may have suffered from the effects of the two gunshot wounds he had received many years earlier.

He contracted the usual respiratory ailments of winter, colds and influenza, but he seldom was too ill to work and never required hospitalization. His longest period away from work because of illness was in 1916 when he was confined to his bed for almost a month with grippe and bronchitis.

In 1918 he was diagnosed with diabetes, and doctors put him on a diet. In a letter written shortly after his death Emma Masterson said he ate only "gluten bread" and could not eat sweets or "any vegetable that grew under the ground." In the winter his feet were so cold that he had to wear woolen stockings in bed at night. Emma described herself as "an invalid," suffering from asthma and "spells" since her "change of life."[14]

One day in October 1921 William S. Hart, one of the top motion picture stars of the day and the unchallenged king of westerns, paid a call on Masterson at his *Morning Telegraph* office. Bat had expressed admiration for Hart's portrayal of frontier characters since January 1910 when he saw him in the play *The Barrier* at the New Amsterdam Theater. The four-act play, adapted for the stage from Rex Beach's popular 1907 novel of the same name, dealt with life in the fictional Klondike gold rush camp of Flambeau. Bat called it "one of the cleverest melodramas" he had ever seen, with none of the "swashbuckler features" so often depicted, but never known in the West. There were no "blood and thunder and notches-on-the-pistol incidents, which the Ned Buntlines and other writers of lurid Western tales told in extravagant detail a generation ago." He thought Hart's portrayal of the main character, Dan Stark, was perfect:

> Any one familiar with the character of the cool, calculating and daring desperado, whose presence was a part of frontier life a generation ago, will instantly recognize in Mr. Hart a true type of that reckless nomad who flourished on the border when the six-shooter was the final arbiter of all disputes between man and man. Mr. Hart looks the part, dresses the part and acts as if he were the real Dan Stark and had stepped out of the book upon the stage. He indulges in none of that sort of bluff and bluster which was characteristic of the tenderfoot who went West to establish a record and was usually buried immediately after his first attempt at playing the part of the bad man.[15]

Pleased and flattered by Bat's remarks, Hart kept the column and quoted from it in his autobiography published almost two decades later.[16]

Undoubtedly Masterson was impressed by Hart's work. Bat seldom commented in his columns on theatrical or cinematic productions, but four years later he noted that Hart had begun filming *The Two-Gun Man* at Santa Monica, California, and again praised the actor for his portrayal of the western gunfighter: "He possesses a finer conception of the Western professional man-killer of pioneer days than any actor who has ever essayed the character. His mannerism, style, voice effect, and dexterity with the pistol admirably fit him for such a part."[17]

When Hart came to New York in 1918 to shoot scenes for a movie entitled *Branding Broadway*, Masterson called at his hotel room to pay his respects. "We talked for two hours and it seemed like five minutes," recalled Hart. Bat, he said, was "the owner of a soft, low voice; the wielder . . . of a virile, audacious pen; a quiet unostentatious gentleman; a great American citizen."[18]

After that meeting Hart made it a point, whenever in New York, to spend some time with Masterson. In the fall of 1921 he was vacationing in New York City and on Friday, October 7, stopped in at the offices of the *Morning Telegraph*. Members of the staff surrounded the movie star, and Louella Parsons, the motion picture editor, pulled him aside for an interview. Hart was polite, but it was clear to Parsons that he had come to pay his respects to Bat Masterson, a man of whom he was obviously in awe. "I play the hero that Bat Masterson inspired," he said. "More than any other man I have ever met I admire and respect him."[19]

Urged by Parsons to write a piece about his feelings for Bat, Hart agreed, and the next day submitted a lengthy article written in longhand on Waldorf-Astoria stationery. Published in the *Morning Telegraph* exactly as written, it was a tribute to both Bat Masterson and his lifelong friend Wyatt Earp, whom Hart also knew and admired.

He himself, Hart said, was "a mere player, an imitation," seeking to re-create on the screen "the lives of those great gunmen who molded a new country for us," men like Earp and Masterson. To students of the frontier, "these two names are revered as none others. They are the last of the greatest band of gun-fighters—upholders of law and order—that ever lived. [Most] have crossed the Big Divide, but Bat Masterson and Wyatt Earp still live and long may they do so!" He thought it ironic that these two men, "gentle-voiced and almost sad-faced, [went] uncheered," while he, the actor, was known and honored by millions. "Let us not forget these living Americans who, when they pass on, will be remembered by hundreds of generations. For no history of the West can be written without their wonderful deeds being recorded."[20]

To memorialize the occasion of Hart's visit, a *Telegraph* photographer snapped pictures of Masterson and the actor, one on the roof of the building, and another in Bat's office with Hart seated at Bat's desk, Masterson standing behind. The photos show Bat nattily dressed as usual in a suit with the omnipresent watch chain draped across the vest, white shirt, starched collar, and tie. In the outdoor shot he is wearing a jaunty wide-brimmed western-style hat. Masterson's clenched hands and rheumy eyes as revealed in the office picture, however, show that he was not well. Eighteen days later, seated in that chair at that desk, he would breathe his last.

A few days after meeting with Hart, Masterson came down with a severe cold and had to take to his bed. He missed two columns the following week. "[He] got better but couldn't seem to get his strength back," Emma said. "But no one could keep him from going out over to his office to write."[21]

He turned out six more columns. On Tuesday morning, October 25, he was seated at his desk writing the column that would appear in the Thursday edition. Several staff members, concerned about his condition, stuck their heads in the doorway and asked how he felt. He said he was "lots better."[22] He completed the column, which contained his often-misquoted observation about the rich getting ice in the summer while the poor got theirs in the winter.[23]

And when he was done, he died. Seized by a massive heart attack,[24] he collapsed over his desk and passed on without a sound. It was, as Damon Runyon put it, "a strangely quiet closing to a strangely active career."[25]

Shortly before noon Sam Taub came into the room to find his boss dead. The *Telegraph* offices were soon in a state of turmoil. None of Bat's shocked colleagues could handle the task of breaking the news to Emma by telephone or in person. She had prepared lunch and was waiting for her husband's return in the apartment a block away. Finally an employee of a messenger service was dispatched to notify her.

Every paper in New York gave prominence to the story of Bat Masterson's death, and the old inaccurate legends were dusted off and published again.[26] Many papers ran editorial tributes to the man and his accomplishments.

Masterson's "career covered two widely separated phases of life and in each he lived hard," noted the *Herald*. His life on the frontier was more thrilling than fiction, and he later became "an authority on many lines of sports."[27]

The *Times* called him "the last of the old time gun fighters," of whom "probably more weird and bloodthirsty tales have been written . . . than of nearly any other man. . . . At one time Masterson was said to have been the best known man between the Mississippi and the Pacific Coast."[28]

A "frontier Cyrano de Bergerac in his youth, [he] improved the world considerably by the people he removed from it," said the *Tribune*. "He died at his desk gripping his pen with the tenacity with which he formerly clung to the hilt of his six-shooter." When he came to New York City, he "brought vigor to the Roaring Forties."[29]

W. E. Lewis, in a *Morning Telegraph* editorial, wrote that "genial, friendly, generous Bat Masterson" was loved by everyone on the paper's staff and would be sorely missed.[30]

Hype Igoe in the *World* said that Masterson "would go through hell for a friend and he would toss an enemy to the regions with little or no compunction."[31]

In his *New York American* column Damon Runyon also emphasized that Bat was a wonderful friend but an implacable enemy. Possessed of "a great sense of humor and a marvelous fund of reminiscence," Runyon found him "one of the most entertaining companions" he had ever known. "The news of Bat's death was a profound shock to all who knew him, and to none did it bring a deeper measure of sincere regret than to the writer of these lines. It was the loss of a personal friend . . . , one of the most indomitable characters this land has ever seen. He was a 100 per cent 22-karat real man."[32] In a wire to the *Telegraph* Runyon said the nation had lost "one of those fine, fearless men that can be illy spared. The world of sport will miss his untiringly honest writing and his constant effort to keep the game clean. He was a magnificent man. We shall never see his like again."[33]

Newspapers across the West reported the passing of the gunfighting legend and ring authority. *Washington Post* correspondent Edwin Bobo Smith found Bat's passing of "melancholy interest" for Washington residents. "Not a living man [could] be found who would not bear willing testimony to the splendid qualities of the deceased."[34]

The Denver papers gave extensive coverage to the story. The *Rocky Mountain News* interviewed police detective Tim Connors, with whom Bat had the polling place skirmish in 1897. Masterson, said Connors, "was always a square shooter—and how fast! He made lots of enemies, but all of the men who really amounted to anything made lots of them. He was quiet and composed, never looking for trouble, but whenever trouble came his way, it was a tough day for Mister Trouble!"[35]

The *Denver Post*, Bat's old journalistic adversary, recounted the hoary legends of his twenty-six killings and fabricated a new, particularly ludicrous, one. Old-timers, it said, called Bat "Patch Pockets," because he shot through his pockets and covered the bullet holes with patches.[36]

Telegrams and flowers poured into the offices of the *Morning Telegraph* from Masterson friends and admirers in the sports, journalistic, and theatrical worlds. Wild Bill Phelon of the *Cincinnati Times-Star* called Bat "the last link between the glorious old West and the life of today." Lou Houseman in Chicago was "inexpressibly shocked." Broadway producer Charles Dillingham mourned the passing of "the thousand per cent American." Vaudevillian Earl "Skater" Reynolds said that all lovers of honest sport would miss Masterson, whose "never-ceasing warfare on crookedness in boxing [had] been the means of saving that sport in America." Louis Siebold of the *New York Herald* said the city had lost "a manly gentleman and a staunch friend." Theatrical press agent Nellie Revell, herself in poor physical condition in St. Vincent's Hospital, wrote: "I haven't had so great a shock since the doctor told me I may never walk again as I did when I read of [Bat's] death. . . . I cried for the first time in months."[37]

Since he had not died at home, the police held Bat's personal effects. Emma complained more than a month later that his ring, watch, and wallet had still not been returned to her, and she expected to have to pay taxes on them.[38] It was the type of bureaucratic nonsense that would have provided fuel for a scathing Masterson column.

Funeral services for Bat Masterson were held at the Campbell's Funeral Parlor, at Broadway and Sixty-Sixth Street, on Thursday, October 27, the day his final column appeared in the *Telegraph*. More than fifty floral displays from friends and admirers surrounded a plain casket covered with a blanket of orchids sent by his associates on the paper.

Damon Runyon was so moved by Bat's passing that he maintained a nightlong vigil beside the casket the night before the funeral. There he had a supernatural experience he could never understand and did not reveal for twenty-four years. Returning from the funeral of President Franklin D. Roosevelt, which he covered in 1945, he finally told the tale. As he sat in Campbell's Funeral Parlor with the body of Bat Masterson that night in October 1921, Runyon said, he fell into a reverie in which he saw all of his friends—past, present, and future—filing past the casket and stopping to gaze at the dead man. In his trance he found himself falling into line. When he looked into the casket he was startled to see not the face of Bat Masterson, but his own. Runyon never forgot that chilling experience, and he never forgot Bat Masterson, who had been like a second father to him.

Five hundred mourners filled the chapel for the funeral services, including William A. Pinkerton, who had come from Chicago; Charlie O'Dell from Savannah; and several of Emma's relatives from Pennsylvania and New Jersey. None of Masterson's Kansas relations attended.

William Muldoon delivered the eulogy. He had known Bat Masterson since the Indian campaigns of the 1870s, Muldoon said, and "in all those years he had never known [him] to do a dishonorable deed, never to betray a friend, never to connive at dishonor, and never to fear an enemy. [He was] a man of the highest moral as well as the highest physical courage. He never hesitated to lift his voice or raise his arm in what he conceived to be a righteous cause." Not hotheaded or quick to anger, he was often "grievously offended but refrained from action because he had a sympathy with weak human nature." He was intolerant of any crookedness in sport and spoke his mind, assuming full responsibility for his language and his conduct.

A brief organ voluntary followed Muldoon's remarks. Then the Reverend Nathan A. Seagle of St. Stephen's Church read a simple Episcopalian ritual. Honorary pallbearers were Muldoon, W. E. Lewis, Tex Rickard, Tom O'Rourke, W. A. Pinkerton, Val O'Farrell, Charles Thorley, Jimmy Sinnott, Frank J. Price, Damon Runyon, and Hype Igoe. Among those attending the funeral were Emma's neighbor and confidante, Nellie Degnan; boxing figures Frank Moran, Dan McKittrick, Jim Buckley, Danny Morgan, Jack Skelly, Al Lippe, and Jimmy Johnston; vaudeville performers Billy Jerome, Jack Farrell, and Pat Casey; and longtime friends George Orlando Weedon, Edward R. Bradley, and Giants owner Charles Stoneham. Burial was in Woodlawn Cemetery.[39]

Bat Masterson left all his earthly possessions to his wife, but there was no life insurance. "Your uncle Bat never believed in life insurance; he was peculiar in some ways," Emma wrote a niece.[40] But even without death benefits Bat left sufficient assets for his widow to live on in New York City in comfortable circumstances for the remainder of her life. She still had a maid in her employ when she passed away quietly, much as Bat had done. She died in her apartment at Stratford House, 11 East Thirty-Second Street, during the early morning hours of July 12, 1932, one day after her seventy-fifth birthday. The maid discovered her body several hours later. Although she had suffered from asthma for many years, her death was attributed to heart disease.[41]

Emma's blood relatives, all residing in Philadelphia and New Jersey, and Bat's closest surviving relatives in Kansas were notified, but it was Madison Square Garden boxing director Jimmy Johnston who took charge and made the funeral and burial arrangements. Emma was interred in Woodlawn Cemetery beside her husband.[42]

GUNFIGHTER IN GOTHAM

AFTERWORD

Biographies published after Masterson's death skimmed over his life in the East and career as a journalist. The first, a monograph published in 1943, devoted scarcely a dozen lines in an appendix to Bat's New York period.[1] Later biographies, appearing in 1957[2] and 1979,[3] provided more information on his later life, but focused primarily on Bat's western adventures. Contributions of other media did little to enlighten the public regarding Masterson's life in New York or his journalistic career.

A low-budget motion picture released in 1943 touched on the subject of Masterson's New York City years. In brief opening and closing scenes of *Woman of the Town*, sports editor Bat Masterson is shown in his *New York Morning Telegraph* office, preparing to leave to cover the Willard-Dempsey fight of 1919. Most of the film, however, is a flashback to early Dodge City and depiction of a fictional romance involving Masterson and beautiful dancehall singer Dora Hand.[4] Later motion pictures, like the 1954 release *Masterson in Kansas*,[5] were typical Hollywood "horse operas," bearing little resemblance to historical reality.

In 1981 director Ivan Passer planned a movie based on Masterson's life in New York. From an original Tom Pope screenplay entitled "The Eagle of Broadway," it was to star renowned Hollywood actor James Cagney as Masterson.[6] After being coaxed out of retirement to play New York City police commissioner Waldo Rhinelander in *Ragtime*, another film depicting early-twentieth-century New York

City, Cagney had won wide acclaim, but it was to be his last role. His health deteriorated, and "The Eagle of Broadway" was never made.

At least three novels based on Masterson's later years have been published. Glendon Swarthout's *The Old Colts*, a wildly imaginative tale supposedly drawn from a long hidden Masterson manuscript, appeared in 1985. The plot has Wyatt Earp coming to New York in 1916 and enlisting Masterson in a scheme to return to Dodge City and rob the bank, but a gang of twentieth-century-style desperadoes beats them to it. Bat and Wyatt, driving Model T Fords and toting Thompson submachine guns, chase down the bandits, and end up heroes.

In 1986 Robert J. Randisi published *The Ham Reporter*, in which the fixed Morris-Flynn fight of 1911 leads *Morning Telegraph* sportswriter Bat Masterson into a web of intrigue and corruption involving early New York City gamblers and racketeers, politicians, and policemen. All of Bat's nerve and investigative skills are required to untangle the mess.

The prolific and highly acclaimed western author Richard S. Wheeler produced a novel in 1999 simply entitled *Masterson*. It tells the story of the respected sports columnist and colorful Broadway figure who, aging and diabetic, faces the fact of his own mortality in 1919 and tries to write the true story of his life in the West. Still conflicted by his own inherent honesty and the legend that he has allowed to grow up around him, he determines to return with his wife to the scenes of his western adventures to find out which Bat Masterson, the true or mythical, should be remembered, or whether it is too late to separate the two. In this book Wheeler captures the character of the real-life Bat Masterson far better than any other fictional writer.[7]

The script of a stage play purportedly dealing with Masterson's later years was published in Canada in 1989 and apparently performed on a few occasions. Any resemblance to factual history or Masterson's true personality was entirely lacking in this nonsensical fable.[8]

In September 1955 the first so-called adult western television series, *The Life and Legend of Wyatt Earp*, with Hugh O'Brien in the title role, debuted on the ABC network. The half-hour series was quite successful and ran for six seasons. Bat Masterson appeared as a regular character during the first two years, which depicted, rather loosely, Earp's experiences as a lawman in Kansas. Actor Mason Alan Dinehart III portrayed Bat as a callow youth following the great Wyatt Earp around like a puppy. The character disappeared in 1957 as the network, prompted by the success of *Wyatt Earp*, decided to introduce another series purportedly based on Masterson's life in the West. The name Bat Masterson became familiar to many Americans through their viewing of the half-hour series that began in October 1958 and ran until September 1961, when both the Masterson and Earp programs ended. In the title role of *Bat Masterson* Gene Barry was a dapper, derbied western gambler and adventurer who roamed the West with cane and pearl-handled pistol, resolving problems with smooth talk when possible, deadly force when necessary. Wyatt Earp never appeared as a character in this series, nor was there a hint that Bat would later live another life, far from the western frontier.

Just as Bat Masterson's western gunfighter notoriety was overblown, his fame as an expert boxing analyst was largely unmerited. In predicting winners of important fights for thirty years, from Sullivan-Kilrain in 1889 to Dempsey-Carpentier in 1921, he was more often wrong than right. He allowed his personal opinion of a fighter's character to influence his professional judgment. Having decided Sullivan was a phony and a blowhard, he backed Kilrain, and it cost him. Soured on Bob Fitzsimmons after the Cornishman stole Billy Woods from him, he foolishly bet against Fitz and erroneously predicted his defeat in matches with Corbett and Gus Ruhlin, and two with Peter Maher. Bat did figure Ruby Bob to defeat Tom Sharkey in 1896, but lost again when Wyatt Earp awarded the bout to Sharkey on a foul. Bat liked Corbett personally, twice picked him to defeat Jim Jeffries, and lost both times. But much as he admired Corbett, he held Charlie Mitchell in even greater esteem, and when the two met in 1894 he bet on the Englishman and again lost. He wrongly chose Jeffries over Jack Johnson, and Fred Fulton, Jess Willard, and Georges Carpentier over Jack Dempsey. There is no doubt that Bat's personal animosity toward Dempsey because of the "slacker" issue prevented him from fully appreciating the fighter's formidable ring skills.

Members of the fistic fraternity might joke about Bat's less than excellent prognosticatory record, but he was almost universally respected and admired for his love of the sport and the honesty and candor he brought to his commentary. Even Jack Dempsey, whom

Bat had criticized unmercifully, did not strike back at Masterson in his autobiography. "Bat Masterson didn't think much of me as champion," he admitted, but he was "a gentleman [and] a sharp observer of the world around him."[9]

But a story related by artist and western history writer Jack DeMattos indicates that long after Bat's passing, the very mention of his name could trigger a visible response of anger—and perhaps apprehension—in the former heavyweight champ. For many years after he left the ring Dempsey operated a popular restaurant on Broadway. In 1968, while chatting with the proprietor, DeMattos asked Dempsey how he rated Bat as a sportswriter. "A look of real disgust came over his face," DeMattos remembered. He "looked like he wanted to kill me." Masterson, growled Dempsey, "didn't know shit about boxing." But DeMattos noticed that as he said these words Dempsey shot a quick glance at the door as if expecting Masterson, who had been dead for forty-seven years, to come walking in.[10]

Despite his generosity with handouts and wagering losses at ring and track, the Masterson bank account remained sufficiently robust to support a well-to-do, if not opulent, lifestyle for Bat and Emma throughout their years in New York, and Bat left his widow in comfortable circumstances when he died. This was in notable contrast to his friend of half a century, Wyatt Earp, whose final years before his death in January 1929 were spent in near poverty and who left his widow with practically nothing of material value.

Although in both his lives Bat Masterson was respected and admired by friends and enemies alike for his honesty and forthrightness and his constant attacks on hypocrisy and sham, his own integrity was not entirely unblemished. He was guilty of giving false testimony in court cases, as in his 1913 lawsuit when, under cross-examination by Benjamin Cardozo, he denied ever having been a professional gambler, when clearly he had followed that trade for twenty years in the West.

He viciously attacked hypocrites and greedy public servants and yet he himself hypocritically held as a deputy U.S. marshal in New York a no-show, grossly overpaid, taxpayer-funded, patronage position for over four years.

But perhaps his most egregious deception was the fiction he maintained throughout his life that he had been born in Illinois, when in fact he was a Canadian by birth and had never taken out naturalization papers. Bat Masterson, the outspoken, unabashed flag-waving jingoist, was therefore not an American citizen, and voted, served as an official delegate to political conventions, and held public office illegally.

He was lax about things he considered of no great consequence, like the year and place of his birth, and the legality of his marriage. He was definitely, as Emma attested, "peculiar in some ways."

Notes

ABBREVIATIONS

GRDJ   General Records, Department of Justice, Record Group 60
GW   *George's Weekly*
NYMT   *New York Morning Telegraph*
TR   Theodore Roosevelt
WBM   W. B. Masterson
WLHU   Widener Library, Harvard University

INTRODUCTION

1. The shooting of the seven was an exaggerated version of the gun battle that resulted in the death of Ed Masterson and Jack Wagner. The "outlaws' heads" story was drawn from an exploit of Colorado frontiersman Tom Tobin, who in 1863 tracked down two bandits named Espinosa and brought back their heads to claim the reward.

2. Masterson's testimony in a civil court case, *R. W. Tarbox v. P. F. Sughrue.*

3. Wright, *Dodge City*, 178.

4. Hoyt, *Frontier Doctor*, 56.

5. Parsons, *James W. Kenedy*, 14.

6. In a widely publicized speech given at a Chicago meeting of the American Historical Society in 1893.

CHAPTER 1. BATTLING MASTERSON

1. Lewis, *Sunset Trail*, 1.

2. Vestal, *Queen of Cowtowns*, 273; O'Connor, *Bat Masterson*, 17.

3. *Dodge City Times*, June 9, 1877.

4. Siringo, *Cowboy Detective*, 316–18.

5. *Dodge City Cowboy*, September 27, 1884.

6. WBM column, *NYMT*, February 6, 1910.

7. *Dodge City Democrat*, May 3, 1884.

8. *GW*, December 2, 1899; WBM columns, *NYMT*, February 6, 1910; October 10, 1916.

9. "Beau Broadway," in *NYMT*, November 20, 1910.

10. *Topeka (Kansas) Commonwealth*, July 6, 1884.

11. *Globe Live Stock Journal*, November 11, 1884.

12. Ibid., November 4, 1884.

13. Quoted in ibid., November 13, 1884.

14. WBM column, *NYMT*, April 26, 1914.

15. *Dodge City Times,* June 16, 1877.

16. Fleischer, "Crusading Scribes."

17. *National Police Gazette*, July 27, 1889.

18. WBM column, *NYMT*, April 26, 1914.

19. Ibid., January 10, 1910.

20. Ibid., July 17, 1913.

21. *Poughkeepsie (New York) Daily Eagle,* March 11, 1927, cited in Penn, "Bat Masterson's Emma," 33.

22. *New Orleans Picayune,* January 15, 1891; *Fort Wayne (Indiana) Sentinel,* January 15, 1891, cited in Penn, "Bat Masterson's Emma," 34.

23. Robertson and Harris, *Soapy Smith,* 106; DeArment, *Bat Masterson,* 332.

24. WBM columns, *NYMT*, February 6, 20, 1910; May 19, 1915.

25. Ibid., February 26, 1918.

26. *Rocky Mountain News,* August 14, 1899.

27. *National Police Gazette,* January 14, 1893.

28. *Illustrated Sporting West,* February 23, 1894.

29. *National Police Gazette,* February 18, 1893.

30. Ibid., April 10, 1893.

31. Ibid., February 17, 1894.

32. *Rocky Mountain News,* June 6, 1895.

33. *New York Tribune,* February 7, 1905.

34. *Rocky Mountain News,* June 6, 1895.

35. Ibid. In 1895, $5,000 was a great deal of money. This was the annual salary of Police Commissioner Roosevelt and Superintendent Byrnes (Morris, *Rise of Theodore Roosevelt,* 821).

36. *Denver Times,* July 9, 1895.

37. WBM column, *NYMT*, July 16, 1912.

38. *El Paso (Texas) Times,* February 4, 1896; *El Paso (Texas) Herald,* February 1, 5, 21, 1896.

39. Quoted in the *El Paso (Texas) Herald,* January 13, 1896.

40. Quoted in Miletich, *Dan Stuart's Fistic Carnival,* 148.

41. *El Paso (Texas) Herald,* March 2, 1896.

42. WBM columns, *NYMT*, October 28, 30, 1917.

43. Quoted in Miletich, *Dan Stuart's Fistic Carnival,* 152.

44. WBM columns, *NYMT*, May 18, 29, June 14, 1919.

45. Ibid., August 4, 1918.

46. *San Francisco Chronicle,* December 3, 1896.

47. *San Francisco Examiner,* December 3, 1896.

48. *San Francisco Bulletin,* December 24, 1896.

49. Lewis, "King of the Gun-Players."

50. *Rocky Mountain News,* February 9, 1897.

51. *Laramie Daily Boomerang*, February 26, 1897.

52. WBM column, *NYMT*, June 10, 1917.

CHAPTER 2. THE WOMEN IN HIS LIFE

1. In response to a written inquiry in 1905 from a Watson Masterson regarding a possible relationship, Bat said that he had been born in Illinois fifty-one years earlier, or in 1854 (WBM to Watson Masterson, December 31, 1905, copy in author's collection). He usually told census takers he was born in Illinois, but when enumerated in the U.S. Census at Dodge City in 1880 correctly reported his birthplace as Canada. The 1900 U.S. Census taken in Denver showed Missouri as his place of birth. His age was consistently reported as a year younger than it actually was, except in 1910 when it was given as two years younger.

2. Lewis, "King of the Gun-Players."

3. *Lincoln (Nebraska) Daily Star*, August 9, 1917; *San Antonio (Texas) Light*, October 9, 1917.

4. Thompson, *Bat Masterson*, 4.

5. WBM column, *NYMT*, March 22, 1910. Ade was amazed to hear that Bat was born in Watseka, just across the state line from Kentland, Indiana, where he was born.

6. *NYMT*, October 27, 1921.

7. O'Connor, *Bat Masterson*, 25.

8. Andrie Raymond, Office of the Prothonotary, St. Jean, Quebec, Canada, to the author, September 30, 1972; Penn, "Note on Bartholomew Masterson."

9. *Olympia (Washington) Record*, February 25, 1905. The piece is filled with many other incorrect assertions: Ed and Jim Masterson were both shot dead in a battle with outlaws. Bat, a city marshal at Dodge City, left town to become a cowboy and was now residing in New York City with his wife "and children."

10. James Masterson to Thomas Masterson, September 26, 1892 (author's collection).

11. As an avid reader, Bat may have read a paperback "penny-dreadful" of 1854 describing the deeds of a murderer named William Masterson and published by M. L. Barclay. The names may have stuck in his mind and led to his adopting them as his own. If this juxtaposition of names is simply coincidence, the question remains, where did Bat get the name William Barclay? (DeArment, "Source for Bat Masterson's Adopted Name").

12. William B. Masterson, Last Will and Testament, August 3, 1907.

13. Thompson, *Bat Masterson*, 47.

14. Bat's fellow frontier lawman, boxing enthusiast, professional gambler and lifelong pal Wyatt Earp lost a wife in childbirth after a documented marriage, but then he and another woman cohabitated for several years without benefit of marriage before Earp left her for a handsome young woman of the stage. No record of a marriage of Wyatt Earp and Josephine Marcus has been

found, but the two lived as husband and wife until his death almost fifty years later.

15. This same census listed Bat's brother Jim, age twenty-four, city marshal, living with Minnie Roberts, a sixteen-year-old concubine. Although Jim and Minnie were never married, she took his name and was known as "Mrs. James Masterson" for many years afterward (DeArment, *Deadly Dozen*, 248, 339). The use of the word "wife" was commonly used in the frontier press as a euphemism for "mistress." The *Dodge City Times* in its edition of November 24, 1877, mentioned the wife of Bat's brother Ed, but Ed was still single when he was killed a few months later.

16. Young, *Dodge City*, 123.

17. Coincidentally, the mothers of Bat and Emma were both named Catherine.

18. Anna Maria was born on June 14, 1854, and Clara Victoria on December 15, 1858 (correspondence to the author from Roy Adams).

19. It has been reported (*NYMT*, October 26, 1921) that Emma's father was the first Civil War veteran buried in Philadelphia, but John Walters, a corporal in the Ninety-First Pennsylvania Volunteers who died of pneumonia at nearby Camp Chase on December 27, 1861, earned that distinction. The similarity of names caused the confusion.

20. Information on the family of Emma Walter Masterson was researched by Lot Grafton of New York City. He drew on Philadelphia city directories, 1840–1910; U.S Census Reports, 1830–1910; the Civil War pension application of Catherine Walter in the National Archives; and the baptismal record of Emma Matilda Walter in the Register, Church of St. Albans, Roxborough, Pennsylvania.

21. Penn, "Bat Masterson's Emma," 26.

22. *Dubuque (Iowa) Herald*, September 24, 1874, cited in Penn, "Bat Masterson's Emma," 27.

23. *New York Clipper*, issues from April to December 1877, as cited in Penn, "Bat Masterson's Emma," 27.

24. *Chicago Inter-Ocean*, August 18, 19, 1879, as cited in Penn, "Bat Masterson's Emma," 28.

25. Penn, "Bat Masterson's Emma," 28.

26. *Rocky Mountain News*, April 21, 1884.

27. Penn, "Bat Masterson's Emma," 29.

28. Quoted in Willison, *Here They Dug the Gold*, 248. A young frontiersman named Rolf Johnson attended the Palace Theater in 1879 and commented, "The dancing and singing of the girls, who were very liberal in showing their legs and bosoms, were of the most 'loud' [lewd?] character. The place was as hard a one as I was ever in. The afterpiece, 'The Mormons,' would raise a blush on the cheek of an Indian, it was so dirty" (Johnson, *Happy as a Big Sunflower*, 183).

29. *Dodge City Democrat*, July 5, 1884; *Rocky Mountain News*, August 12, 1888.

30. *Fairplay (Colorado) Flume*, November 22, December 23, 1888; *New York Clipper*, December 22, 1888, cited in Penn, "Bat Masterson's Emma," 31.

31. Penn, "Bat Masterson's Emma," 31–32.

32. Ibid., 32–33. Interviewed in 1905 Emma said she had begun to call Denver home sixteen years earlier, or in 1889 (*New York Evening Telegram*, March 29, 1905).

33. Quoted in the *Denver Times*, September 16, 1900.

34. *New York Clipper*, October 26, 1889, cited in Penn, "Bat Masterson's Emma," 32.

35. Penn, "Bat Masterson's Emma," 33–34, 42.

36. *Rocky Mountain News*, March 8, 1892.

37. *Emma Moulton v. Edward W. Moulton. Divorce Case 20014 in Arapahoe County, Colorado*, Courtesy Colorado State Archives and Public Records; *Rocky Mountain News*, July 2, 1893, cited in Penn, "Bat Masterson's Emma," 34.

38. Quoted in the *Aspen (Colorado) Weekly Times*, May 13, 1893.

CHAPTER 3. OTTO, REDDY, AND KI YI

1. WBM to Frank D. Baldwin, February 4, 1890, William Carey Brown Collection, University of Colorado, Boulder.

2. Fowler, *Skyline*, 15.

3. *GW*, July 29, 1899.

4. *Denver Republican*, November 19, 1899.

5. *GW*, May 5, 1900.

6. Ibid., February 24, June 16, October 27, 1900. Whatever his faults, Gallagher was not illiterate as Bat charged; in later years he wrote a regular column for the *Denver Post* called "Let 'Er Go Gallagher."

7. WBM to Henry Raymond, July 23, 1899. Copy in Manuscript Division, Colorado State Archives.

8. *Denver Times*, August 22, 1899.

9. Reprinted in *GW*, February 17, 1900.

10. *GW*, February 24, 1900.

11. Reported in the *Denver Times*, April 22, 1900.

12. Ibid., July 15, 1900. For Bat's invention of "Jim Allison," see DeArment, "Jim Allison."

13. *GW*, October 27, 1900.

14. Fowler, *Timber Line*, 118; Fowler, *Skyline*, 15.

15. *Denver Times*, July 31, 1900.

16. *Rocky Mountain News*, July 31, 1900.

17. *Denver Post*, July 31, 1900.

18. *GW*, August 11, 1900.

19. Ibid., April 14, 1900.

20. Lewis, "King of the Gun-Players."

21. *Denver Post*, August 27, 1914. Smith gave an identical story in an interview appearing in the February 7, 1905, issue of the *Denver Times*. James L. Smith was the prototype for Frank Spearman's popular 1906 novel, *Whisper-*

ing Smith, and a 1948 motion picture of the same name starring Alan Ladd. In 1914, when he was seventy-two, Smith committed suicide in the county jail at Boulder, Colorado, where he was being held on bootlegging charges (*Denver Post*, August 27, 1914).

22. *GW*, September 8, 1900.

23. *Denver Times*, April 14, 1900.

24. *NYMT*, May 16, 1900.

25. Ibid., September 7, 1900.

26. *GW*, September 8, 1900.

27. *NYMT*, November 26, 1900.

28. *Denver Times*, September 16, 1900.

29. Ibid., January 24, 1901.

30. Ibid., May 5, 1902.

31. *NYMT*, October 26, 1921.

32. Raine, *Guns of the Frontier*, 253–57.

33. Carberry, "2nd Guess." A single sentence: "[Masterson] died Jan. 21, 1924 .. at the age of 65 without ever . . . having been sick a day in his life," contains three gratuitous mistakes.

CHAPTER 4. A BROADWAY GUY

1. Significantly, no report of the arrest appeared in the *New York Morning Telegraph*, which always championed Masterson. After Bat was cleared, feature writer William Raymond Sill wrote a humorous story for the paper, referring to the arrest of "Col. *Bartholomew* Masterson (June 10, 1902).

2. *New York Times*, June 7, 8, 1902; *New York World*, June 7, 8, 1902; *Denver Times*, June 7, 1902.

3. Before the general use of fingerprints, a system of physical measurements developed by Alphonse Bertillon was the standard procedure in criminal identification.

4. *NYMT*, June 24, 1913.

5. *New York World*, June 7, 1902.

6. Ibid., June 9, 1902.

7. In his suit Bat claimed false arrest and defamation of character. Interviewed later at the Metropole Hotel, he was quoted as saying, "I'll punish Snow if I have to go to the end of the earth to do it. I'll follow him wherever he goes until I get satisfaction. I'm not going to be branded as a crook. I never was and never will be." If Snow lost $28,000 to Leopold Frank and the others, it only showed he was a sucker, said Bat. "He's a sucker all right and was lucky to get trimmed on only $28,000. I'll trim him of $10,000 or eat my hat" (*Durango [Colorado] Democrat*, June 12, 1902).

Detective Sergeant Gargan and his associates on the New York City police force would have done much better and achieved lasting fame had they ignored the alleged criminal Bat Masterson and nabbed instead another legendary western figure who in June 1902 was brazenly walking the streets of their city. In March 1902 the notorious western bank and train robber Harry "Sundance Kid" Longabaugh and his paramour, Ethel "Etta" Place, had sailed from South America, where Longabaugh and his partner in crime, Butch Cassidy, had fled to escape hounding law enforcement, arriving in New York City on April 3. In June, while Masterson was being harassed by New York's finest, the much-sought-after Sundance Kid and Ethel were shopping at Tiffany's jewelry store, when on the 25th they purchased a watch (Ernst, *Sundance Kid*, 137–38).

8. *NYMT* clipping in the Dawson Scrapbooks (Vol. 19, p. 85).

9. Asbury, *Gangs of New York*, 336.

10. *NYMT*, October 30, 1910.

11. WBM column, *NYMT*, December 23, 1920.

12. Asbury, *Sucker's Progress*, 442.

13. *NYMT* clipping in the Dawson Scrapbooks (Vol. 19, p. 85).

14. *New York American*, October 26, 1921.

15. WBM column, *NYMT*, December 28, 1916.

16. Ibid., July 28, 1918.

17. Breslin, *Damon Runyon*, 83–84.

18. Cobb, *Exit Laughing*, 253–56.

19. Clark, *World of Damon Runyon*, 45.

20. Ibid., 119.

21. Ibid.

22. Burke, *Rogue's Progress*, 29–30, 254.

23. WBM column, *NYMT*, July 2, 1911.

24. Ibid., June 6, 1915.

25. Ibid., January 5, 1911.

CHAPTER 5. THE LEWIS BROTHERS, THE *MORNING TELEGRAPH*, AND THE HAM REPORTER

1. *NYMT*, January 10, 1915.

2. Sloane Gordon, "The Man Who Discovered Wolfville," *NYMT*, February 15, 1914.

3. "Diplomacy in Dodge," *Metropolitan Magazine*, April 1904; "An Invasion of Dodge," *Collier's*, April 16, 1904; "The Fatal Gratitude of Mr. Kelly," *Collier's*, September 17, 1904; "The Deep Strategy of Mr. Masterson," *Saturday Evening Post*, December 17, 1904.

4. *National Cyclopedia of American Biography*, 20:184.

5. Smith, "About Bat Masterson's Office Boy," *New York Times*, October 6, 1976.

6. Quoted in Katcher, *Big Bankroll*, 188.

7. Parsons, *Gay Illiterate*.

8. Stuart N. Lake to Wyatt Earp, December 25, 1927, Lake Collection, Huntington Library, Pasadena, Calif.

9. Broun, "Old, Old Telegraph," *Nation*, September 5, 1936.

10. WBM column, *NYMT*, June 18, 1911.
11. Ibid., September 23, 1917.
12. Ibid., June 19, 1910.
13. Fowler, *Timber Line*, 97.
14. WBM column, *NYMT*, March 26, 1911.
15. Ibid., February 18, 1917.
16. Ibid., March 21, 1918.
17. Ibid., May 23, 1918.
18. Ibid., May 5, 1921.
19. Ibid., October 27, 1921.
20. *New York American*, July 14, 1933.
21. *National Inquirer*, February 1, 1977.
22. WBM columns, *NYMT*, January 2, April 15, 1919.
23. Ibid., April 21, 1912.
24. Ibid., July 25, 1916.
25. Ibid., December 23, 1913.
26. Ibid., September 2, 1920.
27. Ibid., July 5, 1921.

CHAPTER 6. A BADGE FOR "OUR HOMICIDAL FRIEND"

1. Morris, *Rise of Theodore Roosevelt*, 374.
2. As stated in a letter to the historian George Otto Trevelyan, quoted in Ball, *United States Marshals*, 217.
3. *Denver Republican*, February 2, 1904; *National Police Gazette*, March 4, 1905; *Washington Post*, January 13, 1910.
4. *Denver Republican*, February 2, 1904.
5. In Lewis's introduction to Masterson's article on Ben Thompson, *Human Life*, January 1907.
6. *NYMT*, February 7, 1905; *New York Times*, April 2, 1905.
7. Lewis to TR, October 16, 1904, WLHU.
8. Henkel to Moody, January 26, 1905, GRDJ.
9. TR to WBM, February 2, 1905, WLHU.
10. *National Police Gazette*, March 4, 1905.
11. *NYMT*, March 29, 1905.
12. *New York Times*, March 29, April 2, 1905. As the wife of the celebrated appointee, Emma was also interviewed by a reporter for another New York paper. When asked if the appointment came as a surprise to her, Emma responded, "Nothing surprises me that happens to him," and added, "He is worthy of the highest honors." She was described as a woman of medium height and "retiring disposition" with "big blue eyes [that] flash out in the fleeting smile which now and then lights her face." But there was on that face "a look of suffering," the reporter noted, for she had been plagued by an asthmatic cough for five months, which explained the lengthy stay of the Mastersons at Hot Springs. While admitting that New York City might not be the best place to live for someone with her health problem, she said she

would follow her husband even if it meant her death for she might as well die "as to be separated from him" (*New York Evening Telegraph*, March 29, 1905).

13. Report of Charles DeWoody, examiner, to the Attorney General, April 27, 1908, GRDJ.

14. WBM to Daniels, April 18, 1905, quoted in DeMattos, "Between Pals," 9–10.

15. WBM to TR, December 7, 1905, WLHU.

16. TR to Remington, February 20, 1906, WLHU.

17. D. D. Rose to TR, February 26, 1906, WLHU.

18. *Weekly Oklahoma State Capital*, November 16, 1907, reprinted from the *Milwaukee Sentinel*.

19. TR to WBM, July 15, 1908, WLHU.

20. Wise to Wickersham, June 16, 1909, GRDJ.

21. Wickersham to Taft, June 23, 1909, GRDJ.

22. Taft to Wickersham, June 29, 1909, GRDJ.

23. Henkel to Wickersham, July 3, 1909, GRDJ.

24. Lewis to Taft, July 4, 1909, GRDJ.

CHAPTER 7. BLUNDERBUSSES AND BADGES

1. *New York Times*, June 7, 8, 1902; *Denver Republican*, June 8, 1902. The number of Bat's supposed victims varied. It had been twenty-six in the original *New York Sun* article in 1881. After his arrival in New York in 1902 it sometimes became twenty-seven or twenty-eight. Perhaps it was believed he had knocked off one or two more after 1881.

2. *Denver Times*, June 15, 1902, quoting the *New York Evening World*.

3. *Kansas City Star*, May 7, 1905.

4. WBM column, *NYMT*, January 2, 1919.

5. WBM to Colt Firearms Co., January 18, February 6, March 25, 1882; March 18, July 24, 1885 (Connecticut State Library), reproduced in DeMattos, "Those Guns of Bat Masterson." Collector Johnny Spellman of Austin, Texas, owns another six-gun Masterson ordered from the Colt Firearms Company on October 19, 1885, and believes that altogether Bat ordered nine or more (Johnny Spellman to the author, October 19, 1985; March 5, 1996).

6. *New York Times*, April 2, 1905.

7. Emma Masterson to Stuart N. Lake, October 10, 1928, Stuart N. Lake Collection, Huntington Library, Los Angeles.

8. *Kansas City Star*, May 7, 1905.

9. The *Herald* interview was picked up and reprinted in many newspapers, including the *Denver Republican* of July 17, 1910, and the *Tombstone Prospector* of August 16, 1910.

10. Lake, *Wyatt Earp*, 41–42.

11. Sutton and MacDonald, *Hands Up!*, 225.

12. Tom Masterson to E. P. Lamborn, November 20, 1933, Lamborn Collection, Kansas State Historical Society, Topeka.

13. For example, see Lewis, *Gun Digest Book*, 79.

14. The article was reproduced in the summer 1960 issue of *Guns Quarterly* and in DeMattos, "Those Guns of Bat Masterson," 14–15, 42.

15. *NYMT*, August 30, 1911.

16. WBM columns, *NYMT*, October 4, 1914; February 23, 1919; January 30, 1920.

17. Parsons, "Bat Masterson."

CHAPTER 8. GOTHAM FEUDS

1. Newspaper report quoted in O'Connor, *Bat Masterson*, 246. Bat's old friend Bill Tilghman knew Plunkett in Oklahoma and also viewed him with a jaundiced eye. He said in 1893 that Plunkett had arrived in the new land-rush town of Perry "with all his pomp, vanity, and some 200 pounds avoirdupois.... He posed as a prizefighter and never tired of telling how he 'put out' this or that notable with knuckle or six-ounce gloves. Strangers were impressed—after a round or two of drinks which Plunkett ordered and the said stranger always paid for" (Shirley, *Guardian of the Law*, 222).
But according to a worshipful article in the *New York Times* of April 4, 1901, "'Colonel' Plunkett arrested hundreds of the most desperate criminals . . . , going up against gun-plays without number, and generally cognizant of the avowed purpose of noted desperadoes to shoot him at sight, has habitually gone with no other weapons than his bare hands or a light bamboo cane and has never yet found it necessary to kill a human being. . . . They shot him many a time, but a few bullets more or less in his powerful frame did not appear to have any effect." The animosity with Bat could be traced back to Creede, it was said, where Plunkett was elected marshal "on a contest with the notorious Bat Masterson, who was backed by all the gamblers and 'bad men.'" In conclusion the article said that "Col. Plunkett has had abundant opportunities for fortune, but all who know him well vouch for it, that he never did a wrong to any human being, and never made a crooked dollar in his life."

2. *New York Herald*, June 23, 1906, under the alliterative headline "WILD WEST AT WALDORF"; *National Police Gazette*, July 7, 1906.

3. *New York World*, June 23, 1906. On October 29, 1919, Plunkett died in New York City, where he had his set-to thirteen years earlier with Bat Masterson. He came from Houston, Texas, the previous August to be operated on for stomach cancer. He was fifty-eight years old. (*Creede [Colorado] Candle*, November 1, 1919).

4. Quoted in O'Connor, *Bat Masterson*, 244.

5. *New York World*, December 11, 1909.

6. WBM column, *NYMT*, January 6, 1910.

7. Quoted in ibid.

8. Ibid., August 8, 1911.

9. Ibid., September 15, 1910.

10. Ibid., September 10, 1911.

11. Ibid., September 17, 1911.

12. Testimony of Leonard Edgren, *Masterson v. Commercial Advertiser Association*.

13. *William B. Masterson, Plaintiff, v. Frank B. Ufer, Defendant*.

14. *Masterson v. Commercial Advertiser Association*,

15. Answer to Am. Compl. at 9, *Masterson v. Commercial Advertiser Association*.

16 Masterson's testimony in this regard was consistent with that he gave in a civil suit in Kansas in 1886 (*R.W. Tarbox v. P. E. Sughrue*). It is significant that in both court cases it was in Masterson's interest to minimize, not magnify, the extent of his bloodletting. Evidently he truly believed he had killed three men.

17. *Masterson v. Commercial Advertiser Association*.

18. O'Connor, *Bat Masterson*, 245; DeArment, *Bat Masterson*, 385.

19. *NYMT*, May 22, 1913. In an appeal Cardozo immediately filed with the Appellate Division he claimed, among other grounds, that the plaintiff "complains, not because he has been defamed, but because he has not been sufficiently extolled." On December 13, 1913, on a three-to-two vote, the Appellate Division reversed the trial court's ruling and ordered a new trial unless the contending parties could agree on a reduced judgment amount of $1,000. This agreement was reached, and Masterson was awarded that amount (*Masterson v. Commercial Advertiser Association*).

20. WBM column, *NYMT*, June 10, 1917.

21. Ibid., January 17, 1918.

22. Ibid., September 2, 1917.

23. Ibid., July 25, 1918.

24. Ibid., May 18, 1919.

25. Edgren made a fortune during the First World War with stock holdings in a leather goods company. After returning to his native state in 1918, he served on the California boxing commission. He resigned due to ill health in 1932 and died in 1939 (*New York Times*, September 11, 1939). Frank Ufer, oil millionaire, died in Los Angeles on April 5, 1942 (*New York Times*, April 6, 1942).

26. WBM columns, *NYMT*, July 11, 30, 1916.

27. Ibid., August 22, 1916.

28. Fowler, *Skyline*, 16.

29. WBM column, *NYMT*, August 10, 1916.

30. Fowler, *Skyline*, 16.

CHAPTER 9. CURMUDGEON OF THE CLUBS

1. Fleischer, "Crusading Scribes," 44.

2. WBM columns, *NYMT*, January 5, 1911; March 21, 1921. In the current "politically correct" culture, sports commentator Jimmy "the Greek" Snyder was quickly banished from television screens in 1988 for mak-

ing similar remarks. He ascribed the superiority of black athletes to their "breeding."

3. Ibid., February 12, 1911.
4. Ibid., June 6, August 11, 1912.
5. Ibid., October 21, 1913.
6. Ibid., December 26, 1915.
7. Roberts, *Jack Dempsey*, 96.
8. WBM column, *NYMT*, April 30, 1916.
9. Ibid., October 9, 1917.
10. WBM columns, *NYMT*, October 9, 1917; March 17, 1918.
11. Ibid., January 25, 1912; October 9, 1917; December 18, 1919.
12. Ibid., May 20, 1915; July 15, 1917.
13. Ibid., September 1, 1912; September 19, 1916; January 27, 1918.
14. Ibid., April 16, 1911.
15. Ibid., July 9, 1911.
16. Ibid., January 15, 1914.
17. Ibid., January 18, 1914.
18. Ibid., September 3, 17, 1911.
19. Ibid., May 26, 1912; June 19, 1913.
20. Ibid., February 16, 1913.
21. Ibid., April 22, 1915.
22. Fleischer, *50 Years at Ringside*, 246.
23. WBM column, *NYMT*, March 20, 1917.
24. Ibid., December 5, 1918.
25. Ibid., March 10, 1921.
26. Ibid.

CHAPTER 10. THE SNAKES OF NEW YORK

1. *NYMT*, December 9, 1906.
2. Quoted in O'Connor, *Bat Masterson*, 249.
3. Ibid.
4. *New Orleans Picayune*, March 29, 1905; *National Police Gazette*, April 15, 1905.
5. O'Connor, *Hell's Kitchen*, 162–63.
6. Earp, "Wyatt Earp's Tribute to Bat Masterson."
7. Bennett, "Frank Canton."
8. *St. Louis Globe-Democrat*, quoted in the *Topeka (Kansas) Daily Capital*, June 26, 1886.
9. Cobb, *Exit Laughing*, 253–54.
10. WBM column, *NYMT*, November 24, 1912.
11. Gilfoyle, *City of Eros*, 207–208.
12. *New York Times*, July 21, 1907.
13. WBM column, *NYMT*, November 2, 1913.
14. Quoted in Morris, *Rise and Fall of Theodore Roosevelt*, 484–86.

15. Masterson's employment in the case may have given rise to the notion that he was regularly engaged in investigative work. "Bat Masterson [is] now a New York detective," former buffalo hunter Charles Dixon was quoted in a 1912 *El Paso (Texas) Times* article ("Old Prospector's Story").

16. *NYMT*, September 27, 29, 1912; WBM column, *NYMT*, November 24, 1912.

17. WBM column, *NYMT*, November 24, 1912.

18. Ibid., May 27, 1917.

19. Ibid., December 1, 1918.

20. Ibid., January 29, 1911.

21. Ibid., December 4, 1917.

22. Ibid., November 29, 1917.

23. Ibid., December 2, 1917.

CHAPTER 11. WHITE HOPES AND WHITE SLAVERY

1. *NYMT*, February 6, 1904.

2. WBM columns, *NYMT*, May 29, 1910; July 2, 1911; January 18, 1914.

3. Ibid., September 14, 1913.

4. Ibid., February 12, 1911; November 25, 1915.

5. Quoted in ibid., April 21, 1912.

6. Quoted in Lucas, *Black Gladiator*, 86.

7. WBM columns, *NYMT*, April 17, June 9, 1910.

8. WBM special dispatch, *NYMT*, July 3, 1910.

9. WBM column, *NYMT*, June 8, 1919.

10. WBM special dispatch, *NYMT*, July 6, 1910.

11. WBM column, *NYMT*, July 24, 1910.

12. Ibid.

13. Ibid., November 20, 1910.

14. Johnson, *Jack Johnson Is a Dandy*, 54.

15. WBM columns, July 30, August 1, October 22, 1912.

16. Ibid., December 28, 1911.

17. Ibid., January 7, 1912.

18. Andre and Fleischer, *Pictorial History of Boxing*, 89.

19. WBM special cables to *NYMT*, March 31, April 1, 2, 3, 4, 1915.

20. Ibid., April 5, 1915.

21. WBM column, *NYMT*, April 13, 1915.

22. Andre and Fleischer, *Pictorial History of Boxing*, 92; Johnson, *Jack Johnson Is a Dandy*, 171–72.

23. WBM columns, *NYMT*, April 20, 1920; July 21, 1921.

24. Ibid., April 11, 18, 1915.

25. Quoted in ibid., May 30, 1915.

26. Ibid., June 19, 1917.

27. Ibid., March 18, 1919.

28. Ibid., April 20, 1920.

29. Ibid., July 25, 1920.

CHAPTER 12. TEDDY ROOSEVELT AND POLITICS

1. The edition of February 6, 1904, ran side-by-side page-one stories of the Masterson visit to the White House. One, written in a humorous vein, quoted Bat; the other was written by Bat himself.

2. Donovan, *Roosevelt*, 5.

3. *New York Times*, April 27, 1908.

4. "How the Great Went Down," March 14, 1909, unidentified clipping quoted in Shirley, *Guardian of the Law*, 331–32.

5. "Bat Shows White Feather."

6. WBM column, *NYMT*, January 25, 1910.

7. Ibid., October 2, 1910.

8. Ibid., December 20, 1911.

9. WBM to TR, December 21, 1911, WLHU.

10. TR to WBM, December 23, 1911, WLHU.

11. WBM to TR, June 1, 1912, WLHU.

12. WBM column, *NYMT*, June 25, 1912.

13. WBM to TR, July 9, 1912, WLHU.

14. WBM to TR, September 1, 1913, WLHU.

15. WBM column, *NYMT*, May 10, 1914.

16. Ibid., June 7, 1914.

17. *NYMT*, June 18, 1916.

18. WBM to TR, May 14, 1917, WLHU.

19. WBM column, *NYMT*, January 5, 1919.

20. Ibid., August 8, 1918.

21. *NYMT*, February 6, 1904.

22. WBM column, *NYMT*, September 15, 1914.

23. Ibid., August 10, 1919.

24. Ibid., February 11, 1920.

CHAPTER 13. WHEN HYPHENATES, HYPOCRISY, AND HYSTERIA RULED THE ROOST

1. Broun, "Old, Old *Telegraph*."

2. WBM column, *NYMT*, January 25, 1910.

3. Ibid., May 16, 1920.

4. Ibid., May 15, 1921.

5. Ibid., February 1, 1917; August 17, 1919.

6. Ibid., February 17, 1917.

7. *Kansas City Journal*, June 16, 1912.

8. WBM column, *NYMT*, November 6, 1910.

9. Ibid., November 2, 1913; February 22, 1914.

10. Ibid., August 20, 23, 1914.

11. Ibid., July 20, 25, 1915.

12. Ibid., October 8, 1918.

13. Ibid., February 4, 1915.

14. Ibid., September 29, 1921.

15. Ibid., June 19, 1910.

16. Ibid., February 13, 1917.

17. Ibid., May 29, August 12, 1919.

18. Ibid., November 30, 1919.

19. Ibid., July 28, 1921.

20. Ibid., May 29, 1919; February 5, 1920; June 19, July 10, 1921.

CHAPTER 14. THE BLACK SOX, THE GARDEN, AND TEX RICKARD

1. WBM column, *NYMT*, October 10, 1916.

2. Ibid., June 2, 1912.

3. Quoted in Burke, *Rogue's Progress*, 142–43

4. WBM column, *NYMT*, April 13, 1920.

5. Ibid., October 30, 1919.

6. Ibid., May 25, 1915; December 6, 1917.

7. Ibid., February 1, 6, 13, 1916; Griffin, *Wise Guy*, 110.

CHAPTER 15. OUT OF THE PAST

1. WBM column, *NYMT*, July 31, 1910.

2. Ibid., October 21, 1910. Strangely, this story is told in neither Foy's autobiography, *Clowning through Life*, nor in any of the histories of Dodge City. Robert Wright, in his *Dodge City: The Cowboy Capital*, tells how the cowboys hazed Foy and dunked him in a horse trough, and Foy repeats the account in his book.

3. WBM column, *NYMT*, December 18, 1910. Bat's tribute was reprinted in the *Chandler (Oklahoma) Tribune* of December 30, 1910. Chandler was Tilghman's home at the time.

4. WBM column, *NYMT*, March 5, 1911.

5. Ibid., December 4, 1910.

6. Ibid. Masterson ran into Miles at Saratoga five years later and was surprised to learn that the general had kept track of the scouts who served under him and knew where they all lived and what they had been doing since the Red River campaign of 1874 (Ibid., August 8, 1915).

7. Dixon, *Life of "Billy" Dixon*, vi–vii.

8. *NYMT*, January 11, 1917.

9. WBM column, *NYMT*, June 3, 1917.

10. Ibid., June 16, 1918.

11. Ibid., October 19, 1916.

12. Ibid., February 26, 1918.

13. Masterson quoted the letter in full in his column of April 7, 1918.

14. WBM column, *NYMT*, July 4, 1920.

CHAPTER 16. ALL WORK AND NO PLAY

1. WBM columns, *NYMT*, February 18, December 7, 1915.
2. *National Police Gazette*, January 24, 1903.
3. WBM column, *NYMT*, July 21, 1921.
4. Ibid., June 18, 1911.
5. Ibid., March 19, 1911.
6. Ibid., March 16, 20, 1913.
7. Brown, *American Spa*, 76.
8. Allsopp, *History of the Arkansas Press*, 168.
9. Quoted in WBM column, *NYMT*, March 23, 1913.
10. Quoted in ibid., March 16, 1910.
11. Ibid., June 7, 1917.
12. Ibid., March 24, 1910.
13. Ibid., March 22, 1910.
14. Ibid., April 18, 1916.
15. Ibid., August 8, 10, 1915.
16. Ibid., August 20, 1914.
17. Ibid., August 17, 1915.
18. Ibid., August 6, 1914.
19. Ibid., August 24, 1915.
20. Ibid., August 17, 1916.
21. Ibid., August 27, 1916.
22. Ibid., July 28, 1918.
23. Ibid., August 11, 1918.
24. Ibid., August 10, 1919.
25. Ibid., August 28, 1921.
26. Ibid., July 28, 1921.
27. Ibid., September 1, 1921.

CHAPTER 17. SLACKERS IN NONSHOOTABLE SUITS AND THE RISE OF JACK DEMPSEY

1. Quoted in WBM column, *NYMT*, June 2, 1914.
2. WBM to M. W. Sutton, June 12, 1917, Masterson Collection, Kansas State Historical Society, Topeka. Masterson often misstated his age; actually he was sixty-four in November 1917.
3. *NYMT*, July 13, 1917.
4. WBM column, *NYMT*, January 3, 1918.
5. Ibid., October 20, 1918.
6. Ibid., May 27, 1917.
7. Ibid., July 5, 1917.
8. Ibid., November 1, 4, 1917.
9. Ibid., December 2, 13, 1917; January 13, March 12, April 18, May 2, 26, 28, 1918.
10. Ibid., September 15, 1918.
11. Ibid., October 6, 1918.

12. Ibid., November 12, 1918.

13. Ibid., November 14, 1918.

14. Ibid., November 12, December 12, 15, 1918.

15. Ibid., July 27, 1919.

16. Ibid., January 3, 1915.

17. Ibid., March 18, 1917.

18. Quoted in ibid., November 6, 1917.

19. Ibid., January 18, June 15, October 29, November 7, 1916.

20. Ibid., January 11, February 4, 1917.

21. Ibid., February 28, 1918.

22. Ibid., March 10, 1918.

23. Ibid., March 21, 1918.

24. Dempsey, *Dempsey, By the Man Himself*, 92.

25. WBM column, *NYMT*, May 21, 1918.

26. Ibid., March 19, 26, July 7, 1918.

27. Ibid., July 30, December 3, 1918.

28. Ibid., August 1, 8, 1918.

29. Ibid., July 16, 1918.

30. Ibid., March 5, May 7, 26, 1918.

31. Dempsey, *Dempsey, By the Man Himself*, 121.

32. WBM columns, *NYMT*, September 1, 3, 1918.

33. Ibid., December 21, 1919; January 4, 15, 1920.

34. Ibid., September 18, 1918.

35. Ibid., July 22, 1917.

36. Ibid., January 6, March 7, July 28, 1918.

37. Ibid., March 20, 1919.

CHAPTER 18. THE BATTLES OF MAUMEE BAY AND BOYLE'S THIRTY ACRES

1. Samuels, *Magnificent Rube*, 209.

2. WBM columns, *NYMT*, June 5, 8, 12, 17, 19, 22, 1919.

3. Ibid., June 22, 24, 1919.

4. *Toledo (Ohio) News-Bee*, June 30, 1919.

5. WBM column, *NYMT*, October 19, 1920.

6. WBM special dispatch, *NYMT*, June 26, 1919.

7. Ibid., July 1, 2, 3, 1919.

8. Ibid., July 1, 1919.

9. WBM column, *NYMT*, February 6, 1921.

10. Ibid.

11. WBM special dispatch, *NYMT*, July 1, 1919.

12. *Toledo (Ohio) Times*, July 2, 1919.

13. Dempsey, *Dempsey*, 101; Clark, *World of Damon Runyon*, 197. Clark reported Harris gave Runyon 100-to-1 odds, but 10-to-1 is much more likely.

14. WBM special dispatch, *NYMT*, July 4, 1919.

15. WBM column, *NYMT*, August 15, 1920.

16. Dempsey, *Dempsey*, 106–107.

17. WBM special dispatch, *NYMT*, July 6, 1919.

18. WBM column, *NYMT*, July 8, 1919.

19. Ibid., July 13, 1919.

20. Ibid., January 27, February 6, June 26, 1921.

21. Ibid., February 6, 1921.

22. Ibid., April 21, 1921.

23. Ibid., January 11, February 8, 1921.

24. Ibid., September 21, 23, 1919; January 11, 22, 27, February 1, 3, 1920; May 24, 1921.

25. Ibid., January 18, 22, 1920.

26. Ibid., February 8, 11, 1920.

27. Ibid., August 3, 1920.

28. Ibid., October 17, 1918; July 29, 1920; July 8, 1921.

29. Ibid., December 21, 1919.

30. Ibid., May 5, June 19, July 3, 14, 1921.

31. Ibid., May 29, June 21, 1921.

32. *NYMT*, July 3, 1921.

33. WBM column, *NYMT*, July 3, 1921.

34. Ibid., July 3, 5, 14, 17, 1921.

CHAPTER 19. "A STRANGELY QUIET PASSING"

1. WBM column, *NYMT*, October 14, 1919.

2. Ibid., April 12, 1917.

3. *New York Times*, April 2, 1905.

4. 1920 U.S. Census. The maid at that time was Hannah Simon, a single white woman, age twenty-three.

5. WBM columns, *NYMT*, September 19, 1920; September 18, 1921.

6. Ibid., June 19, 1917.

7. Ibid., July 3, 1917.

8. Ibid., July 27, 1919.

9. Ibid., August 3, 1911.

10. Ibid., March 22, 1917.

11. Ibid., March 19, 1918.

12. Ibid., March 13, 1921.

13. Ibid., April 10, 1919; July 8, 1920.

14. Emma Masterson to Nellie Cairns, November 26, 1921, Kansas State Historical Society, Topeka.

15. WBM column, *NYMT*, February 1, 1910. Rex Beach patterned "Flambeau" after Rampart, a gold rush camp on the Yukon River, where in 1897–98 he wintered with Frank Canton, a legendary western lawman in the Bat Masterson mold. Many believed the character "Dan Stark" was a depiction of Canton (DeArment, *Alias Frank Canton*, 312).

16. Hart, *My Life East and West*, 182.

17. WBM column, *NYMT*, June 14, 1914.

18. Hart, *My Life East and West*, 272.

19. Quoted in Louella Parson's column, "In and Out of Focus," *NYMT*, October 30, 1921.

20. *NYMT*, October 9, 1921.

21. Emma Masterson to Nellie Cairns, November 26, 1921.

22. Ibid.

23. In *Guns of the Frontier*, 257, for instance, William MacLeod Raine called Bat's comment "cynical" and quoted him as saying that he had observed "that we all get about the same amount of ice. The rich get it in the summer-time and the poor get it in the winter." This is a paraphrase that turns Masterson's personal view on end.

24. Official cause of death was chronic myocarditis and angina pectoris (William B. Masterson, Certificate of Death, October 25, 1921).

25. *New York American*, October 26, 1921.

26. The *Morning Telegraph* (October 26, 1921) was as inaccurate as the rest. The date and place of Masterson's birth were wrongly reported, as was the name of his mother. Among other errors was the assertion that Masterson "was never known to take a drink of strong liquor."

27. *New York Herald*, October 26, 27, 1921.

28. *New York Times*, October 26, 1921.

29. *New York Tribune*, October 26, 1921.

30. *NYMT*, October 26, 1921.

31. *New York World*, October 26, 1921.

32. *New York American*, October 26, 1921.

33. *NYMT*, October 26, 1921.

34. Ibid., October 28, 1921. Edwin Smith was a double first cousin of Bat's old Denver pal Jefferson "Soapy" Smith.

35. *Rocky Mountain News*, October 26, 1921.

36. *Denver Post*, October 25, 1921.

37. *NYMT*, October 26, 1921.

38. Emma Masterson to Nellie Cairns, November 26, 1921.

39. *NYMT*, October 28, 1921; *New York American*, October 28, 1921; *New York Tribune*, October 28, 1921. All the newspapers incorrectly reported the year of Masterson's birth as 1854 and his tombstone is so marked. Emma Masterson evidently never knew when Bat was born; the "date of birth" box on his death certificate is blank. Incorrectly shown is his place of birth (United States) and his mother's name (Mary Kirk), rather than the correct Catherine McGurk.

40. Emma Masterson to Nellie Cairns, November 26, 1921.

41. The examining physician listed coronary sclerosis and chronic myocarditis as the cause of death (Emma Masterson, Certificate of Death, July 12, 1932).

42. *NYMT*, July 14, 1932; *New York Tribune*, July 13, 1932. Emma's will, signed on April 17, 1925, directed her executor, the Empire Trust Company, 120 Broadway, New York City, to set aside $200 of her estate for income to

cover care and upkeep of the Masterson graves at Woodlawn. Another $200 was bequeathed to Emma's friend of long standing, Nellie Degnan. After payment of doctor's fees and funeral expenses, the balance of the estate went to Emma's sister, Annie (Walter) Adams, nephew Lewis T. Ferguson, grand niece Bertha Ferguson, and May Masterson, C. B. Masterson, Cora (Masterson) Land, and Madeleine (Masterson) Dixon, children of Bat's brother Tom. Emma's estate at her death was valued at almost $3,000, a substantial sum in the depths of the Great Depression. Most of the assets were in two $1,000 bonds issued by the American Telegraph & Telephone Company and the Consolidated Gas Company; $758 was in a savings account at Empire Trust (Emma Masterson, Probate of Will, March 1, 1933).

AFTERWORD

1. Thompson, *Bat Masterson*, 47.

2. O'Connor, *Bat Masterson*.

3. DeArment, *Bat Masterson*.

4. The film starred Albert Dekker as Masterson, Claire Trevor as Dora Hand, and Barry Sullivan as King Kennedy (Jim Kenedy). It was independently produced by Harry Sherman, and directed by George Archainbaud. Aeneas McKenzie wrote the screenplay from a story by Norman Houston.

5. *Masterson in Kansas*, directed by William Castle, starred George Montgomery as Bat Masterson. Nancy Gates had the female lead. For once, Wyatt Earp and Doc Holliday were depicted in roles secondary to Masterson.

6. Harry Haun's column, "Off the Grapevine," *Toledo (Ohio) Blade*, July 21, 1981.

7. Wheeler's novel won the Western Writers of America prestigious Spur Award in 1999.

8. Ballantyne, *Bat Masterson's Last Regular Job*.

9. Dempsey, *Dempsey*, 107.

10. Jack DeMattos to the author, April 28, May 10, 1995.

Bibliography

MANUSCRIPTS AND OTHER UNPUBLISHED MATERIAL

Bennett, Edward Burnett. "Frank Canton, the Sheriff." Local History Collection, Johnson County Library, Buffalo, Wyo.

Dawson Scrapbooks, Colorado Historical Society, Denver.

Theodore Roosevelt Collection, Widener Library, Harvard University, Cambridge, Mass.

O. W. Wright Collection, Kansas State Historical Society, Topeka.

GOVERNMENT DOCUMENTS

U.S. Census

1870: St. Clair County, Ill.; 1880: Dodge City, Kans.; 1900: Denver, Colo.; 1910: New York City, N.Y.; 1920: New York City, N.Y.

Charles Rath and Company v. The United States and the Cheyenne, Kiowa and Comanche Indians. U.S. Court of Claims, Indian Depredation Case Files, Case 4593, Charles Rath and Company Claimants. MS Record Group 123, National Archives, Washington, D.C.

General Records of the Department of Justice. File No. 33 S. 31, Record Group 60.

Masterson, Emma, Certificate of Death, July 12, 1932, No. 16437, Department of Health, City of New York.

Masterson, Emma, Probate of Will, File No. P-1810 (1932), Surrogate's Court, County of New York, March 1, 1933.

Masterson, William B. Masterson, Certificate of Death, October 25, 1921, No. 24516. Department of Health, City of New York.

Masterson, William B., Last Will and Testament, August 3, 1907, filed in Surrogate's Court, New York County, New York, November 3, 1921, and admitted to probate December 6, 1921.

Masterson, William B., Probate of Will, File No. P-2310 (1921), Surrogate's Court, County of New York.

William B. Masterson, Plaintiff, v. Commercial Advertiser Association, Defendant. Supreme Court of New York, Case 21082.

William B. Masterson, Plaintiff, v. Frank B. Ufer, Defendant. Supreme Court of New York, Case 20670.

R. W. Tarbox v. P. F. Sughrue. 1886–87, Supreme Court of Kansas Case 3940, Series H, Folder 3, Archives Department, Kansas State Historical Society.

Walter, Catherine, Application for widow's pension, Philadelphia, Pa., October 1, 1866, File 2266 (Pa.), National Archives.

Walter, John, certification of death, signed by Captain W. C. Cameron, May 1, 1863, National Archives.

NEWSPAPERS

Aspen (Colorado) Weekly Times, May 13, 1893.

Barber County (Kansas) Index, December 4, 1885.

Chandler (Oklahoma) Tribune, December 30, 1910.

Colorado Chieftain (Pueblo), August 2, 1888.

Creede (Colorado) Candle, November 1, 1919.

Denver Daily News, September 22, 1886.

Denver Post, March 12, 1895; July 31, 1900; August 27, 1914; October 25, 1921; August 5, 1929; November 13, 14, 16, 1937; August 8, 1938; September 22, 1944; September 14, 1958.

Denver Republican, April 9, 19, November 19, 1899; January 14, 21, April 14, June 10, 1900; April 28, 1901; June 8, August 3, 1902; February 2, 1904; July 17, 1910.

Denver Times, July 9, 1895; August 16, 22, 1899; April 13, 22, 24, May 3, 6, 23, 25, June 7, 14, 15, July 15, 31; September 2, 7, 16, October 2, 4, December 2, 1900; January 24, 1901; January 8, May 5, June 7, 15, 1902; February 7, 1905.

Dodge City Cowboy, September 27, 1884.

Dodge City Democrat, May 3, July 5, 19, 1884.

Dodge City Times, June 9, 16, September 29, November 24, 1877; August 3, 17, 1878.

Dubuque (Iowa) Herald, September 24, 1874.

Durango (Colorado) Democrat, June 12, 1902.

El Paso (Texas) Herald, January 13, February 1, 5, 10, 21, March 2, 1896.

El Paso (Texas) Times, February 4, 1896.

Fairplay (Colorado) Flume, November 28, 1888.

Ford County (Kansas) Globe, November 22, 1881; June 24, 1884; August 11, 1885.

Fort Wayne (Indiana) Sentinel, February 8, 1890.

George's Weekly (Denver), July 1899–October 1900.

Globe Live Stock Journal (Dodge City, Kansas), November 4, 11, 13, 18, 1884; July 7, October 27, 1885.

Guthrie (Oklahoma) Daily News, August 6, 1893.

Idaho Daily Statesman (Boise), June 30, 1907.

Illustrated Sporting West, February 23, 1894.

Kansas City Journal, February 7, 1905; June 16, 1912.

Kansas City Star, December 10, 1897; May 7, 1905.

Kansas City Times, March 8, 1938; December 5, 1947.

Laramie Daily Boomerang, April 24, 1894; February 26, March 4, 1897.

Lincoln (Nebraska) Daily Star, August 9, 1917.

Medicine Lodge Cresset, December 3, 1885.

National Inquirer, February 1, 1977.

National Police Gazette, July 27, 1889; October 10, 1891; January 14, February 18, April 1, December 30, 1893; February 3, 17, December 1, 1894; June 1, July 20, 1895; February 22, 1896; January 24, February 7, October 31, December 12, 26, 1903; February 13, 27, 1904; March 4, April 15, 1905; July 7, 1906.

New Orleans Picayune, January 15, 1891; March 29, 1905.

New York American, October 26, 28, 1921; July 14, 1933.

New York Clipper, December 22, 1888.

New York Evening Telegraph, March 29, 1905.

New York Evening World, December 11, 1909; June 2, 1917.

New York Globe, March 25, 1907.

New York Herald, February 1, 1904; June 23, 1906; May 17, 1907; October 26, 27, 1921.

New York Morning Telegraph, 1900–1921; July 14, 1932.

New York Sun, November 7, 1881.

New York Times, April 4, 1901; June 7, 8, 10, 1902; October 22, 1904; February 7, March 29, April 2, 4, May 7, 1905; April 27, 1908; September 18, 20, 1912; December 24, 1914; October 26, 27, November 11, 1921; September 11, 1939; April 6, 7, 1942; October 6, 1976.

New York Tribune, July 6, 1902; February 7, 1905; October 26, 28, 1921; July 13, 1932.

New York World, June 7, 8, 9, 1902; June 23, 1906; October 26, 1921.

Olympia (Washington) Record, February 25, 1905; December 11, 1908.

Poughkeepsie (New York) Daily Eagle, March 11, 1927.

Reno Evening Gazette, June 28, 1910.

Rocky Mountain News, April 21, 1884; October 5, 1886; August 12, 1888; March 18, 1892; June 6, 1895; February 9, 1897; August 14, 16, 1899; July 31, 1900; October 26, 1921; November 14, 1937.

San Antonio (Texas) Light, October 9, 1917.

San Francisco Chronicle, December 3, 1896.

San Francisco Bulletin, December 24, 1896.

San Francisco Examiner, December 3, 1896.

San Francisco Post, August 26, 1899.

Toledo (Ohio) Blade, June 6, 30, July 4, 1919; July 21, 1981.

Toledo (Ohio) News-Bee, June 30, 1919.

Toledo (Ohio) Times, July 2, 1919.

Tombstone Prospector, August 16, 1910.

Topeka (Kansas) Commonwealth, July 6, 1884.

Topeka (Kansas) Daily Capital, June 26, 1886; January 3, 1915.

Vox Populi (Dodge City, Kansas), November 1, 1884.

Washington Post, January 13, 1910.

Weekly Oklahoma State Capital (Guthrie), November 16, 1907.

ARTICLES

Alexander, David. "The Fabulous Car Barn." *Turf and Sport Digest*, October 1964.

"Bat Shows White Feather." *Santa Fe Magazine*, July 1909.

Carberry, Jack. "The 2nd Guess." *Denver Post*, September 14, 1958.

DeArment, Robert K. "Bat Masterson and the Boxing Club War of Denver." *Colorado Heritage*, Autumn 2000.

———. "Bat Masterson in New York City." *Wild West*, June 2001.

———. "Bat Masterson Myths." *Wild West*, June 2004.

———. "Bat Masterson's Femmes Fatales." *True West*, October 2001.

———. "Jim Allison: Deadly Gunfighter." *Wild West History Association Journal* (February 2009).

———. "Masterson Interviews." *Wild West History Association Journal* (February 2010).

———. "The Night Bat Masterson Stayed at the Secor Hotel." *Bend of the River*, February 2003.

———. "The Source for Bat Masterson's Adopted Name?" *Quarterly of the National Association for Outlaw and Lawman History* (January–March 1999).

———. "That Masterson-McDonald Standoff." *True West*, January 1998.

DeMattos, Jack. "Between Pals: A Missive Between Presidential Gunfighters." *Quarterly of the National Association for Outlaw and Lawman History* (July–September 1993).

———. "The President and the Gunfighter." *True West*, February 1976.

———. "Those Guns of Bat Masterson." *Frontier Times*, March 1977.

Earl, Phillip I. "The Fight of the Century." *Nevada*, March–April 1997.

Earp, Wyatt. "Wyatt Earp's Tribute to Bat Masterson, the Hero of 'Dobe Walls.'" *San Francisco Examiner*, August 16, 1896.

Farhood, Steve. "The 100 Greatest Title Fights of All Time." *Ring Magazine*, Holiday issue 1996.

Fleischer, Nat. "Crusading Scribes." *Ring Magazine*, June 1941.

"A Good Bad Man." *San Francisco Evening Post Magazine*, August 26, 1899.

Hinkle, Milt. "The Earp and Masterson I Knew." *True West*, December 1961.

Jay, Roger. "Bat Masterson, Paladin of the Plains." *Wild West*, August 2009.

Lewis, Alfred Henry Lewis. "The King of the Gun-Players, William Barclay Masterson." *Human Life*, November 1907.

———. "William Barclay Masterson: An Adventure Story with a Live Hero." *Texas Magazine*, March 1913.

Manz, William H. "Benjamin Cardozo Meets Gunslinger Bat Masterson." *New York State Bar Association Journal* (July–August 2004).

Manzo, Flouroy D. "Alfred Henry Lewis: Western Storyteller." *Arizona and the West*, Spring 1968.

Masterson, W. B. "Alfred Henry Lewis Lived in Action He Penned." *New York Morning Telegraph*, November 11, 1917.

———. "Billy Tilghman." *Human Life*, July 1907.

———. "Doc Holliday." *Human Life*, May 1907.

———. "Famous Gunfighters of the Western Frontier: Ben Thompson." *Human Life*, January 1907.

———. "Luke Short." *Human Life*, April 1907.

———. "Roosevelt? He's the Real Thing." *New York Morning Telegraph*, February 6, 1904.

———. "The Tenderfoot's Turn." *Guns Quarterly*, Summer 1960.

———. "William F. Cody." *Human Life*, March 1908.

———. "Wyatt Earp." *Human Life*, February 1907.

"The Old Prospector's Story." *Frontier Times*, September 1944.

Palmquist, Bob. "Who Killed Jack Wagner?" *True West*, October 1993.

Pardy, George T. "Old Time Tales of the Squared Circle." *New York Morning Telegraph*, September 12, 1915.

Parsons, Chuck. "Bat Masterson: A Gun and a Cane." *Westerner*, Spring–Summer 1987.

Pegler, Westbrook. "Bat Masterson's Writing Career." *Kansas City Times*, December 5, 1947.

Penn, Chris. "A Note on Bartholomew Masterson." *English Westerners' Brand Book*, April 1967.

———. "Bat Masterson's Emma." *Wild West History Association Journal* (April 2011).

Reel, William. "Old Pal of Bat Masterson Still Knows the Ropes." Unidentified clipping dated August 25, 1978, in Masterson file, Western History Department, Denver Public Library.

Runyon, Damon. "Shanley's and a Memory—Bat Masterson's Table—His Strange Court—Fighters, Et Cetera—A Tale of Broadway." Undated Damon Runyon column clipped from the *New York American*. Gary Roberts Collection.

Rybolt, Bob. "The Search for 'Whispering Smith.'" *Quarterly of the National Association for Outlaw and Lawman History* (Fall 1986).

St. John-Brenon, Algernon. "Alfred Henry Lewis: An Appreciation of the Late Novelist." *New York Morning Telegraph*, January 10, 1915.

Siau, Sandra M. "Big-City Life Lured Bat Masterson." *Kansas City Star*, November 8, 1969.

Snell, Joseph P., ed. "The Diary of a Dodge City Buffalo Hunter, 1872–1873." *Kansas State Historical Society Quarterly* (Winter 1965).

BOOKS AND PAMPHLETS

Abernathy, John R. *In Camp With Roosevelt, or, The Life of John R. (Jack) Abernathy*. Oklahoma City: Times-Journal, 1933.

Allsopp, F. W. *History of the Arkansas Press for 100 Years and More*. Little Rock, Ark.: n.p., 1922.

Andre, Sam, and Nat Fleischer. *A Pictorial History of Boxing*. Secaucus, N.Y.: Castle Books, 1975.

Asbury, Herbert. *The Gangs of New York: An Informal History of the Underworld.* New York: Alfred A. Knopf, 1929.

———. *Sucker's Progress: An Informal History of Gambling in America from the Colonies to Canfield.* New York: Dodd, Mead, 1938.

Baker, T. Lindsay, and Billy R. Harrison. *Adobe Walls: The History and Archeology of the 1874 Trading Post.* College Station: Texas A&M University Press, 1986.

Ball, Larry D. *The United States Marshals of New Mexico and Arizona Territories, 1846–1912.* Albuquerque: University of New Mexico Press, 1978.

Ballantyne, Bill. *Bat Masterson's Last Regular Job.* Toronto: Playwrights Canada Press, 1989.

Black, Jack. *You Can't Win.* New York: Macmillan, 1926.

Breslin, Jimmy. *Damon Runyon.* New York: Ticknor & Fields, 1991.

Broun, Heywood Hale, ed. *Collected Edition of Heywood Broun.* New York: Harcourt, Brace, 1928.

Brown, Dee. *The American Spa, Hot Springs, Arkansas.* Little Rock, Ark.: Rose Publishing, 1982.

Burke, John. *Rogue's Progress: The Fabulous Adventures of Wilson Mizner.* New York: G. P. Putnam's Sons, 1975.

Byrnes, Thomas. *1886 Professional Criminals of America.* New York: Chelsea House, 1969.

Chafetz, Henry. *Play the Devil: A History of Gambling in the United States from 1492 to 1955.* New York: Clarkson N. Potter, 1960.

Chidsey, Donald Barr. *John the Great: The Times and Life of a Remarkable American, John L. Sullivan.* Garden City, N.Y.: Doubleday, Doran, 1942.

Churchill, Allen. *Park Row.* New York: Rinehart, 1958.

Clark, Tom. *The World of Damon Runyon.* New York: Harper & Row, 1978.

Clarke, Donald Henderson. *In the Reign of Rothstein.* New York: Vanguard Press, 1929.

Cobb, Irvin S. *Exit Laughing.* New York: Bobbs-Merrill, 1941.

Corbett, James J. *The Roar of the Crowd: True Tales of the Rise and Fall of a Champion.* New York: Gosset & Dunlap, 1925.

DeArment, Robert K. *Alias Frank Canton.* Norman: University of Oklahoma Press, 1996.

———. *Bat Masterson: The Man and the Legend.* Norman: University of Oklahoma Press, 1979.

———. *Deadly Dozen: Forgotten Gunfighters of the Old West, Volume 3.* Norman: University of Oklahoma Press, 2010.

———. *Knights of the Green Cloth: The Saga of the Frontier Gamblers.* Norman: University of Oklahoma Press, 1982.

DeArment, Robert K., and Jack DeMattos. *A Rough Ride to Redemption: The Ben Daniels Story.* Norman: University of Oklahoma Press, 2010.

DeMattos, Jack. *The Earp Decision.* College Station, Tex.: Creative Publishing, 1989.

————. *Masterson and Roosevelt*. College Station, Tex.: Creative Publishing, 1984.

Dempsey, Jack, as told to Bob Considine and Bill Slocum. *Dempsey: By the Man Himself*. New York: Simon and Schuster, 1960.

Dempsey, Jack, with Barbara Piattelli Dempsey. *Dempsey*. New York: Harper & Row, 1977.

Dixon, Olive K. *Life of "Billy" Dixon: Plainsman, Scout and Pioneer*. Dallas: P. L. Turner, 1914.

Donovan, Mike. *The Roosevelt That I Know*. New York: B. W. Dodge, 1909.

Ernst, Donna B. *The Sundance Kid: The Life of Harry Alonzo Longabaugh*. Norman: University of Oklahoma Press, 2009.

Fleischer, Nat. *50 Years at Ringside*. New York: Fleet Publishing, 1958.

————. *The Heavyweight Championship: An Informal History of Heavyweight Boxing from 1719 to the Present Day*. New York: G. P. Putnam's Sons, 1949.

————. *Jack Dempsey*. New Rochelle, N.Y.: Arlington House, 1972.

Fowler, Gene. *Skyline: A Reporter's Reminiscences of the 1920s*. New York: Viking Press, 1961.

————. *Timber Line: A Story of Bonfils and Tammen*. New York: Blue Ribbon Books, 1933.

Foy, Eddie, and Alvin F. Harlow. *Clowning through Life*. New York: E. P. Dutton, 1928.

Gilfoyle, Timothy J. *City of Eros: New York City, Prostitution, and the Commercialization of Sex, 1790–1920*. New York: W. W. Norton, 1992.

Gorn, Elliott J. *The Manly Art: Bare-Knuckle Prize Fighting in America*. Ithaca, N.Y.: Cornell University Press, 1986.

Griffin, Marcus. *Wise Guy*. New York: Vanguard Press, 1938.

Hart, William S. *My Life East and West*. Boston: Houghton Mifflin, 1929.

Haywood, C. Robert. *Cowtown Lawyers: Dodge City and Its Attorneys, 1876–1886*. Norman: University of Oklahoma Press, 1988.

————. *The Merchant Prince of Dodge City: The Life and Times of Robert M. Wright*. Norman: University of Oklahoma Press, 1998.

Heller, Peter. *"In This Corner . . . !: Forty Champions Tell Their Stories*. New York: Simon & Schuster, 1973.

Hickey, Michael M. *The Death of Warren Baxter Earp—A Closer Look*. Honolulu: Talei Publishers, 2000.

Horan, James D. *The Authentic Wild West: The Lawmen*. New York: Crown Publishers, 1980.

Horan, James D., and Howard Swiggett. *The Pinkerton Story*. New York: G. P. Putnam's Sons, 1951.

Hoyt, Edwin P. *A Gentleman of Broadway*. Boston: Little, Brown, 1964.

Hoyt, Henry F. *A Frontier Doctor*. Boston: Houghton Mifflin, 1929.

Isenberg, Michael T. *John L. Sullivan and His America*. Urbana and Chicago: University of Illinois Press, 1988.

Jackson, Kenneth T., ed. *The Encyclopedia of New York City.* New Haven, Conn.: Yale University Press, 1995.

Johnson, Jack. *Jack Johnson Is a Dandy: An Autobiography.* New York: New American Library, 1970.

Johnson, Rolf. *Happy as a Big Sunflower: Adventures in the West, 1876–1880.* Lincoln: University of Nebraska Press, 2000.

Katcher, Leo. *The Big Bankroll: The Life and Times of Arnold Rothstein.* New York: Harper & Bros., 1958.

Kimmel, Michael. *Manhood in America: A Cultural History.* New York: Free Press, 1996.

Kramer, Dale. *Heywood Broun: A Biographical Portrait.* New York: Current Books, 1949.

Lake, Stuart N. *Wyatt Earp, Frontier Marshal.* Boston: Houghton Mifflin, 1931.

Lardner, John. *White Hopes and Other Tigers.* Philadelphia: J. B, Lippincott, 1951.

Laurie, Joe, Jr. *Vaudeville: From the Honky-tonks to the Palace.* New York: Henry Holt, 1953.

Lewis, Alfred Henry. *The Sunset Trail.* New York: A. S. Barnes, 1905.

Lewis, Jack. *The Gun Digest Book of Single Action Revolvers.* Northfield, Ill.: DBI Books, 1982.

Logan, Andy. *Against the Evidence: The Becker-Rosenthal Affair.* New York: Mc-Call Publishing, 1970.

Look, Al. *Unforgettable Characters of Western Colorado.* Boulder, Colo.: Pruett Press, 1966.

Lucas, Bob. *Black Gladiator: A Biography of Jack Johnson.* New York: Dell, 1970.

Lukas, J. Anthony. *Big Trouble.* New York: Simon & Schuster, 1997.

McGinnis, Edith B. *The Promised Land.* Boerne, Tex.: Toepperwein, 1947.

Miletich, Leo N. *Dan Stuart's Fistic Carnival.* College Station: Texas A&M University Press, 1994.

Miller, Nyle H., and Joseph W. Snell. *Why the West Was Wild: A Contemporary Look at the Antics of Some Highly Publicized Kansas Cowtown Personalities.* Topeka: Kansas State Historical Society, 1963.

Morris, Edmund. *The Rise of Theodore Roosevelt.* New York: Coward, McCann & Geoghegan, 1979.

National Cyclopedia of American Biography. New York: James T. White, 1921.

O'Connor, Richard. *Bat Masterson.* New York: Doubleday, 1957.

———. *Hell's Kitchen: The Roaring Days of New York's West Side.* Philadelphia: J. B. Lippincott, 1958.

———. *Heywood Broun: A Biography.* New York: G. P. Putnam's Sons, 1975.

———. *Young Bat Masterson.* New York: McGraw-Hill, 1967.

Paine, Albert Bigelow. *Captain Bill McDonald: Texas Ranger.* New York: J. J. Little & Ives, 1909.

Parsons, Chuck. *James W. Kenedy: "Fiend in Human Form."* London: English Westerners Society, 2001.

Parsons, Louella A. *The Gay Illiterate.* New York: Doubleday, Doran, 1944.

Raine, William MacLeod. *Guns of the Frontier: The Story of How the Law Came to the West.* New York: Houghton Mifflin, 1940.

Randisi, Robert J. *The Ham Reporter: Bat Masterson in New York.* Garden City, N.Y.: Doubleday, 1986.

Rice, George Graham. *My Adventures with Your Money.* 1913. Reprint, Las Vegas: Nevada Publications, 1986.

Rickard, Mrs. "Tex," with Arch Oboler. *Everything Happened to Him: The Story of Tex Rickard.* New York: Frederick A. Stokes, 1936.

Roberts, Randy. *Jack Dempsey, the Manassa Mauler.* Baton Rouge: Louisiana State University Press, 1979.

————. *Papa Jack: Jack Johnson and the Era of White Hopes.* New York: Free Press, 1983.

Robertson, Frank G., and Beth Kay Harris. *Soapy Smith: King of the Frontier Con Men.* New York: Hastings House, 1961.

Roosevelt, Theodore. *Theodore Roosevelt: An Autobiography.* New York: Charles Scribner's Sons, 1926.

Root, Jonathan. *The Life and Bad Times of Charlie Becker.* London: Secker & Warburg, 1962.

Rosa, Joseph G. *The Gunfighter: Man or Myth?* Norman: University of Oklahoma Press, 1969.

Sammons, Jeffrey T. *Beyond the Ring: The Role of Boxing in American Society.* Urbana and Chicago: University of Illinois Press, 1988.

Samuels, Charles. *The Magnificent Rube: The Life and Gaudy Times of Tex Rickard.* New York: McGraw-Hill, 1957.

Samuels, Charles, and Louise Samuels. *Once Upon a Stage: The Merry World of Vaudeville.* New York: Dodd, Mead, 1974.

Schoenberger, Dale T. *The Gunfighters.* Caldwell, Idaho: Caxton Printers, 1971.

Secrest, Clark. *Hell's Belles: Denver's Brides of the Multitudes.* Aurora, Colo.: Hindsight Historical Publications, 1996.

Shirley, Glenn. *Guardian of the Law: The Life and Times of William Matthew Tilghman.* Austin, Tex.: Eakin Press, 1988.

Sifakis, Carl. *The Encyclopedia of American Crime.* New York: Smithmark Publishers, 1982.

Siringo, Charles A. *A Cowboy Detective: A True Story of Twenty-Two Years with a World-Famous Detective Agency.* Chicago: W. B. Conkey, 1912.

Smith, Jeff. *Alias Soapy Smith: The Life and Death of a Scoundrel.* Juneau, Alaska: Klondike Research, 2009.

Somers, Dale A. *The Rise of Sports in New Orleans, 1850–1900.* Baton Rouge: Louisiana State University Press, 1972.

Stephens, John Richard, ed. *Wyatt Earp Speaks!* Cambria Pines by the Sea, Calif.: Fern Canyon Press, 1998.

Sullivan, Edward Dean. *The Fabulous Wilson Mizner.* New York: Henkle, 1935.

Sutton, Fred E., and A. B. MacDonald. *Hands Up! Stories of the Six-Gun Fighters of the Old Wild West.* Indianapolis: Bobbs-Merrill, 1926.

Swarthout, Glendon. *The Old Colts.* New York: Donald I. Fine, 1985.

Tefertiller, Casey. *Wyatt Earp: The Life behind the Legend.* New York: John Wiley & Sons, 1997.

Thompson, George G. *Bat Masterson: The Dodge City Years.* Topeka: Kansas State Printing Plant, 1943.

Thrapp, Dan. L. *Encyclopedia of Frontier Biography.* 4 vols. Glendale, Calif.: Arthur H. Clark, 1988–94.

Vestal, Stanley. *Queen of Cowtowns: Dodge City.* Lincoln: University of Nebraska Press, 1972.

West, Richard. *Television Westerns: Major and Minor Series, 1946–1978.* Jefferson, N.C.: McFarland, 1987.

Wheeler, Richard S. *Masterson.* New York: Tom Doherty Associates, 1999.

Willison, George F. *Here They Dug the Gold.* New York: Reynol & Hitchcock, 1946.

Wright, Robert M. *Dodge City: The Cowboy Capital and the Great Southwest in the Days of the Wild Indian, the Buffalo, the Cowboy, Dance Halls, Gambling Halls, and Bad Men.* Wichita, Kans.: Wichita Eagle Press, 1913.

Young, Frederic R. *Dodge City: Up through a Century in Story and Pictures.* Dodge City, Kans.: Boot Hill Museum, 1972.

Zornow, William F. Kansas: *A History of the Jayhawk State.* Norman: University of Oklahoma Press, 1957.

MISCELLANEOUS

W. B. Masterson photograph-clipping file, Western History Department, Denver Public Library.

Philadelphia City Directories, 1840–1910.

New York City Directories, 1902–1921.

Emma Matilda Walter, Baptismal Record, Register of the Church of St. Albans, Roxborough, Pa., October 5, 1866.

BIBLIOGRAPHY

Index

279

INDEX

Times Square, 59, 60, 67, 125, 126, 128, 167, 231
Tinker, John, 57
Titus, George, 57
Tobin, Tom, 249n1
Toledo, Ohio, 216–25, 227, 230
Toledo Times, 219
Tombs Prison, 131
Tony Denier's "Humpty Dumpty" (theatrical co.) 36, 37
Trevor, Claire, 268n4
Trinidad, Colo., 43, 62, 68, 148, 174
Trinidad News, 12
True, Margaret T., 54
Tulsa, Okla., 108
Tunney, Gene, 230
Turner, Frederick Jackson, 6
Tuthill, Gus, 45
"Two-By-Six Kid," 138
"Two-Gun Man, The," 237

Ufer, Frank B., 102–104, 107, 142, 169, 259n25
United States Congress, 83, 156, 157, 177
United States Senate, 83
United States Supreme Court, 104, 155
Updegraph, Al, 5, 105

Vallinsky, Harry. *See* Vallon, Harry
Vallon, Harry, 129–31
"Valley of the Vapors." *See* Hot Springs, Ark.
Vanderbilt, Reginald, 190
Vanderbilt, William, 169
Variety, 72
Verdict (weekly), 69
Villa, Pancho, 63, 143
Villepigue, Jim, 66
Virgie Colmalobo Meteors (theatrical co.), 38
Volstead Alcohol Act, 161
Vox Populi, 12, 148

Wagner, Jack, 4, 5, 105, 249n1
Wahle, Charles F. G., 131
Walcott, Joe, 110, 135
Waldorf-Astoria hotel, 99, 237
Waldo, Rhinelander, 128, 233, 243

Walker Act (boxing), 120
Walker, Alf, 4
Walker, James J. "Jimmy," 65, 120, 229
Wall Street Journal, 72
Walter, Anna Maria, 35, 252n18
Walter, Catherine Bantom, 35, 252n17, 252n20
Walter, Clara Victoria, 35, 2252n18
Walter, James, 35
Walter, Jane, 35
Walter, John, 35
Walters, John, 252n19
Warburton, William H., 199
Warfield, David, 201, 233
Warner, Jack L., 65
Washington, D.C., 69, 71, 84, 148–49, 157, 176, 240
Washington, George, 157
Washington Post, 240
Watrous, Mart, 20
Watseka, Ill., 32–33, 251n5
Watson, Lester A., 136
Wayne County, Ill., 32
Webber, Bridgey, 129–31
Weedon, George Orlando, 242
Welch, Jack, 143
Welsh, Freddy, 108
Wenck, Fred, 74, 119
West Philadelphia, Pa., 35
Wheeler, Richard S., 244
"Whispering Smith," 254n21
Whispering Smith (Spearman), 253–54n21
White, Charlie, 75, 102, 110, 174, *182*
White House, 79, 80, 84, 86, 129, 148, 149, 176, 262n1
White, Johnny, 110
White Rats (actors' social club), 175
White Slave Traffic Act. *See* Mann Act
White, Stanford, 124, 169
Whitman, Charles S., 106–107, 129, 131, 155
Whitman, Nelson, 14
Whitney, William C., 71, 195
Wichita, Kans., 175, 178
Wickersham, George W., 85–86
Willard, Jess, 65, 142–45, 172, 207–209, 213–27, 243, 245
Williams, Christy, 108, 136

Also by Robert K. DeArment

Bat Masterson: The Man and the Legend (Norman, Okla., 1979)
Knights of the Green Cloth: The Saga of the Frontier Gamblers
    (Norman, Okla., 1990)
George Scarborough: The Life and Death of a Lawman on the Closing
    Frontier (Norman, Okla., 1992)
(ed.) *Early Days in Texas: A Trip to Hell and Heaven* (Norman, Okla.,
    1992)
Alias Frank Canton (Norman, Okla., 1996)
Bravo of the Brazos: John Larn of Fort Griffin, Texas (Norman, Okla.,
    2002)
Deadly Dozen: Twelve Forgotten Gunfighters of the Old West (Norman,
    Okla., 2003)
(ed. and anno., with William Rathmell) *Life of the Marlows: A True*
    Story of Frontier Life of Early Days (Denton, Texas, 2004)
Jim Courtright of Fort Worth: His Life and Legend (Fort Worth, 2004)
Broadway Bat: Gunfighter in Gotham : The New York City Years of Bat
    Masterson (Honolulu, 2005)
Ballots and Bullets: The Bloody County Seat Wars of Kansas (Norman,
    Okla., 2006)
Deadly Dozen, Volume 2: Forgotten Gunfighters of the Old West
    (Norman, Okla., 2007)
Deadly Dozen, Volume 3: Forgotten Gunfighters of the Old West
    (Norman, Okla., 2010)
A Rough Ride to Redemption: The Ben Daniels Story (Norman, Okla.,
    2010)
Assault on the Deadwood Stage: Road Agents and Shotgun Messengers
    (Norman, Okla., 2011)